Praise for

The Bullpen Gospels

"After many minutes, hours, days, weeks, months, and years spent in the bullpen, I can verify that this is a true picture of baseball."

—Tim McCarver

"There are great truths within, of the kind usually unspoken. And as he expresses them, Dirk Hayhurst describes himself as 'a real person who moonlights as a baseball player.' In much the same manner, while *The Bullpen Gospels* chronicles how all of us face the impact when we learn reality is both far meaner and far richer than our dreams—it also moonlights as one of the best baseball books ever written."

—Keith Olbermann

"A bit of Jim Bouton, a bit of Jim Brosnan, a bit of Pat Jordan, a bit of Crash Davis, and a whole lot of Dirk Hayhurst. Often hilarious, sometimes poignant. This is a really enjoyable baseball read."

—Bob Costas

"Fascinating . . . a perspective that fans rarely see."
—Trevor Hoffman, pitcher for the Milwaukee Brewers and baseball's all-time leader in saves

"The Bullpen Gospels is a rollicking good bus ride of a book. Hayhurst illuminates a baseball life not only with wit and humor, but also with thought-provoking introspection."
—Tom Verducci, *Sports Illustrated*

"Dirk Hayhurst has written a fascinating, funny, and honest account on life in the minor leagues. I loved it. Writers can't play baseball, but in this case a player sure can write."
—Tim Kurkjian, senior writer, *ESPN The Magazine*, and analyst/reporter, ESPN television

"*Bull Durham* meets *Ball Four* in Dirk Hayhurst's hilarious and moving account of life in baseball's glamour-free bush leagues."
—Rob Neyer, ESPN.com

"If Holden Caulfield could dial up his fastfall to 90 mph, he might have written this funny, touching memoir about a ballplayer at a career—and life—crossroads. He might have called it 'Pitcher in the Rye.' Instead, he left it to Dirk Hayhurst, the only writer in the business who can make you laugh, make you cry, and strike out Ryan Howard."
—King Kaufman, *Salon*

"*The Bullpen Gospels* is a funny, bone-tickling, tear duct-stimulating, feel-good story that will leave die-hard baseball fans—and die-hard human beings, for that matter—well, feeling good."
—Bob Mitchell, author of *Once Upon a Fastball*

the Bullpen Gospels

Major League Dreams of a Minor League Veteran

DIRK HAYHURST

Citadel Press
Kensington Publishing Corp.
www.kensingtonbooks.com

CITADEL PRESS BOOKS are published by

Kensington Publishing Corp.
119 West 40th Street
New York, NY 10018

All Kensington titles, imprints, and distributed lines are available at special quantity discounts for bulk purchases for sales promotions, premiums, fund-raising, educational, or institutional use. Special book excerpts or customized printings can also be created to fit specific needs. For details, write or phone the office of the Kensington special sales manager: Kensington Publishing Corp., 119 West 40th Street, New York, NY 10018, attn: Special Sales Department; phone 1-800-221-2647.

CITADEL PRESS and the Citadel logo are Reg. U.S. Pat. & TM Off.

First printing: April 2010

10 9 8 7 6 5 4 3

Printed in the United States of America

Library of Congress Control Number: 2009937074

ISBN-13: 978-0-8065-3143-4
ISBN-10: 0-8065-3143-6

To Bonnie,
for loving the man beneath the jersey.
And to my family,
for supporting him while he reached for it.

A Note from the Author

It's no easy undertaking to write a book. It's especially hard to write a book about professional baseball while playing it. Thanks in large part to the exposé-style works that have come out in the past, any book about baseball from a player/author is met with incredulity and paranoia. Despite the rough-and-tumble, thick-skinned persona needed to survive in this industry, telling a story about what happens behind the scenes is a sensitive subject.

That said, I'd like to tell the reader that this book's purpose is to entertain, not to name names; pull the cover off the bare ass of drug use; show cheaters, adulterers, or tax dodgers; or do any other whistle-blowing. If you are looking for someone's dirty laundry, you won't find it here. I know it stands to reason that if those things didn't exist in the sport, there would be no paranoia—and I hear ya—I'm just saying, it's not in this book.

Names have been changed at the request of some players and at my discretion, to give them more of a character feel as well as to protect identity. Some characters within are composites blended together for ease of reading. Everything in this work is based on actual occurrences, though I have attempted to conceal identities for the benefit of those who may not want to deal with any extra drama this book may bring their way. Mind you, I was a teammate before I tried my hand at writing, and I hope to be one long after this book is published.

Furthermore, I believe there is more to the game than steroids and scandals. I also believe there is more to the game than just baseball. For all the great things baseball is, there are some things it is absolutely not. And that is what this story is all about.

the
Bullpen
Gospels

Prologue

When we won the division in the first half of 05, I had nothing to do with it. Hell, I was lucky to be employed. I was deadweight on a team full of prospects—a dud, a smudge on an otherwise crystal squad. We may have been guaranteed a spot in the postseason, but I didn't know if I'd be around when we got there.

I was the team's long relief man. A nonglorious pitching role designed to protect priority pitchers. If the starting pitcher broke down or the game got out of control, I came in to clean up so the bullpen wasn't exhausted. Despite feel-good semantics supplied by the organization, my main job was mopping up lost causes. Why waste a talented pitcher when there was a perfectly useless guy for the job? I could pitch five innings in a blowout or face one batter in the seventeenth inning. Put it this way: if I could have done any other role successfully, I wouldn't have been the long man.

I had been struggling all year, inadvertently serving as the league's batting practice thrower. I floundered as a starter and was demoted. Then I brought the kind of relief that made starters moan, "Jesus, *I* could have given up my own runs—no need to bring in this guy!" The way the season was shaping up, it would take a witch doctor to resurrect my career.

I didn't pitch very often, which didn't bother me at all. I knew I couldn't make it to the big leagues if I didn't get out on the mound and show the world what I had, but, at the time, I didn't feel I had much. All I could think about is how bad things could go, even worse than they were.

It's hard to pitch with fear. It was as if baseball's Grim Reaper was watching every time I took the mound. Most of the time he'd show up in little incarnations, like a black cat or a double that landed exactly on the foul line just when I thought I was going to have a clean outing. Lately though, it seemed as if the Baseball Reaper had season tickets for front row seats to every park I played in. He never missed me pitch, sitting silently in the stands, sipping a Red Bull while waving a foam finger that said #1 Fan! From the way he looked at me, I knew he couldn't wait to reach out and snatch my baseball career.

Maybe I'm being a little dramatic, but I had never struggled before. I imagine a lot of guys who get drafted aren't used to struggling. I always knew it would happen eventually, but I envisioned it to be more like turbulence than a fiery plane crash.

The only solution I had was to bear down and work through it. I spent hours on the practice mound refining my delivery. I tried to bend my breaking ball, hasten my fastball, and change my changeup. I even tried sports meditation, which had me standing on the mound with my eyes closed visualizing myself pitching better. I'd picture myself standing on the mound in the heat of battle, with my hair being tussled by a breeze blowing purely for the sake of making me look sexy. At my feet would be the corpses of dragons, ninjas, and Chuck Norris. My pecs would barely fit into my uniform, and I would pitch with a huge sword strapped to my back. I would laugh at batters as they feebly limped to the plate, my voice deep like thunder. I would crush the hitters, see them driven before me, hear the lamentations of their dugouts. I enjoyed the visualizations, maybe a little too much, and would stop only when I felt I'd centered myself—or after one of my teammates hit me in the nuts with the rosin bag while my eyes were closed.

Come the second half of the season, things were still going bad. My voice was no deeper, and it was all I could do to keep the Baseball Reaper's blade from my neck. The only positive note was that all the team's prospects were promoted to Double-A. A fresh pack of less talented replacements were promoted, filling in vacant spots and allowing me to blend in.

In our first month together, the new squad fell apart. We tumbled from first place in the league all the way to dead last on a twenty-game losing skid. Our manager tried every combination to reverse the streak, but we thwarted them all. We lost on errors and home runs, in extra-inning heartbreakers and first-inning blowouts, and on bad calls and blown saves. We even managed to walk in the winning run. Sometimes it was bad luck, other times we looked like the Lake Elsinore circus.

Fans stopped sitting down the first baseline because the short-stop threw so many balls into the stands. The pitching staff agreed we might as well pitch to the backstop since all our efforts ended up there anyway. We hit so badly you'd think the batting coach had Tourette's. Mix in a lion tamer and a tightrope, and we could have put a tent over the place.

Other guys began to see the Baseball Reaper as well. Haunted and paranoid, we strugglers took refuge in the rear of the bullpen discussing what we'd do after being released. I told everyone I was going to join the circus because it'd remind me of life in the minors. Another guy said he was going to become an executioner because at least he'd feel like he was getting even.

No matter how badly we did, we were still on course for the playoffs. We looked forward to it like a root canal. The second half of the season was a disaster we couldn't wait to see end. Instead of looking at the postseason as a chance to win some jewelry, a chance for redemption, it was extra days of ass-kicking. We were phonies who hadn't earned our own playoff berth being rewarded for the efforts of the first-half guys who weren't even around any-more.

When we arrived in our first playoff series, the most amazing thing happened: we won. My only explanation was that we had nothing to lose. We hit well, we pitched well, and we made fewer mistakes than the other team, which was unheard of. Suddenly, we were a brand-new team.

The only negative to be mentioned was during the last game of the first series. Our starter got hurt. About the third inning, he stopped pitching, grabbed his arm, and began to cuss under his breath. The trainer and the manager ran out to assist him. I don't know how, but he had incurred a stress fracture in his wrist from throwing. I, as was my role, came in to replace him. The team held the lead and won the game. We swept the Lancaster Jethawks and clinched a spot in the championship series versus the San Jose Giants.

After the game on the bus back to Lake Elsinore, the air was alive with music and celebration. The front office furnished us with enough booze to hammer an elephant. You would have never guessed that a few days previous none of us wanted to be a part of the postseason. Everyone was brimming with confidence and excitement. Someone peed on my backpack, and I still don't know who it was.

On came the Giants, and we won the first two games with the same ease with which we swept the Jethawks. After the second win, the coaches pulled me aside to tell me Luke, the starter who got hurt, would be out for the remainder of the season. They said I, being the long man, would fill in for him if there was a game five. Then they slapped me on the back and told me not to worry about it, as if it were some piece of trivial fine print. They said if we kept playing the way we were, we wouldn't need a game five. We immediately blew the next two games.

The night before game five, the biggest game of my pro career, I lay in bed staring at the ceiling, sleepless. There was nothing I could do to prepare; it was too late. I thought about standing on the mattress and doing some blind visualization, but my roommate was already convinced I was nuts because of my conspiracy references to the Baseball Reaper. I do some of my best thinking when I'm in bed, but all I wanted to do that night was turn my mind off. A river of anxiety was running through my brain. Sleep would be an escape from the lashing of anxious thoughts. Finally, during the dark, forgotten hours of the morning, I went under. I dreamed I was Captain Ahab chasing a big, white, baseball-shaped whale. And I was naked.

The day of game five, my teammates repeatedly approached me asking if I was ready. What a stupid question, of course I wasn't ready. How could I be? I was tossed into this role about forty-eight hours ago, expected to pitch a gem after hurling nothing but turds the entire season! I didn't say that though; I just looked my inquirers in the eye and in my confident, competitor's voice, said, "Oh, you know it, baby." They'd smile, kneed my shoulders, or slap me on the ass, then tell me we were going to get 'em today. It made me wonder if they were faking it too.

I used all my cellular minutes talking to any positive voice that would pick up. I prayed every panic-induced prayer I could think of, being sure to remind God of each and every nice thing I'd ever done. Then I panicked and prayed for something wonderful to happen, like Armageddon, so the game would get postponed. I wrestled with the event I was about to spearhead until I had explored all possible contingencies and I was still feeling nauseous.

By the time I walked out to warm up, I was a mental and emotional ruin, and I hadn't thrown a pitch yet. The stands were packed, and sure enough, there was the Baseball Reaper sitting in the beer garden—the smoking section—running a sharpening stone over his scythe in between lustful looks at senior citizens. He waved when he saw me. I pretended not to notice.

I warmed up, spinning my arms like propeller blades, contorting my legs at odd angles—toe touches, twists, nervous dry heaving. Then before it was time to start throwing, I flopped on the ground and closed my eyes. I had to—some force beyond my understanding made me do it. Twenty minutes before the biggest game of my life, I lay, stretched out like a snow angel with no snow in the middle of the outfield grass.

I was tired of thinking about the end of my career or the meaning one game had over my life. All this time spent being a prisoner of results. I wasn't even having fun anymore. There was no assurance all the work I'd put in would pay off in improved pitching numbers or a win. I'd spent most of the season trying to fix whatever was wrong with me. Even if I'd figured it out, I could take the mound and get shellacked regardless. That's the thing about baseball: every game is a roll of the dice. Once the ball leaves your hand, what happens next is out of your control. Veteran baseball people will tell you the same thing—hard work can only take you so far, the rest is luck and opportunity. Well, I had put in my hard work and landed an opportunity, for better or worse. Now it was time for luck to show up.

I can't explain what it's like to pitch an amazing game. I always wanted to be a superhero when I was a kid, and when I pitch well, it's as if I am, and everyone watching knows it. Still, it's something you need to feel to understand. Words can't tell you how fulfilling, empowering, and relieving it is, all at the same time. How it makes you feel like some great champion, the master of the battlefield. How it justifies all the work you put in to capture it, even though you know it's something so wild and free it can't truly be contained. In the brief moments you hold on to it, it frees you from your bondage, each perfect pitch erasing a speck of self-doubt. It's a feeling you'll gladly endure a season of hell to experience. It's why you compete.

I was a champion that day. I was a king among men. I was all that and a bag of chips. I carried a one hitter through six before talented pitchers came into relieve me. In my last inning, I struck out the side for good measure. A whole season of treading water justified by one stellar performance. I felt as if a weight was lifted from my chest. The shackles were unlocked, and I was free to believe in myself again. All year I had been a failure, blasted in the media as a letdown and on his way out. But in that moment, I was the hero.

Then minutes after I exited, somewhere between congratulatory butt slaps and getting my arm in ice, my relievers handed the game away. A hit batsman, a walk, a single, a sacrifice . . . We lost the game three to one.

The movie theme music screeched to a halt, the dream burned up like flash paper. When the last out was made, we watched as the other team surged onto the field, dancing around like wild men. They screamed and hugged and waved their jerseys overhead. Fans roared, music blared, cameras clicked to immortalize it. All we could do was sit in silence, too crushed to speak. That was supposed to be us; I was going to be the star.

Long after everyone made his way into the locker room, I remained sitting in the dugout, staring into nothing. I was too numb to move. It wasn't supposed to end up like this, but once the ball leaves your hand . . .

In that moment, I got my first taste of hate for the game I loved. My entire life I had been told that hard work and hustle could get you anywhere you wanted to go. There were always obvious exceptions to the rule, top-dollar assholes who fueled ESPN showcasing how they squandered their talent and resources, but I blocked them out. I thought baseball was a pure thing, magical, bigger than the men who made it. I thought it was fair. Turns out that baseball is a lot like gambling. I had gone all-in with my beliefs. I bet the house on that championship start, and in those final innings, when it looked as if I was going to win everything back and then some, I got beat on the river.

A manager once told me, you don't have to be a big leaguer to play a big-league caliber game. He said players all through the minors play like big leaguers while some players all through the big leagues play like minor leaguers. On any given day spectacular things can happen in this profession. It's a game of luck and opportunity. Thus, we work hard so that we can make the most of things when they fall in our favor, have no regrets when they don't. Sometimes a player puts it together at the right time even if he isn't the most talented, and sometimes the most talented players fall apart when the spotlight is on them. Call it luck, call it opportunity. The bottom line is, you always have a chance if you have a jersey on your back. What you do with that chance, is a different story.

Chapter One

I toed the rubber, turning my foot to that unique angle that marks my set position—a deep breath, shoulder wiggle, and complete focus. Ball in glove, locked and loaded.

Inner Dirk was talking, *"You're a winner, you're a tiger, a champion. You can do this, you will do this."* I felt awesome. I felt invincible. I felt as if I should be in a sports drink commercial. I was dominating this team, a complete force of nature punishing them from all angles, like throwing to blindfolded children. A grand symphony should have been playing in the background for my display of pitching mastery. At one point I could actually see myself from the outside, really digging myself, like an out-of-body moment of baseball Zen.

I adjusted my hat and took the sign from the catcher. I didn't like it, so I shook. I didn't like the next one either, or the next one, or the . . . "Come on man, I don't even throw a three, why do you keep putting three fingers down?" I shouted.

"I'm sorry, the other guys use three as their curve ball," he whimpered back. He didn't come out for a mound visit, yelling at me from across the expanse that separated us.

"Great. Thanks. Just *tell* the guy what I'm throwing why don't you! Besides, no one uses three for a curveball! Three is always a slider!" I said. The batter stood awkwardly, looking back and forth between the two of us, confused.

"Sorry, you don't have to throw it. We could throw your—"

"Use your fingers, not your mouth, okay?" *Stupid rookie.*

He squatted back down and adjusted his mask. I reloaded on the mound. *"I'm a winner. I'm a champion. I will do this. There is no try, only do or do not do. Wait, how did Yoda get in here? I'll bet he has a filthy changeup, a Jedi mind trick or something . . . What am I doing? Focus Hayhurst! You're a tiger. . . ."*

I set my feet again slowly. Then for the coolness effect, I lifted my head to lock on with the catcher's fingers. Fastball. Just what I wanted. Why waste good breaking stuff on these losers when all I needed was good old numero uno to sit them down?

I nodded, then started my windup—left foot back, hands up over head, rock, pivot, knee up, and then a ferocious uncoiling down the slope to where I let loose.

In slow motion you'd see the batter's hands go back taking the bat to its proper position. You'd see my front foot land in the precise location I practiced repeatedly in front of a mirror. You'd see my torso rotate, level and clean with no balance issues. You'd see the batter's foot go up as he began to channel his weight for max power. You'd see my elbow give way to my hand as it snaps a screaming fastball into motion. It would all look so flawless, so magical, so poetic. It would leave you scratching your head, wondering how in the hell I could look that good and still drill a poor high school kid in the ribs at around ninety miles per hour.

You know that dull thud sound—the one a blunt object makes when a person gets hit real good? It made that sound. He went down hard, convulsing between screams of pain as he writhed on the floor.

"Ah, Jesus," I whispered behind my face-covered glove. "I'M SORRY!" *I knew I should have made him sign that liability waiver. . . . Way to go, Jedi Master.* The kid was crying now. Not all-out tears but enough water was leaking out to show he was feeling all four seams. I thought we were going to have to put him down, shoot him like a lame horse.

The catcher, continuing his streak of helpfulness, came to the rescue with the comment, "Don't rub it."

"Nice job, meat," Mazz said from the next cage over. He'd been tossing batting practice to one of his clients, a big, beefy, future lesbian, the entire time I was throwing live batting practice to this group of high schoolers. This was his place, the perfect extension of his personality.

The joint was a run-down, former machine shop converted into a baseball lessons facility. The walls of the place had grease stains, and metal shavings littered the floor. The windows were old and single paned, holding in little heat. Mazz turned the heaters on only rarely, kept the minimal amount of lights, and didn't think painting over the dismal gray walls was cost-effective.

The track record for indoor baseball facilities in the area was poor. Mazz had been doing great because he only worried about the necessities. No paint, dim lighting, heaters kept slightly above freezing—it all averaged out to less overhead. He was a Scrooge with his own economic rules, which I called Mazzenomics. He was a good hitting coach, but a ruthless businessman, which is why he made such good money doing lessons. A little extra money and the place could look respectable instead of the baseball equivalent of punching beef in a meat locker, but with lessons second to none, people put up with the substandard conditions.

Mazz played pro ball for several years, then coached it, and then coached college ball. Currently, he was coaching an independent team called the Washington Wild Things when not peddling lessons. Since his life had been spent in the game, his default tone was that of the thick-skinned ballplayer crowd where "What's up assbag?" is just as good as hello. He's never been away from the game long enough to be in any danger of civilizing himself, so screwing up in front of him still warrants high school, bully-style chastisement.

"I wasn't trying to hit him. It was an accident," I said.

"I know you didn't mean it. That's why you've got a career 7.00 ERA—poor command."

"It's not a seven, it's . . . well it's not a seven."

"It's a six, you're right. That's *way* better."

I never played for Mazz, but he told me I would soon. "Don't worry," he'd say, "you can still be the ace of the Wild Things after you get released this year." He tells me that every year, mercifully, as if the thought of him as my manager should somehow make me feel blessed.

"You know, it probably wouldn't have stung so bad if you'd turn on the heat in here."

"You guys are here to train. Exercise makes its own heat. If you were working hard, you wouldn't even feel the cold," came the Mazzenomics principle in response. The boy continued moaning on the ground.

"Just like if my lungs were tough from working hard, I wouldn't feel the iron shavings chewing them up?"

"Exactly." Mazz nonchalantly flipped another ball to the war club of the she hulk.

I walked over to the boy I drilled, who, with the help of his coach, was on his feet now and trying to walk it off. The blow was to his ribs, but baseball law requires players to walk off all wounds, even those not related to walking. When I got beside him, I slapped him on the butt and said, "You alright kid?"

"Yeah, I'm okay," he squeaked, trying to act tough. I probably scarred him for life, and he was only a sophomore. He'd never crowd the plate again, that was for sure.

He and the rest of the high schoolers, whom I subjected to this face-off, didn't realize what a favor they were doing for me. I wasn't going to tell them I needed them or that I felt bad about the beaning. I'm a pro; I have an image to maintain. I had to remain strong and impassive like some general. Part of war is casualties, and part of baseball is hit batsmen. If I acted too concerned, it would look as if I weren't in control.

"Hey man, my bad," I offered magnanimously. "I just wanted to brush you back. I was afraid of your power. Didn't mean to come in that far." No need to tell him the pro guy missed his spot by four feet. "If I gave up a hit to you, I'd never hear the end of it." And I'd feel like a complete joke. If Opie here got a knock off me, I might as well call the Padres and tell them I'm done and save them the trouble. Pro pitchers should never give up hits to fifteen-year-olds who weigh as much as the bat they swing.

Now that we were talking, I tried a little misdirection, some smoke and mirrors to change the subject from potential lawsuits. "Go grab a Gatorade, it's free today," I said, squeezing his shoulder as if we were pals. Sugar still distracts kids up to at least age eighteen. I think.

"No, it's not!" Mazz said, cawing from his cage. He was still sacrificing balls to the she-wolf, but he never missed a beat of my conversation.

"I'll pay for it you cheap bastard."

"Then I'll take it out of your next lesson," A buck fifty spent to make a wounded soldier feel better, and he was itemizing it like Satan's CPA.

The boy walked over to grab a cold one out of Mazz's mini fridge. The big softball orc smiled at him. From the way she looked him up and down, I couldn't tell if she thought he was cute—or edible. The rest of the group followed suit, grabbing more Gatorades that I also ended up paying for. Mazz said happy customers are good for business, but he was only saying that because I was paying for their happiness.

I wanted to keep throwing to hitters, but the boys lost their nerve after watching one of their own reduced to tears. I only had a week before spring training, and this would be my last chance to pitch to live bats before shoving off. However, with no one brave enough to stand in, I had to settle for a standard practice session, tossing openly discussed pitches to the genius behind the plate for the remainder of our time

As I threw, the boys stood sipping their Gatorades outside the cage, watching me do my thing. Their coach pointed at me during key points in my delivery, going as far as to mimic my motion at certain points. Some of the other boys followed suit. It's a good thing they didn't know much about the business of baseball, or they'd see something completely different.

One year had passed since that 3–1 loss in the Cal League finals. During the following season of 2006, I managed to climb up to Double-A, even a short stint in Triple-A. I was, on paper, a Triple-A pitcher, something I could proudly declare whenever asked about my level of experience.

What I couldn't say, however, is that I earned it. My promotions were gilded. Dig a little and you'll discover I really didn't have any tangible success last year. I had poor stats in Double-A. Atrocious ones in Triple-A, and despite my good ERA in High-A, I had a win/loss record of 1–7. I didn't move up because I was a prospect—quite the opposite actually.

Injuries and call-ups drained all the talent from the system. I, not being a priority guy the club felt like focusing on anymore, was the perfect choice to hop around the system and mop up spilt innings. At one time, the Padres may have kept me securely planted on the developmental track. That was back when I was an All-Star in the Midwest League and a choice conversational piece for media covering up-and-comers in the Padres organization. I was someone to watch out for then. Now four years into my pro career, I was tagged with lines like washout, roster filler organizational guy. The only all-star team I belonged on was the winter batting practice bruisers who bean high schoolers in rusty machine shops. Maybe not even that.

In four years, I'd failed to impress the people who do the promoting. I was a cold product, and folks who knew the game from the inside, folks like Mazz, knew where a guy like me, an aging, senior college signee with a small bonus and unattractive career numbers, was headed.

Mazz understood how the game works. He knew the outward appearance of success was just that, the appearance of it. He knew I was trying desperately to make sure people didn't know the rest of the story, and he loved to call me out on it.

Sure, the game isn't fair and guys who don't deserve it move up all the time. Several players in my situation have hopped up levels, paying no thought to the opportunity or to the way they got it, only to have a run of unprecedented success. I wish I could say I was one of those players.

The vast majority of people who love this game care only for big-time players with big-time numbers. I wasn't one of those, but I was faking it as best I could. The way I carried on, you'd never know I was back in the same situation I was a year ago, standing at the edge, staring into the pit of my career's end. For all the Gatorade-sipping boys knew, I was shooting through the system. Three levels in one year. Triple-A time was just a step away from the big leagues. Sounds impressive, especially when presented in a way that, again, misdirected attention from the whole truth. Yet, no matter how much smoke, mirrors, or sugary sports drinks I used, I couldn't misdirect the truth away from myself. Every opportunity I had last year, I failed to impress. I was on my way out barring something inexplicable. As soon as the organization found a younger guy to do my job better, I'd get chopped, and there's always a younger guy.

The boys' coach pointed at me, "Watch his finish. See how he gets through each of his pitches?" He bent over in imitation, balancing on one leg.

"Yeah, he's going to look great in a Wild Things uniform isn't he?" Mazz said. He had finished his lesson and now came to mock.

"Why don't you grab a bat and stand in here, Mazz," I called to him.

"No thanks, I don't want to embarrass you in front of your fans," he said. "I might be older, but I can still turn on your eighty-six."

"I thought you said you threw ninety-two," the coach said.

"Whoops," Mazz said, tittering.

"I, uh . . . well . . . *I can*. I mean, I don't right now because it's cold and I'm still getting into shape and . . ." I stammered out some hyperbole on pitching that ended with, "Besides, velocity isn't everything, you know."

"Neither are K's or Wins, which you also don't have. Funny how that works." If I did have Jedi powers, I would use the Force to choke Mazz until his head popped off.

I ended my practice session with a dazzling array of big, loopy curve balls. The kids oohed and aahed over them; Mazz yawned. Finished, I strolled over and addressed my crowd. "Thanks for coming in tonight guys. I appreciate your time."

"It was our pleasure. I think the boys really learned a lot from hitting off you." I nodded and told him they looked good and had a lot of potential, which I would have said regardless. "Hey!" the coach said, forming his hand into a pistol and shooting me as he talked. "If you make it to the big leagues, we expect tickets!" If

I had a dollar for every time I got gunned down with that comment, I wouldn't need to make it to the bigs.

They left, and I went back to my cage to keep throwing, trying to make my pitches obey. Fastballs that wouldn't go down and away, curves you could hang on a coatrack, and a slider I had been tinkering with for years with no luck. I was trying to get better today, but I felt worse than when I came in. The ball felt wrong in my hand, and all the grips were like math problems I couldn't solve. The game didn't even feel right to me anymore.

Mazz, done for the night, said, "I'm leaving. Lock the place up, turn off the lights—"

"And turn off the heat, and enter the alarm, and make sure there's no penny unaccounted for, I know. I'll take care of it Ebenezer."

Mazz stopped and looked at me. In an extremely rare moment of genuine care, he dropped the surly routine and said, "Easy Dirkus, you can't force it. Relax."

"All the same, I'm going to stick around for a while and see if I can." It was kind of him to let me keep working. I won't deny, he did support me in his roundabout, borderline abusive way. Maybe he wasn't that bad after all.

"Well don't blow your arm out. The Wild Things can't use you if you have a bum arm."

Then again, maybe he was.

"I'll remember that—top of my priority list." Right under leaving the door unlocked, turning the heat all the way up, and dumping the rest of his Gatorades.

Away he went, turning out all the lights save for the one cage I was in. I stayed, who knows how long, alone in a cold, dark building, throwing sliders that wouldn't slide into a worn, plastic tarp, trying to figure out more than just pitching.

Chapter Two

When I woke up the next day, my arm was sore from throwing. I lost count of how many sliders I peppered into Mazz's tarps, but the big knot by my scapula and the stiffness in my elbow told me it was far too many for this time of year. I would've loved to have fallen blissfully back to sleep, let my body mend the way God intended it too, but the unholy antics of my housemate wouldn't permit me.

Considering how old my grandma was, you would think her house would be shaped more like a pyramid than a split-level with a leaky basement. God knows how long she'd been up, watching over her precious bird feeders. I honestly didn't think she slept. She just waited, hanging upside down in her room at night, devising more ways to make my life a living hell come sunup. Pounding on the storm door at squirrels at the crack of winter dawn was just the latest development on a long list of tortures.

I rolled over and read the alarm clock: 6:30 A.M. The sight of those cruel digits incited instant fury. Lying with my arms spread wide on the air mattress, my angry face aimed toward the heavens, I screamed at the top of my lungs, "SHUT UP, GRANDMA!"

She continued to bang. She'll pretend she didn't hear me when I ask her, but her hearing is never an issue when she stands outside my door, eavesdropping on my phone calls. In an attempt to drown out her noise, I pressed a pillow over my ears. That didn't work, so I tried to suffocate myself with it instead. That didn't work either.

Moments later she burst into my room. "Where's that gun of yours?"

"Why?" I asked, pulling the pillow from my face. "Are there terrorists in your bird feeders?"

"I'm going to shoot 'em! Give me that gun," she said, referencing my pellet gun. I'd shoot up soda cans with it every now and then to blow off steam. Sometimes pretending the cans were her face. She'd taken it before, while I was sleeping, and tried to shoot the squirrels but ended up shooting up the whole neighborhood because her hands shook so badly. My parents had to confiscate the old shotgun she brandished for the same reason.

"I'm not giving you that gun. The squirrels aren't hurting anyone."

"They're plotting something. I know it."

I stared at her blankly. "You've lost your mind."

"Oh, you are good for nothing! You get out of that bed and get those things out of my feeders if you're not going to give me that gun."

"No. It's six thirty in the morning! Let them finish breakfast and they'll leave." I rolled over, but she remained standing there, burning holes in my back. I couldn't sleep with her hexing me, so I rolled back to face her. "I know. Why don't you throw one of the seventy chocolate cakes you bought on sale out there? Try and make friends."

"I bought those cakes for you!" she wailed.

"The squirrels can have my share as a peace offering."

She shook her head at me in a disdainful manner. "The way you talk to me," she seethed, "after all I do for you."

And boy, does she do a lot for me.

My laundry, for example. She still uses a wringer washer, a testament to the time period she's stuck in, in which she threshes my clothes. The wringer sits in the basement like some beast lurking in the dark, waiting for her to feed it my wardrobe with a tall, cool jar of lye soap to wash it down. To date, that machine has mangled melted, or consumed enough fabric to cover a third-world country.

She cooks for me too, mainly because I am forbidden to use the kitchen. She's appointed herself my personal chef, which is more akin to kitchen dictator. She oppresses me with bacon-grease-injected marathon meals chanting, "You're a growing boy, calories aren't going to hurt you!" The grease I don't consume is repurposed into the soap used in her first charitable act.

Some days I don't eat. I can't risk getting her started. She pumps out food like a munitions factory during the war effort—high-calorie rounds of biscuits and gravy aimed directly at my heart. She'll hold me hostage until it's all finished, but it's never finished. At any given time, you can find six gallons of milk, fourteen boxes of cereal, and about one hundred pounds of canned fruit spread throughout the house's three refrigerators and eight pantries. There's enough freezer-burned meat to reconstruct a mastodon.

She shops on my behalf because she says she's such a *great* bargain hunter. She nabs great deals, and by "nabs" I mean she takes everything on the shelf in one swoop. She'll come home with a trunkful: eight chocolate cakes, seventeen loaves of bread, and six gallons of orange juice, all "marked down for a limited time." You could sit her down and explain it all to her, that we beat the commies and the local supermarket won't be destroyed by a nuclear attack, but it makes no difference—she won't stop. When turkeys go on sale, it'll be Thanksgiving at her house for the next nine days. It'll be for me anyway, and as long as I keep eating it, she'll keep buying. I'd gladly invite you over to help me get it all down, but she hates you.

She hates pretty much everyone I know and is never shy about telling why. She hates all the presidents, all her doctors, the family, the guy packing groceries at the Food 4 Less, my girlfriends. None of them can do anything right. She hates the neighbors enough to aim that shotgun I told you about out the window when they set foot on her property. She's developed colorful nicknames for the folks on the block, like the endearing bunch across the lawn she commonly refers to as "that no-good pack of lying, hillbilly Satanists!"

The Satanic hillbillies, who own three large, friendly dogs, used to mow my grandma's yard for free until she stepped in dog poop. You should have heard the rant that started. She swore the hillbillies were training the dogs to hold their poop and leave it in great big piles in her yard—mountainous piles, dinosaur turds that suck your foot in like a tractor beam.

She threatened to call the cops on the dogs. Then she threatened to call the cops on the neighbors. Next, she threatened to kill the dogs. Then she threatened to kill the neighbors. It wouldn't be long until there was freezer-burned dog in the fridge.

She provided a roof over my head, and for that I'm thankful, but my life with her is far from fantasy. She'll tell you she treats me like a prince. She'll tell you a lot of things. Like how she saved Einstein from the Nazis or the stretch of Underground Railroad beneath the house. What she won't tell you is how she keeps me in the sewing room, on an air mattress, with nothing but a card table and a suitcase.

My princely suite is filled with her precious treasures: heirlooms; boxes and boxes of worthless, bought-on-sale heirlooms she plans to pass on to us when she dies. I asked her if I could move a few of her artifacts out of "my" room in the meantime, and she told me no. I said I'd do all the work and she wouldn't have to lift a finger, but it was still a no. One day I decided to move one single thing: a broken exercise bike about ten years older than me. She called a lawyer when she found it was missing. She was going to sue me for the cost of one dilapidated early 1970s exercise bike. She said she was going to use it, and I had no right to throw away her things. I asked her how much long-distance biking she planned on doing at ninety-one years of age, and she told me to go to hell.

There is a real bed in the house, in one of the other junk-stuffed rooms. It's wedged in next to an old flannelgraph and books on how Stalin is the Antichrist. The bed is brand new, but I can't sleep on it. Not that she won't let me; rather, I can't because she won't let me take the plastic off the mattress or the pillows. Ever sleep on Saran wrap? Try it sometime—really opens the pores. I told her princes didn't sleep on plastic, and she told me to go to hell.

She said taking the plastic off was how things wore out and got dirty. I told her everything eventually wore out and got dirty. She said her things were still around because she took care of them. I told her some things had life expectancies on them, like people, hint, hint.

She told me to go to hell.

"All those things you do for me. . . ." I said, being sure to look her straight in the eyes as I spoke. I learned long ago that you can't show weakness when you speak to her or she'll attack. I recounted the list of her services, including, but not limited to, bacon fat, lye soap, the Antichrist, lack of sleep, exercise bikes, and bullet holes. "Chocolate cakes are supposed to make it all better?"

Her face flushed red, and I thought her head would spin around like something from *The Exorcist*. Anger didn't help her looks much. Permanently hunched over like some evil scientist's assistant, if she wore a hood, she could get a job haunting bell towers.

She grabbed my door's handle and just before slamming it screamed, "If you've got it so bad, you can just move out!"

"Good luck with those squirrels."

"You can go to hell!" came her retort. See, I told you she could hear me through the door.

"Pretty sure I'm already there. . . ." I sighed, and flopped back onto my makeshift bed.

Five minutes later, I reluctantly got up and chased the squirrels out of her feeder in my underwear and pair of snow boots. She asked me what I wanted for breakfast as reward for my good deed. I told her I could really go for some chocolate cake.

We fight about the bedding, the food, the clothes, the neighbors, the squirrels, Harriet Tubman, and whatever else she can think up—every day, one futile battle after the next, always ending the same way. You know, Grandma's house, Grandma's law. If I don't like something she does, she tells me I can just move out, and, of course, she knows I can't.

This is my life now. I'm a poor twenty-six-year-old professional athlete who lives on the floor at his grandma's. I don't make enough money during the minor league season to afford living any other way in the off-season, and as long as I want to keep chasing my dream, I'll have to sacrifice. She's about as sweet as the living dead, but she's my sugar momma, and no matter how bad she treats me, I'll always keep crawling back to her.

My days start with mornings full of obscenities aimed at woodland creatures banging and screaming. I trudge through the snow and run the squirrels off, but they come back—rinse, lather, repeat. It appears the squirrels and I have a common enemy. I guess maybe we should work together. Someday I could leave the door unlocked and let them in when she's sedated, watching Judge Judy. They could ambush her. I'd act as if I didn't know anything. I'd feign devastation to the authorities and make a good sound bite for the local news. As soon as it all passed by, I'd throw the rest of the birdseed out, burn those feeders, and drive off into the night cackling maniacally. But, and this is no joke, she already suspects we're up to something.

Something about lying in my underwear with snow boots on while my right arm throbbed got me thinking. Suffice to say, this was not how I pictured my life as a professional baseball player. Me shacking up with the withered old puppet of evil I called grandma, hanging on to a crumbling dream while the world passed me by, is not how things were supposed to go.

There is so much you don't know when you get into the baseball business. You think you know it all. You've certainly seen enough of it on television to form an educated guess. But the stuff that happens on television isn't real, no matter how bad you want it to be. I thought signing a contract to play was going to be my promotion into the glamour lifestyle. I would walk down the street and people would whisper, "There goes Dirk Hayhurst, professional baseball player." Maybe they'd stop me for an autograph or ask me what it was like to be so awesome. I was going to live the big-league dream life. What the hell happened? Where were all the millions? Where were the luxury cars? Where was my first-class jet to paradise? Where was my dignity?

Instead, my career has crash-landed me on the floor of Grandma's sewing room. If this is a dream come true, then dreams come packed in mothballs, smell like Bengay, and taste like lard-flavored turkey leg. My dream has made me into a commodity, a product, only as valuable as the string of numbers attached to my name—like some printout stuck in the window of a used car. The reality of my professional baseball player's life is that most people have no idea who I am, nor do they care. The pay sucks, the travel sucks, the expectations suck, and, recently, I suck. Instead of gaining ground in life through my dream job, I've lost it. I'm further behind than when I started.

People always say they'd do anything to play professional

baseball. The feel of the grass, the smell of a hot dog, and all that other Disneyland bullcrap. Don't lecture me about the magic of the game; I'm all magicked out. I've heard every cliché, read every quote, watched every Disney movie about overcoming. I know what Hollywood fabricates the sports life to look like, and this ain't it. In real life there are no symphony scores playing in the background while we go through our moments of doubt. There aren't always coaches pulling for us or family members spouting inspirational soliloquies. Sometimes there's just you, your bed on the floor, and a mean old lady telling you to go to hell.

Sure, I smell the hot dogs, and I feel the grass, but I also smell the scent of urine splashed on the walls of the minor league tour bus while the coach seats dig into my ass. I see sugar-crazed gremlins lining park fences, begging for baseballs. I say no, and those cute, innocent, dreamy little faces cuss me out like the drill sergeant in *Full Metal Jacket*. Every two weeks my minor league paycheck affords me another round of value meals, and if I stay in the game long enough, I just might make as much as the high school dropout messing up my order.

I don't have a slick car or a nice condo. I don't have a designer wardrobe or a good investment strategy. I've been slaving away at this job for the last four years, heading toward my fifth, and the only thing I have to show for it is an uncanny ability to hit squirrels with snowballs.

This is my question—my giant, dinosaur-turd-sized question: How much longer do I want to keep living this *dream*? Truthfully, not very much. I know folks would say that walking away from such a great opportunity would be a mistake. But what if giving up some of the best years of your life for something that may never happen is the mistake? There comes a moment in life, no matter what your line of work is, when you have to step back and wonder if you're heading in the right direction.

Most baseball players are content to play until they have absolutely no chance left. In fact, I'd say that's the basic mindset: keep pitching, until your arm falls off or they tear the uniform from your back. However, I'm not most baseball players. I realize that if this doesn't pan out, I'm not going to have anything to show for it except boring stories of glory days.

While I lay there on my air mattress, some unremarkable Tuesday morning with snow and squirrels and screaming, I decided I'd start taking the necessary preparations to make my peace with baseball. I didn't want to quit, but I'd run out of good reasons to keep playing. I couldn't go on living like this, which wasn't really living at all. I needed to get out before too much of my life had collected alongside the other broken-down relics in Grandma's house. I just had one problem: I wasn't the only person wrapped up in this dream.

Chapter Three

Though my parents' house was only a few miles away in Canton, I didn't visit it very often. When I did, I didn't have to be there long before I was reminded why I stayed away. Yet, I had to come home, they deserved to know what I was thinking. My parents were there at the start of my baseball career, and they should know how it would end.

My dad sat at the kitchen table, smoke streaming up from the cigarette pressed in his off hand. I took a seat across from him and waited for a chance to talk. A gray smog had collected in the air above us, hanging there, dimming the light. He was so silent, one might suspect he was dead, stuck in place save for the way the smoke-filled air moved when he breathed.

I didn't know how long he was like that—minutes, hours, or days perhaps. The only way to measure was to check how much ash had accumulated in the tray in front of him. If I had to guess, he'd been motionless for about two hours.

Stomping could be heard upstairs. My mother and brother were moving about. The thumps came and went with long breaks in between—water running, toilet flushing, someone taking a shower. It was just a matter of time before they crossed paths.

I tried to think of something to say to my father as we sat, but how to begin? Small talk? Something light before telling him I really wanted to quit my dream and ruin the family's big hope of something better for just one of its members? What was there to say?

He had no life, nothing to chat idly about. On the off chance we did speak, he'd regurgitate television programs he'd watched. Some show on how things were made. That's all he did now. Unemployed, angry, unmotivated to live, he sat in front of the television or in the silent haze of a cigarette. We've passed a lot of hours like this: neither of us talking, both sitting in front of his television drug.

My mother's voice broke in above us. The sound of my brother's retort followed—yelling ensued, foot stomps, more yelling. Refreshed, they'd awoken to resume the fight. As much my mother's fault as anything, she couldn't let it go. I'm not sure I blame her, but since she was unwilling to lock him up, the fighting would just meet the same result it always did.

Today was Saturday. My brother was probably drunk last night. Came home late to my mother, who stayed up to ambush him about his debauchery. They fought, maybe something got broken, maybe someone got hit, maybe both. My dad, unwilling to stay in bed and listen, would get up and start screaming at the both of them in a voice that made you wish the world would end. Then, when he couldn't take it anymore, he'd implode, start to cry, and wish he were dead—maybe more than wish, maybe try again. He'd say he hated his life, hated the family, hated everything. Upon losing her ally, Mom would turn on Dad. She'd say he needed to toughen up, quit being a baby, and act like the man she used to know.

Vindicated, my brother would laugh mockingly, calling them both fuckups, horrible parents, the reason for his drinking. And then there would be more screaming, more breaking, and more hitting, followed by a call to the cops, not to make an arrest, but to scare away the drunk. He'd leave, wreck his car, stumble back, and pass out on the floor in his own vomit. Come morning, when he was hung over, the fight would continue.

My dad sighed at the sound, lifted his head from his hands, and snuffed his cigarette into the ashtray. He was both as sad and angry as a person could be; you could see it when you looked at him, the way his body worked as if under some heavy, invisible weight.

Acting on the urge to leave, he reached down to put his shoes on. His crippled hands grabbed at them with all the finesse of a rusty wrench. Next, he reached for a wooden spoon, his makeshift shoehorn. He attempted shoeing his feet into his Velcro shoes, but the simple motion was too complex and he dropped the spoon. He tried to pick it up, but his fingers would not grab as instructed. Extreme frustration trumped the sadness that kept him in check and he exploded.

"Goddamn worthless fucking hands!" he screamed. Then he began clubbing his hands into the table with the same force someone would smash dry tree limbs. He couldn't feel the blows, the same reason he couldn't feel the shoes or the spoon. Repeatedly, he beat his hands until the frustration gave way to sadness again; then he began to sob. He slumped back into his chair defeated, head in broken hands, heaving.

At one time he built million-dollar machines. Perfect lines of metal intersecting in perfect mathematical harmony. He drafted things, complex mechanical things that would themselves build more complex mechanical things. All of it, pristine, flawless, designed never to break. Now the man behind all that perfection was broken. He couldn't even tie his shoes, Velcro shoes.

I said nothing. I hadn't spoken the entire time I was there—not even hello. I was a spectator in my own home. I was slowly remembering what drove me out in the first place to fight my way toward the big leagues into a better life.

The battle above us stopped. My mother must have detected my father's outburst. She made her way downstairs, rounded the corner into the kitchen, and stood with her hands on her hips, staring at him, a puzzled look on her face. I could see the remnants of compassion in her eyes, deeply buried beneath a layer of resentment, as if her emotions moved away years ago, leaving the place to deteriorate.

She surveyed the two of us. Then, looking to me, she asked, "What's wrong with him?"

I shrugged.

"Sam," she said, turning to my father, "what's the matter?"

No answer.

"Sam, tell me what's wrong."

"Nothing, just leave me alone."

"Tell me what's the matter. What happened? What was all the banging?" At one time, she asked the question in a sweet and caring way. Now, after years of no change, she was tired of being Mary Poppins about it. She asked in a sterile, near annoyed way.

"Nothing, goddamn it, just leave me alone!" my father roared.

My mother sighed. "What's wrong with him?" she asked, looking at me.

"He couldn't get his shoes on," I said, but that wasn't what she was really asking.

"All this screaming and banging because you couldn't get your shoes on? Jesus, Sam."

Anger began to win over my father again. He was so volatile—explosive one moment, despairing a second later. One more push and he'd blow, and this little family reunion would turn into chaos.

My brother began his way down the steps. His footfalls were much heavier than my mother's. He rounded the corner, nudging her out of the way with his beer belly. Full of attitude, he now stared at the head of the house, laughing to himself like some movie villain at the failed attempts of those who would overthrow him. "What the fuck's your problem?" he asked.

I'll answer that one. My dad fell from the roof of our house while he was laying shingles. He fell headfirst, dropping twenty-odd feet before crashing into the rough ground below. He shattered his nose and blew out disks in his neck and back.

I can remember it all, like a memory recalled at the site of a scar. I was the only one home at the time. I heard my father shout, tumble, and hit. I ran from the house to see what had happened and found my father motionless, a pool of blood forming around his face. I asked him if he was okay, even though I knew he wasn't, but what else is there for a thirteen-year-old son to ask?

He told me, in gurgles and gasps that he couldn't feel his body, that he couldn't move. He told me to walk away, to leave him because he was dying, and he didn't want me to have to see it. I ran into the house and punched 911.

He wouldn't walk again for two years. After all the rehab, when he could finally stand on his feet without assistance, he was a different man. A shell of one, not the father we had grown to love.

Outsiders would tell me I should be thankful he could walk, what a blessing it was, and all that jazz. I didn't feel that way about it. Maybe I should've, but it wasn't like the feel-good stories used to sell bracelets with trendy slogans. My dad could walk, but he did so like Frankenstein. He couldn't feel his hands or his feet. His bowels didn't wait for his consent to go. His vision suffered and his flexibility disappeared. He couldn't tell whether he cut his legs or whether he was bleeding. He slept with constant discomfort and medicated himself heavily. When the pills stopped working on their own, he began mixing them with alcohol. The mighty perfectionist was unequipped to deal with his new imperfections. He was disgusted with everything, including himself.

For a time, things plodded along. It seemed as if, despite all of my father's issues, the family would survive. Things were hard, but we were getting the hang of it. Then dad lost his job—the salary, the benefits, the sense of purpose were all gone. His hands, cumbersome and mangled, could not work the computer keys like they once did. When the company he worked for restructured itself, my dad was restructured by a fresh college graduate with no experience for half the salary.

The termination snuffed out the last remaining pieces my father had to build with. He could not work and so he felt useless. Having already reconciled the demise of his sports hobbies, no longer a softball or basketball player, he was at least a valued member of his work team. Now he was nothing. Coming from the generation that did not require degrees to get a job, any hope my handicapped, undereducated father had of competing in the present market was gone. He had lost his employer and the rest of his identity.

My mother's job supported us while my father looked for work. Then she too was fired. Suddenly, we had nothing but a few waning months of unemployment. My dad had to take manual-labor jobs and simply could not keep up with the work pace. He was let go from all of them.

My brother turned to the bottle to help him cope. He fell into alcoholism about as hard as my father fell from the rooftop. He was a mean drunk, violent and irrational. He'd toss my crippled father aside like a rag doll. He'd smack my mother, choke her, and knock her down. He'd flat out beat the shit out of me. He put my head through picture frames, through coffee tables, and into hospital beds. He hated me because I was the family golden boy, sheltered by the success sports had brought me. I was the enemy—a relationship I'd become accustomed to.

My brother spent a lot of his early life getting into trouble. He had a poor self-image. ADD and a cleft pallet can do that to a person. When he grew up, failed relationships and drunk-driving charges galvanized him. He was convinced he was a bad egg because all his endeavors met with disastrous results. He dreamed as big as any kid, yet always found himself in situations where no one understood what he was dealing with. *Why isn't he normal? Why doesn't he look like the other kids? Why can't he stay on task?* And, maybe worst of all, *Why can't he be more like his brother?* He would come to wear judgment around his neck like a scarlet letter. The only time he felt relief was when he was drunk.

And so it went. Some days were worse than others, but so common was the domestic violence that the neighborhood cops knew us on a first-name basis. They'd show up and ask if anyone wanted to press charges, and my parents would both say no. When we got hurt, they'd lie about it. We wanted everyone to think we were normal, to keep up appearances. We had a great athlete in the family from a functional home. Nothing was wrong.

Once, when I was so tired of getting my head busted, I made up my mind I was going to lock up my brother and get it over with. I would put an end to the drama. My mom got on her knees and wept at my feet, soaking my ankles with her tears, begging me not to. I told her I had to. It needed to be done because we couldn't keep living in fear of him. She told me I was just as bad as my brother and threw me out. I grudgingly dropped the charges, but I refused to live at home again. I packed up my tiny ship of dreams and set sail for the horizon. Instead of a bright future, I ran aground on the other side of the city, minutes away from my high school, employed in a run-down machine shop, living under the roof on my grandma's asylum.

Today I made a pilgrimage back my parents to talk baseball or rather to talk about quitting baseball. Yet watching them tear each other apart, I didn't have to ask why I should keep playing. If I did it for no other reason than just to escape my home life, it was reason enough.

I stood up from the chaos and walked through their battlefield, out the door, and into the winter wind. I stood in the drive, listening to the echoing shouts, watching them through the window, wondering how to fix it.

There had to be more than this, more to life than titles and jobs and roles to fail at. My father was a broken heap without a purpose. My brother was a drunk and branded a failure—my mother, a victim. What title would brand me? Was I to be the baseball player who didn't make it? Would I always wear the jersey of a career minor leaguer? Would I be remembered as a washout, a failure, or a nonprospect?

I wanted to find out what I should do with my life from here on. I wouldn't find it in the chaos of my family. I wouldn't find hope there either, just a reason to put my key in the ignition and drive on.

Chapter Four

That night, after I met with my family, I lay on my air mattress at Grandma's, flicking a baseball up into a cloud of swirling thoughts. I sent the ball back spinning in tight, four-seam revolutions, trying to see how close I could make it come to the ceiling without striking it. Next, I tried to make the ball spin like a slider, seams forming a tight, red dot, indicative of a well-spun punchout pitch. The ball clumsily wobbled up and thunked against the ceiling, then wobbled back down. I caught it on the return; then, irritated, I heaved it into an open suitcase across the room. My bags were packed, though I had no idea why. I couldn't fix my slider, I couldn't fix my career, and I couldn't fix my family. Spring training was around the corner, and the only reasons I had for going was it was better than being at home.

Someone once told me a great way to take your mind off your own problems was to help people with theirs. I'm sure it was some great spiritual leader who said it, the kind who frequents mountaintops and deserts for perspective. I could use some perspective myself. Unfortunately, Ohio doesn't have any topographical features that lend themselves to enlightening breakthroughs. Even so, the idea of helping someone was appealing to me, if not for perspective, then at least to know that there were some things in the world I could fix.

The next day, after a lard-soaked marathon breakfast, I made my way to a homeless shelter on the eastern edge of Canton called the Total Living Center, or TLC. It sits in a run-down area on the tip of the city's sprawl, surrounded by project homes and government housing. Cops patrol the streets at all hours, and I swear I always hear emergency sirens echoing in the distance when I drive through the area.

I should tell you, this wasn't my first time volunteering at TLC. I started doing it a few months before because, to be perfectly honest, I thought it would make me look good. I can't blame all my actions on the institutionalizing of pro baseball, but one thing a public opinion–based job had taught me was that appearances meant something. Just like people assume things when they hear the words "pro baseball player," they assume things when they hear "volunteers at a homeless shelter." The words conjure visions of caring and self-sacrifice: humility, mercy, and charity.

All I did was take names. I sat at a desk by the door, signing people in, making sure too much warm air didn't escape, doing a job a pencil on a string could have managed. I was a regular Mother Theresa. Originally, I wanted to fly over to Calcutta and help heal people who got bitten by tigers or by whatever they had over there. I didn't research the topic that well; I just thought I should go. When I found out how much it would cost to buy a plane ticket, I had to settle for working at the shelter a couple miles from my house. It wasn't exactly playing baseball with the kids from the "just seven cents a day" style commercials, but it was better than sitting on my hands, I guess.

The experience was a letdown, actually. Taking names at the local shelter wasn't as dramatic or as awe inspiring as picking fleas off people who speak in clicks and pops. No witch doctors grabbed my head and prophesied my fastball's future. No women with rings in their noses fell in love with me. No one thanked me for saving his life with my semicelebrity presence, and I didn't walk away from the place transformed, ready to market Kabbalah water.

Today I sat at the shelter's door, lethargically making clicks and pops with my pen. Most of the folks who came for the shelter's meal and grocery handouts had already shuffled in. I signed them in, as usual, directed them to the meal, and then closed the door so the winter air didn't leak in. There wasn't much else for me to do except twiddle my pen, wrestle with my thoughts, and wait for the remainder of my time playing benevolent saint to pass.

In hopes of jump-starting an enlightening experience, I brought a collection of my minor league baseball cards. I had this ingenious idea to bring cards so I could sign them for the people who frequented the place. I got the notion because a lot of people asked me for cards once they found out what I did. Some thought it would be worth money someday, if I made it big. Some wanted a card to commemorate their brush with a quasi-famous person. Most wanted it so they could pass it on to their kids. Whatever the reason, there was an undeniable ego stroke from doing it. Someone was asking me to sign a picture of myself like a person would ask a movie star or Pamela Anderson. I thought every smiling face that asked for one of my cards would inspire me to keep soldiering on in my career.

In the same pocket I kept my cards, I kept the meal tickets—nothing more than worthless shards of scrap paper you could forge at home. In my boredom, I plucked one of my cards free and looked it over. It wasn't a great picture of me, my face was puffed out like a blowfish and my hair desperately needed a cut. I wished I had a more impressive picture, let alone stats. I didn't even bother reading the back side where words like "Hayhurst ranked among the top 200 pitchers in the Cal League in ERA and mound visits" were inscribed.

I placed the card back into my jacket pocket and resumed clicking my pen. The door of the center opened, and the room filled with a gust of frigid air. In hobbled a ragged, old man. His face was worn, weathered like cracked leather. His eyes were dull and gray, sunk into his face. He looked like some old prospector who lived his life on the edge of humanity back during the years when the West was wild. Multiple layers of clothing, all of them stained with what looked like dirt or grease, made a patchwork outfit that shielded him from winter's bite. His scraggly beard was matted and tangled in clumps and knots. A green stocking cap covered his head, the top pulled up high like a cartoon elf. His pants were filthy, splattered with road salt toward the bottom and well into the later stages of fray. Slung over his shoulder was a stuffed sack, bulging with lumps on every side. He pushed his forearm across his face and snorted.

"Good afternoon," I said with a big beaming smile. I was clean, well dressed, and ready to sign for such an obvious charitable cause.

This was his lucky day, and I knew it. He didn't respond to my greeting, but walked over to the desk in a side-to-side motion, continually smearing his hands on the sides of his outfit as he came. He took my offered pen, hunched over the table, and began to sign.

"Will you be dining with us tonight, or just here for some groceries?" I asked in a saccharine-sweet voice.

The ragged man coughed, finished scribbling his name, then let the pen drop. He mumbled to himself, wiping his hands on his sides again.

"Will you be eating with us today, sir?" I repeated.

"Yeah, yeah. What ya havin'?" He traced the architecture of the room as he spoke, like an animal measuring its cage.

"We are having yummy roasted chicken with noodles," I said.

Then I added in the same camp counselor voice I used earlier, "It's mmm-mmm good."

"Shit, ain't as if it matters. . . ." His voice trailed off and he returned to mumbling to himself.

"Well, Phyllis and the girls are fantastic cooks, and I'm sure you'll love it." I beamed back at him.

It was as if I were Willy Wonka. Everything I said was uttered with an über-excited ring, as if eating chicken and noodles were orgasmic. "Well, you certainly seem excited about it," the ragged man said. "Can I have my tickets now?"

"Oh, right." I reached into my pocket and grabbed for the meal tickets. I felt a baseball card's stiff, cardboard backing, and I pulled it out instead.

"I don't know how to tell you this, but, *I* am a professional baseball player. I pitch in the minor leagues with the San Diego Padres." I'm surprised I didn't brush my nails on my shirt after I said it.

"Uh huh."

"I brought some of my cards with me. I can sign one for you if you like."

"*You* are a professional baseball player?" the man asked.

"Yes, sir, I am," I said, as if I were allowing him admission to a very elite club.

The ragged man reluctantly took the card from my hand, looked at both sides as if it were a shiny rock, then tossed it back down in front of me. I watched the card as it twirled down and spun on the table.

"There," he said, as if he had done me a favor.

"Do you, uh . . . do you want me to sign one for you? A lot of people like that kind of thing."

"No."

"Are you sure? I mean, I am a real pro athlete."

"No."

"I'll go ahead and sign one for you and you can give it to your wife or son or . . ."

His eyes came out of the dark clefts of his dense silver eyebrows. His face, so worn and beaten, still had such intensity. "Look at me kid. What in the hell am I going to do with a goddamn baseball card?"

"I, uh . . . I just thought it would make you feel good," I said, and then smiled.

"Make me feel good?" he heckled. "I live on the goddamn street!"

"Well, I know, but—"

"Do you know why?" he interrupted. I did not, and my blank expression proved it.

"'Course you don't, why the hell would you bother to find out?"

" . . ."

"My wife got sick. I lost my job, and our insurance went with it. With no insurance, we couldn't afford to keep her in medicine. Then"—if he was remorseful, it was buried in his frustration—"she died, 'cause I couldn't get a job to pay for treatment. We were married twenty years. Twenty years! I lost everything trying to keep her with me and now she's gone. I got nothing and nobody. I walk around, and everyone thinks I'm on the street 'cause I'm some crackhead or something. I live handout to handout, and you think you're just gonna fix it all with your goddamn baseball card?" He stared right through me, his words stealing the noise out of life around us. Then he picked my card up and looked at it again. "Oh, you look real good underneath that jersey, don't you? Not a care in the world." Then he crumpled the card in his dirty hand, and tossed it at me. "You can keep your bullshit card."

All I could muster was, "I'm sorry."

"You can keep that too!"

I sat at the table, trying to escape his gaze.

"Can't a man just get a meal here?" he bellowed. "I gotta get preached to before I can eat so I started comin' late. Now, I gotta listen to your bullshit about how great your life is?"

I fumbled in my pocket and pulled out his meal ticket as ordered. As I plucked it free, the entirety of my pocket's contents poured forth. Baseball cards and meal tickets splattered on the floor. Cards, worthless cards, with glossy pictures of an inconsequential idiot littered the space at our feet along with precious meal tickets written with a ballpoint pen on nothing more than shards of scrap printer paper.

I bent down on one knee and picked up the mess as fast as I could. The ragged man watched me labor at his feet. He wore black workman's boots that were falling apart. One boot had duct tape wrapped around it and both soles looked like blown-out tire treads.

"Looks like those shoes have had it?" My voice was back to normal. I must have found my natural tone somewhere in the mess on the floor.

The ragged man kicked out one shoe. "These pieces of shit? Bought 'em at the Super Walmart just a month ago. One month! They's already fallin' apart."

"Why didn't you take them back?"

"Won't let me. Didn't believe me, and I didn't keep the receipt neither—I finally got enough money to buy me some decent shoes and this is what I got." He mumbled curses, looking down at his feet.

This time of year in Ohio, the cold weather turns from snow to rain almost every other day. The ragged man's feet had to be wet; there was no way, with so many standing puddles of slush-filled water, he was keeping his feet dry.

I looked to my feet. I was wearing Bass Company boots, fancy leather workman's boots but not for working—they were too dressy. I got them a few years back with some extra Christmas money and kept them in fine condition, only wearing them when the weather necessitated.

"What size are your boots?" I asked.

"They're a ten."

It was in my brain. Something was pulling at me. Maybe it was always there, and I just did my best to tune it out. My mouth started talking, "You wanna switch?"

"What?"

"I'm asking you if you wanna swap shoes?"

The ragged man frowned at me as if I were playing a cruel joke. Then as if this was a bet he couldn't afford not to take, he wiped his face, tugged his matted beard, and said, "I'll switch, but you're the one getting the raw end of the deal here, pal."

"I'll be alright."

"Okay then," he said, and he wasted no time kicking off his mangled boots. I unlaced mine, slipped them off, grabbed the pair together gently above the tongue, and handed them to him. He kicked his across the floor to me to complete the trade. He placed my boots on his feet and tied them up.

"How do they fit you?"

"Real good, these are real good, and"—he took some steps—"fit perfect, like they was made for me." Reaching down, he pressed the tip of the boot to indicate where his toe snugly stopped. Then he almost began to smile, but stopped himself and eyed me with suspicion.

"Enjoy man. They're all yours."

His eyes and face changed, almost softening. The wildness left his countenance. He seemed like a person, like a man, a broken one but no longer disconnected. As cracked and cold as it was, his face began to warm. Maybe it was the way I viewed him now, maybe he was always that way.

"Thank you," he said, in voice of the most genuine appreciation I'd ever heard. "This is a great kindness you're doing." The rough grains of his voice had smoothed out, and for a second I thought he might tear up. Instead of speaking, he reached out a dirty hand. Without hesitation, I took his hand in mine, and we shook.

"Thank you," I said, stunned by it all. I gave him his meal ticket, and out of my life he walked in his dry, new boots, enroute to a chicken noodle meal that was mmm-mmm good.

Having nothing else to wear, I put on the ragged man's old boots. They were, as I expected, soaked through. The damp soles discharged icy water into my socks on contact, and I almost tripped when the blown-out soles caught the corner of the steps. Wet, cold, blown apart, those boots were the best shoes I'd ever worn.

I didn't know that man in rags, and he didn't know me, but we knew how to treat each other because of the clothes we wore. Yet, something deeper than stained rags, dirty hands, glossy pictures, and clean uniforms took place between us. In that moment, both awkward and perfect, something happened I didn't quite understand. For a moment the burden of baseball left my shoulders, and I wasn't a player to be labeled. Though I didn't understand it all right there, I knew my life in the game was going to change.

Chapter Five

My grandma didn't exactly come to see me off as much as she came to stare eerily at me one last time for good luck. She lurked by the open garage door, safe from the harmful rays of direct sunlight, watching me like some carrion bird, as if I might take a dump in her yard. I threw my big suitcase and my Padres-issued equipment bag in the back of the cab and smacked the top of the trunk signaling I was ready to go. Then, despite myself, I managed to play good grandson long enough to hug my grandma even though the risk of being bitten on the neck was considerable.

At the airport check-in counter, I was informed that my bags were both overweight by about ten pounds. It's hard to pack six months of stuff in one suitcase and an equipment bag. As I forked out one hundred dollars for the overages, I promised myself I'd ship my stuff next year. Then I recalled, I'd promised myself I'd do that last year.

Airplanes can be depressing, especially when you wind up with a middle seat between two chubby businessmen. When I boarded they followed me in, squeezing into the seats on the left and right of me and forcing me into that awkward game of chess involving armrest space. If this were a team flight, my compatriots and I would be smacking each other on the back of the head by now, ringing call buttons, annoying the stewardesses, and generally making asses of ourselves. There is safety in team numbers, a confidence not present when you're alone. As it was, I pretended I was a mime, and flipped open *SkyMall* magazine while the business brothers broke out their BlackBerrys.

While I marveled over *SkyMall*'s life-changing ingenuity, the brothers sparked up a conversation, speaking through me as if I were invisible, rambling on about widget sales and gross national product or something. Suddenly excited, they hit on some bar they knew in the area they were headed to and how they were going to get ripped, how there was a dancer there, and how if their wives knew about all of it, they'd be in the doghouse—again. They laughed very mischievously, like the Dukes of Hazzard business edition, and might have shared high fives if my head wasn't in the way.

I gave up on *SkyMall* and made a break for my iPod. I had to rummage through my carry-on to get at it, dredging up all the items I had packed in the process, including the worn chunk of leather I passed for a glove. When I took out my mitt, the Duke Brothers took interest.

"You a ballplayer?" Bo Duke asked from the window seat. He motioned toward my glove.

"Yeah,"

"College?"

"No, professional"

"Really?"

"Yeah, I'm reporting to spring training today."

"Oh, right on, man. What position do you play?"

"I'm a pitcher."

"Righty or lefty?"

"Righty, unfortunately."

"How long you been playing?"

"This is my fifth year."

"Hey Luke, this guy plays professional baseball, how about that?" He called to his buddy, but there was no way he couldn't have heard me as tightly as we were packed in.

"Oh yeah?" Luke Duke said from the aisle seat. "What position do you play?" he asked me, but the guy by the window answered.

"He's a pitcher"

"Righty or lefty?"

"He's a righty who wishes he were a lefty," Bo said.

"How long you been playing?"

"He's been playing for five years, Luke." I didn't even know the guy sitting next to me and already he was talking as if he edited my Wikipedia page.

"Got any time in the big leagues?"

"No, no time yet." I answered for myself.

"So you're just a minor leaguer then?"

What's that supposed to mean? "Just a minor leaguer?" *What are you, just a vacuum cleaner salesman?* "Yes, sir, I'm *just* a minor leaguer." I exhaled.

"Well, keep playing, never give up. You'll hate yourself for the rest of your life if you do. You'll wake up every day and feel terrible about it." He said it, and then sighed, shaking his head as if I just brought up a dead relative.

How was I supposed to respond to that statement? Did he really need to drop the "hate yourself for the rest of your life" line? There are a lot of people out there with sports-themed regrets, but this was a tad excessive. I nodded very mime-like.

"I'd still be playing today if I hadn't had kids," he continued, forcing an empty laugh before elbowing me in a "know what I mean" type way, but I didn't.

"Did you play pro for a while?" I asked.

"No, I got my girlfriend pregnant in high school and had to quit ball to get a job. The kid ruined my dreams of playing. Don't have kids. They wreck your life!" Again he laughed in an inside-joke kind of way, and again I didn't feel as if I was on the inside. I laughed with him to make him feel better.

"Yeah," he continued, "I was one of the best players on my high school squad. I was looking at colleges and was going to try for the pros, but life gets in the way, you know?"

"Yeah, that's a shame," I said. "Someone should really tell life to quit doing that."

"I had a knockout curve," he continued, staring off into dreamland, "and I had to have been throwing at least ninety miles per hour. We didn't have radar guns or nothing, but all the guys told me I was throwing real hard."

"Oh. Wow," I said, highly doubtful but mastering it.

"Yeah, she said she was on birth control, but I don't believe it. She knew I was going to be something special. She thought she'd just lock me down, you know?"

"Hmmm."

"My advice to you, buddy, don't trust women." He stopped and looked at me with a queer smile. "I'll bet a guy like you gets women after him all the time, what with being a ballplayer and all." He stared at me as if I had the power to possess women with my uniform. I thought about the only woman in my life, my grandma, and felt the urge to tell him she was available. Instead I said, "Oh you know it, man! *All the time*," and elbowed him back.

"Attaboy! Don't ever give it up son, trust me. Say, you know my cousin's kid has one hell of an arm. Do you think you could get me in touch with a scout to come watch him? I think he's got what it takes. I've been working with him. Taught him the old hook." He wrung his arm as best he could in our tight seating to demonstrate.

"Looks like a good one."

"Yeah, it's nasty."

"I'll bet."

"So, can you get me in touch with a scout?"

"Yeah, sure. We do that all the time." We never do that.

"What do I do, just give you my info then?"

"Yeah, I'll pass it on to the Padres for you."

"Ooh, the Padres?" he cringed.

"Yeah, why?"

"Um . . . I was hoping you could get the Yankees."

" . . ."

I spent forty-five minutes I'll never get back listening to Luke's life story before the plane touched down in Chicago. He handed me his card as we exited the plane. I threw it away as soon as he was out of sight.

The long connector flight to Phoenix had me sitting next to a senior couple. They wore big, Terminator-style sunglasses that covered up their whole head. They had to use the bathroom every fifteen minutes and kept complaining about how much they hated today's music compared to the good ol' days when you could understand lyrics and women didn't dress like hussies. When they saw my mitt, they asked me if I was a ballplayer. I told them it was a present for my kid brother in Arizona. I told them he was having an operation due to a rare disease called turf toe, and he was going to be off his feet for a while. Baseball was his favorite sport, so I got him the glove from this really nice, caring, and handsome pro pitcher named Dirk Hayhurst, who played for the Yankees. They said they'd keep an eye out for him. I told them my name was Eric Heater. They said it was shame I didn't play baseball with a name like that.

Chapter Six

Car after car came buzzing around the Phoenix terminal while I lingered in the shade, hiding from the high-voltage sun. Cops made people who loitered too long move; families hugged hello and good-bye. I stood curbside with my luggage looking for the Padres shuttle van, a plain, white, eighteen-passenger van, with one small sign that read Padres printed out on standard computer paper and taped to the bottom right of the windshield. About a half an hour after I landed, it scooped up me and a few others and whisked us to our team hotel.

The Padres' spring training hotel is a Country Inn and Suites nestled right up against the highway about fifteen minutes from the Peoria Sports Complex. It's a nice place, and everyone who was with the Padres before it relocated to the Inn and Suites says it's a palace compared with the dump the team used to be put up in.

I liked the hotel because it had free, fresh-baked cookies in a glass jar at the front desk. This year, the hotel desk also featured an eye-candy dish courtesy of a well-stacked blonde sporting a tight Padres' T-shirt. She smiled as I approached, my luggage in tow. Undoubtedly, she would become the object of regular player attention, fielding stupid questions, direction requests, package inquiries, pillow-fluffing needs, mattress-fluffing needs, and other after-hours activities.

I, for example, led off with, "Hi, I'm a player with the Padres. Can you tell me where the check-in is?" even though there were a series of bold signs clearly directing new arrivals, besides my previous years of check-in experience. Nevertheless, she gave me thorough directions in a giggly, bouncy voice that made it completely worth it.

I hefted my luggage to the conference room as directed. Inside were members of the organization's training staff, which doubled as secretarial staff this time of year, imprisoned behind stacks of papers.

Checking in for spring training can be a hassle. There's a heap of paperwork to be signed, answering questions ranging anywhere from "Do you have drug allergies?" to "Does it feel like razor blades when you pee?" I'm sure it's important to the organization to get all urinating habits out in the open, but the biggest part of check-in is getting a room and roommate.

There are only so many suites in the Country Inn and Suites, and a smart player spends the whole year kissing up to trainers to make sure he can score a suite with his buddy the following year. So when I hit the check-in room and met two new faces, I didn't see new trainer friends, I saw a year's worth of ass-kissing out the window.

"Name?"

"Hayhurst, Dirk." Upon my utterance, the questioner sifted through a pile of names and sheets, found my information, and marked me off as arrived.

"Do you have any suites left?" I asked, as he worked.

"I don't think so," he said, absently shuffling, "I think we gave them all out."

"Well, I hate to play the seniority card, but I've got five years in this hotel, and if I was ever going to use seniority to get a perk, it would be on this issue. I've been looking forward to a suite all off-season, and believe me, if you spent a whole winter at my grandma's, you'd look forward to it too. Besides, there can't be that many older guys in-house this year?" Most of the other guys in my age bracket were at big-league camp, found places outside the hotel, or were fired.

The trainers sighed and cycled through the rooms. I'd been grinding it out for half a decade, and if I wasn't going to make it out of this camp, at least I could have a nice winter vacation in Arizona in a room with a refrigerator and a goddamn microwave.

"We've got one left. Do you know Leroy Davis?"

"Yeah, I know Leroy. He snores like a semi truck—"

"It's the only one left. Him or no suite."

"Usually there are more, especially on the first day."

"This is the only one left. Yes or no?"

This may seem trivial, but in reality, it's pure economics. Players don't get paid in spring training; we get meal money. We get $20 a day, $120 a week after "clubbies" (clubhouse attendants) take their share. If you eat decent meals, you'll be broke by the end of the week. Even if you get a doggy bag, you can't bring it home with no place to store it. No suite means you'll have to go into your own pocket for food. Fine for a high draft pick, debt for everyone else.

There was a SuperTarget within walking distance of the hotel. With a suite, I could pick up a Pyrex bowl and buy pasta, soup, milk, and cereal. I'd be set. Spend forty bucks, pocket the rest, and come out of spring training in the black.

However, I also needed to sleep. Leroy didn't just snore; he had the septum of a wood chipper. He also has other "unique" tendencies that've earned him the nickname Larry the Cable Guy. For one, he looks just like him. For two, he acts just like him. His body is a refinery for dip, grease, domestic beer, and redneck humor. Larry, as we always referred to him, is not a drunk, but he's consistent. He's the type of guy who says he likes to have a beer with dinner and then a few for dessert. The more beers he has, the more he transforms into Larry the Cable Guy in looks and demeanor, and the louder his snoring gets.

He's a hell of a guy, as nice as a big friendly dog, with a streak of that country boy, do-anything-for-ya hospitality a mile wide. He's hard not to like, or at least laugh at, but living with him would require ear plugs and a strong tolerance to the smell of dip spit. Yet having lived with worse, I opted for the suite.

I parked my suitcase in the front part of my new home, where a table, a couch, and a kitchenette were located, but no Larry. In the rear part of the suite, where the beds were, I could hear a television turned to the unmistakable sounds of ESPN's *SportsCenter*. Littered across one of the beds was an empty Gatorade bottle containing a brown gravyesque liquid, a can of Kodiak, a Carl's Junior Bag, and a crumpled up sandwich wrapper. A Western Bacon Six Dollar Burger had been murdered here.

Like a trained detective, I knew the routine. The modus of minor league meals: get food, eat food, put in dip (the official diuretic of baseball), place hand down pants, watch *SportsCenter*, take a dump. This would explain why the suite's bathroom door was shut with the fan whirring from the inside.

Without disturbing the evidence, I made my way to the bathroom and knocked. No answer. I opened the door and immediately wished I hadn't. There, splattered all over the porcelain of the toilet bowl was the body of the Six Dollar Burger. The murderer had escaped without flushing.

It was getting late, and Larry still wasn't back yet. I was looking forward to seeing him, and reminding him what the little lever on the top of the toilet was for. He was probably out with some of the other boys, having a cold one, or four, to commemorate another spring training in the grind. A few beers would mean snoring, so I made a preemptive strike and dragged one of the mattresses from the bedroom portion of the suite into the living room portion and threw it on the ground—just like Grandma's. So accustomed was I to sleeping on floors at this point that I didn't know if I'd even be able to fall asleep without the ambient sounds of pissed elderly women beating on doors.

Sometime before midnight, Larry blasted the suite's door open and nearly stepped on my head. "Jesus man, what the hell are you doing on the floor?" My eyes had trouble adjusting to the light from the hall. Larry stood in the doorway, and between my sleep-dilated eyes and the bright backlighting, he looked like a big redneck angel—an angel with a spitter and a goatee.

"Hey, Larry. Good to see you too."

"Good to see you man, but seriously [spit], why in the hell are you out here on the floor?"

"Well, the rumor is you snore pretty bad. I'm a light sleeper and figured I wouldn't take any chances." I smiled at him, sincerely. He looked at me as if I were fucking retarded.

"Dude, you're fucking retarded."

"I think it's pretty smart! This way we both sleep fine."

"Why didn't you just buy earplugs? [spit]"

Why didn't I just buy earplugs? "Well, Target was sold out. I'll get some tomorrow," I said, knowing I was lying.

"Well, what if I wanna sit out here? Your bed's takin up all the room!"

"Don't give me shit about the bed, not after what you did in the bathroom. I came in today, and it looked like a scene from the *Exorcist* in there. I had to call maintenance to come and force it down because it scared the maids."

"Ha-ha, my bad, rommie," he said, but you could tell he was proud of his bowels. "I got a phone call from one of my good buddies and forgot all about it."

"I don't see how you could forget an experience like that."

"Actually, I thought it was one of my better ones."

"You're disgusting."

"Now wait a minute." He looked at me, suddenly serious possibly offended. "Who said I snored?"

"Everyone who has ever lived with you."

"Everyone?"

"Everyone, Larry."

"Well, hell [spit], then maybe I do!" He stepped over me and went into his room. "Well, I'll let you get back to sleeping on the kitchen floor, smart guy. Good to see you again!"

"You too, Larry."

Chapter Seven

The next day, bright and early, I rolled off the mattress and onto the floor. I lumbered into the bathroom to greet the morning with a nice, long whizz, when I remembered I couldn't. Nothing was clogged or jammed. Rather, today was testing day, and I would need to save the sample for scientific reasons.

The entirety of testing day is dedicated to getting things stuck in and extracted from my person, along with running for time, being pinched for body fat, and enduring cold, awkward hands while coughing with my pants down. Chief on the list of nuisances is filling a plastic cup under the scrutinizing gaze of Dr. Fondle, whose wonderfully relevant job was to "make sure it comes out of me properly" by standing over my shoulder in a bathroom stall like some lonely trucker.

White, Padres' passenger vans would be running players from the hotel to the complex every half hour, on the dot. I took the first one, bright and early, under the pretense that the sooner I got there, the sooner I could get it all over with.

The familiar scenery of my spring home passed by as the van rolled down the highway to the complex. The desert was in bloom. There had been enough rainfall to turn the rocky hills of the Phoenix landscape green with bursts of brightly colored flowers. The morning was a cool sixty degrees, with soon-to-be extinct rain clouds hovering in the air. It was a beautiful scene. In a month the sun would be back from its winter break to chase the clouds away and turn the landscape a burnt tan.

When the Padres' van pulled into the parking lot, nothing had changed. It was as if time stood still in spring training. The cars of the big-league squad were already there. The big-league invitees arrived two weeks ago, their luxurious rides lined up in the choicest parking locations. The remaining spaces, closest to where foul balls landed most frequently, were left for the minors players.

Our eighteen-passenger taxi halted outside the minor league doors. I got out, produced my ID, and headed to the piss testers. They gave me a cup. My piss-test partner and I went into a toilet stall and did our best imitation of rookie inmate hazing. I closed my eyes and pretended I was Harry Potter casting a spell. *"Expelliamus!"* I thought.

During my early days of pro ball, before I'd adjusted to whizzing with random dudes staring at my junk, I couldn't go no matter how bad I had to. I'd just stand there, holding my wand, trying to talk myself into it. I'd hum "Eye of the Tiger" to myself. The professional meat gazer would flush the toilet in hopes the sound of running water would help ease the tension and give me some momentum. When that didn't work, he'd try asking me questions about my hobbies and goals, as if we were speed dating. No questions about my personal interests would diffuse the fact I had my pants down and my shirt around my neck while I held a cup under my twig and berries. I'm glad it went well this time.

"Well look who it is!" the booming voice of Ox Bundy said. He bumped into me as I was walking down the hallway, zipping my pants up after a job well done.

"Hey bud, good to see you!" I replied. Ox gave me a playful shove as a greeting. I tried to shove him back, but he was too thick to move, and I ended up bouncing off him like a toddler running into his father's leg.

Ox was a fellow pitcher. A boldface, all caps, type-A male. A big, solid, man-boy with a perpetual five o'clock shadow that made his face part Wookie, part lumberjack. He loved hard rock, cheap action movies, and chicks with big boobs. He ate red meat like Pez candies and never stopped to think about what was good for the environment. He was a savage, but a lovable one, and like most guys with tough exteriors, he was a softy deep down—very deep down.

"How ya been pal?" he asked.

"I'm good. Happy to be back, I think. You?"

"Fucking one more year in the grind." He shrugged his shoulders.

"Well you look good man. You look strong, *strong like bull.*" With so much emphasis on shape and strength, this is the one place where it's cool for guys to compliment each other on their looks. "Your ass looks great this year," I continued. "You must have decided to get off it once or twice in the off-season."

"No, but thanks anyway. You look good too."

"Oh, it's my sexy hair." I tossed my long, wispy locks.

"No, that's not it."

"Then it's my chiseled physique. Let me tell you man, I know it's in to give Billy Blanks a bad rap, but that Tae Bo crap really works."

"No, that's not it either."

"Then what is it?"

"Actually, you look like shit, but I figured since you said I looked good, I'd be nice."

"Thanks, pal."

"Don't mention it."

"Dirk!" A new voice joined the scene, that of Drew Macias. Drew was a perennial center fielder who became my friend during our first full season. He's one of the few position players with a personality compatible with pitchers. Maybe it's that position players swing clubs for a living or maybe they're just born that way, but many of them seem a little too serious and macho to loosen up like the collection of loony tunes that comprises a pitching staff. Drew, on the contrary, had an aura about him of pure fun. He had thick, dark hair that shot out at crazy angles, an infectious laugh, a charismatic personality, and a sense of humor that provided a quick joke or a good retelling of after-hours exploits. His creativity was always in motion, doodling up someone's caricature, designing some crazy invention, or planning a practical joke. He also knew a fair share of magic tricks that earned him the nickname Drewdini.

We exchanged a "man hug," a male-sanctioned, completely heterosexual embrace consisting of a half backslap, a half chest bump, and a three-quarter handshake.

"Drew, what's up buddy—wait! Look at you! Is that a big-league uniform?"

"Yeah, they have me backing up over on the other side."

"Nice. Get you a little Big-League Camp action. How was your off-season?"

"Good, bro. Played some guitar, mastered some new magic tricks, learned ninjitsu."

"Sounds productive. You still drawing?"

"Yeah, you should see the one I did of Bonvechio!"

"It's outstanding dude," Ox said. "Looks just like him, the freckles, bald spot, even the extra ass cheeks."

"I'll show it to you later. How was your off-season?"

"Worked on my slider, grew my hair out, refrained from killing my grandmother."

"Sounds productive."

"Not really, I should have done it."

"Hey guys, what's happening?" Another friendly face hit the scene. It seemed there was suddenly a party in front of the bathroom. I'm sure all the excitement made the other guys trying to squeeze out some specimens a little nervous.

The newest voice was that of Brent Carter. He strolled up to us in a pair of khaki shorts, a polo, and deck shoes, with a friend sporting the same. Though I didn't know Brent's friend, he was most likely a pitcher and left-hander, like Brent, as they both had medical tape wrapped around gauze on their right arms, indicating blood extraction. Everyone shook hands and exchanged courtesies. Brent's friend went by the nickname Frenchy.

Brent was a Southern Comfort gentleman. His smooth voice had a slight drawl, which, when combined with sir or ma'am, always made him sound respectful. Typically adorned in deck shoes and polos, he looked as if he were perpetually on his way to the golf course. Though he didn't know the rest of the pack that well, we were good friends from last year, splitting a season together. Initially, we didn't have much in common, but once we discovered a mutual enjoyment of imitating our pitching coach, the rest was history.

Frenchy, as it turned out, was drafted from the same college as Brent, which explained their connection. He did not share the accent, though they could have shared wardrobes. This was Frenchy's first spring training with the club, so the experience was foreign. Most new guys follow an older acquaintance around until they learned the ropes. Brent was playing chaperone, and any friend of Brent's was a friend of mine. Taller than Brent, Frenchy lurked at the edge of the circle, looking over shoulders and listening to how players who had some time interacted.

"What tests have y'all done so far?" Brent asked.

"I've done the blood test, and I only did that so I could eat." This was Ox.

"What about the piss test?" I asked.

"I made the mistake of taking a piss when I got up this morning. Now I gotta wait to go again. I'll do it last."

"I wouldn't expect a ten-year vet like you to make such a rookie mistake."

"It's only been eight years, asshole, I ain't that old," Ox barked.

"I don't know Ox. How many Advil does it take you to get through the day again?" Drew asked.

"Kiss my ass, Mr. Big-League Backup."

"You should draw a picture of Ox with a cane and a walker, popping Advils, listening to Metallica, and cussing at children."

"Save it, cockface. I hope Grady sees that wannabe Jesus hair you got and fines your ass five hundred dollars."

"They can fine you that much?" Frenchy asked.

"I don't know, but I hope he starts with this guy." Ox fingered me in the chest with one of his thick, caveman digits.

"Hey man, if I were Jesus, I'd raise my career from the dead."

"Shit, if you were Jesus, you could start with healing me," Ox said, extending his notoriously cranky right arm out.

Drew chimed in, "I think healing what's wrong with you would take a miracle even Jesus couldn't perform, Ox."

Brent and Frenchy both laughed, but stopped abruptly when Grady Fuson himself walked into the locker room. Carrying a clipboard and a coffee cup, he made his way past, stopping to look at us in a detached and uninterested way before unclenching a very sterile "boys" in a voice like a cross between Lou Brown from *Major League* and Tom Waits.

We looked back at him like dogs about to get whipped. "Grady," we harmonized. He locked eyes with me. "Hayhurst, good to see you. Get your fucking hair cut by tomorrow or pay the fine." Then he walked away.

"What are the chances?" I said, when I was sure he was out of range.

"Wear that, fucker!" Ox belched.

"Why me? Your hair is just as long as mine!" I said to Drew.

"I'm in a big-league uniform. I can do whatever I want."

"Immunity," Brent casually noted, nodding his head casually as if Drew's uniform were irrefutable law.

"Great way to start off my spring. Now Grady thinks I'm a rebel."

"Have you seen some of the guys in this organization? We gave a kid who bit a bouncer three million dollars and you're worried about your haircut?"

"So you think he'll fine me three million dollars?" I joked.

"Hope so," Ox said, angling past me with a stiff shoulder. "I'm gonna try to piss. See you on the other side, boys."

Drew patted his pockets. "Wanna borrow my Whizzinator?" A Whizzinator, in case you've never seen one, is a fake plastic penis connected to an extraneous bladder where a clean specimen is stored. The Whizzinator slips "inconspicuously" over your own package and makes it seem as if you are really whizzing your own pee. Color options include, Black, Latino, and Flesh. So utterly ridiculous, it has become a joke among most athletes.

"No thanks, I got my own."

"Don't be surprised if the piss testers act disappointed with your package, Ox. I'm a tough act to follow," I yelled after him.

"That's surprising, considering you sit down to pee."

It was good to see friendly faces and joke around, but spring training was no joke. This wasn't a vacation, and our job wasn't to come into the office and play nine to five around the watercooler. This was a competition, and starting tomorrow, we'd begin fighting for spots. I may have come here with mixed emotions, but now that I was here, I had a job to win if I wanted to go any further. It was baseball in the driver's seat from here on. To feel even like I'd a shot at something resembling a future in this game, I needed to make the Double-A squad out of camp, no small feat. After all the laughter, roles would be won, at any cost, even if it meant taking it from the best of friends.

Chapter Eight

"Alright men, let's bring it in." Wyatt Earp, so everyone called him, was our high-voiced field coordinator. His order to group up meant our first morning meeting was ready to start. The players stopped loitering by the field six fencing and crowded in on Earp's command, forming a semicircle around him. He told us to take a seat, which we did Indian style in the morning dew atop manicured Arizona sod. The coaches and trainers remained standing, spread out before us like they were going to read to us like kindergarteners. Today would mark day one of camp, a day of intros and rules.

Earp led things off, reintroducing himself, though he needed no introduction. He was already infamous. He was a decision maker, like Grady, which meant he held our futures in his hands. The slope to the top of the game is so steep, it's hard to like the folks who decide who makes it there. Statistically speaking, the decisions they make you probably won't like. You learn fast who they are and pander accordingly.

Though Grady was hard to read, Earp was obviously biased. Everyone who'd been around him for any length of time knew he was obsessed with high numbers on the radar gun. He carried said gun with him everywhere, hence his nickname. Since the vast majority of pitchers didn't generate the kind of numbers that turned him on, it was generally assumed Earp didn't like anyone. Even if you pitched a great game, he'd bring up that you weren't throwing hard enough. He always touted this character trait as honesty, but it was a blunt, unhelpful kind of honesty that made you wish he'd just lie to you for a change.

He gave the floor over to Grady, who choked out a greeting to us in his raspy, two-pack-a-day voice. "Gentlemen, welcome to camp. If you take a look around you'll notice there are a lot more of you than we have roster spots for. I'm sure I don't have to explain what that means."

"Way to kick things off on a hopeful note," I murmured to Brent, sitting next to me alongside Frenchy.

"Yeah, seriously. There are like a million new faces here this year."

"I'd like to introduce some of our coaching staff," Grady continued. He turned to face the line of coaches and trainers behind him. The coaches had on their baseball uniforms. Aside from their uniforms, the one thing they all had in common were stopwatches hanging out of their back pockets. The watches weren't for timing sprints, but to keep track of groups between station rotations. Everything in spring training ran on a tight schedule. Beyond that, some coaches had fungo bats for hitting ground balls, gloves for fielding, clipboards for clipping. Most of the coaches stood in clumps with their friends, just like we players sat in clumps with ours.

A few decision-making individuals sat on golf carts: the "Brass," as we called them. You could usually find Grady and Earp sitting comfortably in one. It was easier to make rounds on the complex's seven fields via cart than it was to hoof it in the hot sun. Over the years, golf carts became a symbol of disdain with the players, since a cart was always occupied by some member of the Brass who didn't talk to you, but could make or break your career.

Grady asked the coaches and trainers to introduce themselves, which they did, in no particular order. They broke ranks and explained their title and previous year's coaching locations, then fell back in line. I knew some staff better than others, Randy Ready, Rick Renteria, Wally Whitehurst, Tom Tornincasa, and several others whose names weren't alliterated. I knew almost all the pitching coaches, including Steve Webber, at whom Brent and I giggled like school kids when he spoke, and Glenn Abbott, who labored to teach me a slider for half a season in Double-A.

The trainers introduced themselves next, followed by some front-office staffers whom we'd most likely never see again after today and ending with the clubbies. It was all very quaint, if not boring, and I spent most of my time picking up loose wads of grass and tossing them on other nearby players, pretending Frenchy was responsible.

Grady ended his portion of the morning with, "We have high expectations for this camp, and your job is to make our decisions at the end of it as hard as possible."

Earp took the floor again, pulling a sheet of paper from his pocket. "Alright men, let's go over some rules for camp. First, if you're late for anything, it's fifty bucks plus a dollar for each minute after that. If you don't tie your shoes in the weight room, you'll be thrown out. Don't be in there without the proper gear on. Don't be jack'n around when you are in there. . . ."

I looked over at Frenchy who was trying his best to act as if it were as serious as Earp made it out to be, "Hold on, it gets better," I said.

"What do you mean?"

"The hotel hot tub is not a washing machine," continued Earp. "Don't try to wash your laundry in the hotel whirlpool or you'll pay for it to be cleaned."

"What? Is he kidding?" Frenchy asked, smiling as if it were one of those jokes speakers mix in just to see if you're still paying attention.

"No. About two years back, we had a guy in camp who honestly tried to wash his clothes in the hot tub. He took detergent and his dirty drawers and threw them in. I think he was trying to hand wash them when he was busted. They had to drain the whirlpool and clean out the jets. The hotel billed the Padres, and they were pissed."

"Was this guy retarded?"

"No, but he was from a very undeveloped part of the world."

"Wow, that's unbelievable."

"Oh, just wait—"

"No cooking in the hotel bathrooms. In fact, no cooking in the rooms at all."

"What does he mean no cooking? If you got a suite, can't you use your microwave?"

"You got a suite? How the hell did you get a suite? It's your first year!"

Frenchy shrugged. "So can I cook or not?"

"The microwave is fine," I resumed. "He's talking about something that happened when a couple of guys tried to make food in the bathtub. They almost set the place on fire, and the heat melted some of the plastic in the tub."

"The room caught on fire?"

"No, just part of it."

"What were they making?"

"Rat, or something. Hell, I don't know. They were making it in a damn bathtub."

"Stay off the hotel computer. Every year we have problems with this, so this year we are just banning it from the start. Stay off the hotel computer, or else it's a two hundred and fifty dollar fine. No excuses." Earp was referring to the hotel lobby's computer. There was only one computer in the hotel that guests could use for free. It was located by the front desk, next to the entrance, and was a common gathering site for players to look up things they shouldn't.

"That won't last," I said.

"What do you mean?"

"Every year, fine or no fine, there are people on it. And every year, someone gets caught looking up porn and leaving the links open for other guests to stumble on. It's never your standard porn, either. It's always make-you-gag fetishes with barn animals and stuff. Honestly, I don't want to know who is looking that stuff up because I gotta shower with the dude. Maybe I already have?"

"Barn animals? That's disgusting," Brent said.

"It was you, wasn't it?" Frenchy accused, nudging Brent.

"Yeah, right. Even if I did look at porn, I wouldn't do it in the hotel lobby, and I wouldn't look up *that* crap."

"I'd say that too, if I was doing it, Brent," I said.

"It's probably one of you guys," he countered.

I sighed heavily, "It's me; I admit it. Nothing like a little barnyard love to get me ready for a day at Padres Spring Training 2007!"

"No beef in the team hotel," Earp said, not referring to either burgers or barn animals. He was talking about minor league groupies or random encounters at the bar. "You get caught bringing beef back to your room, it's gonna cost you five hundred dollars. Go to her place instead."

"Or just do it in the lobby, I guess," Frenchy said.

"No, seriously, go back to her place because it's cheaper that way. If you get busted for curfew it's only two hundred and fifty dollars—half the price."

"Where's Hayhurst at?" Earp shouted suddenly.

"Jesus, they caught me!" I said, winking at the boys. I put my hand up.

"Stand up, Hay!" Earp commanded. I got up as ordered and

stood awkwardly in front of the entire Padres minor league troupe as well as its coaches, trainers, and staff.

"Did you wear your cup today Hayhurst?"

"Sure did," I said, knocking on it.

"You ever think about not wearing it anymore?"

"No chance."

"You can all thank Hayhurst here for a fifty-dollar fine if we catch you not wearing a cup out here. How hard was that line drive that almost knocked your beans off?"

"Ninety-four they said." There was a collective groan by the audience.

"Damn." Earp adjusted himself uncomfortably. He laughed in that strained way a person does when confronted by something really painful but still funny. The coaches just shook their heads, obviously believing my choice not to wear a cup was well beyond stupid—which it was.

Earp turned back to us. "Alright, fifty dollars if you don't wear a cup, got it?"

I sat back down while he was putting the price on the threat. I didn't want to relive that experience any more than I had to, but thanks to Earp's callout, I'd be explaining it for the rest of the day. Yes, I got hit in the nuts with a ninety-four miles per hour line drive while not wearing a cup. I just didn't like the way a cup felt when I pitched, so I didn't wear one. Never did, not even in college. People would always joke it was going to catch up to me, but I didn't buy it. Turns out, I was wrong. Now one of my nads has a seam mark on it. It was the worst pain I'd ever felt in my life, ripping through my body like a chainsaw, not letting up for twenty-four hours.

"Did you lose one?" Frenchy asked.

"No, but I was dangerously close. I remember praying I would never think another impure thought if God would just let me keep them!"

"So does everything work down there?"

"I think so. I haven't tried to have kids yet, but everything seems to function like it's supposed to."

"Well, you should be ashamed of yourself, if you ask me," Brent said.

"Why is that?"

"Promising God no more impure thoughts and then looking up sheep porn on the lobby computer, it's just wrong."

"Alright," Earp said, resuming his lecture. He had folded up his notes and was about to end the meeting but was looking to go out on a bang. "Anyone got any good jokes?" He looked over the crowd, but no one felt courageous. "Lars, I know *you* got something."

Lars Maynard, a right-handed closer drafted the same year as I was, may best be introduced as the one person in the organization who could walk up to Grady and tell him to go fuck himself without batting an eye. He was, without a doubt, the most interesting person I ever played the game with, and thanks to his eccentric personality, he stood out among peers and coaches. Sometimes it almost seemed as if he were from another world.

To give you an idea of what kind of guy Lars was, you need to know what Tommy John surgery is, which Lars underwent a little over a year before. Named after the pitcher who the surgery was tested on, Tommy John is the reconstruction of the ulnar collateral ligament, or UCL, located in a pitcher's throwing arm. It's major surgery requiring holes to be drilled in bones and the harvesting of a replacement ligament sewn through said holes. The goal is to repair the damaged throwing arm and save the career of the pitcher who receives it.

Normal recovery time for the operation is about a year. It takes months to get the necessary range of motion back in your elbow, fighting through layers of scar tissue. But that was just too long for Lars.

After surgery, Lars walked into the doctor's office for a consultation and he asked the doctor how long it would take to get full mobility back in his arm. The doctor told him the usual, months of rehab. Lars asked why, a question most people would hold off on, content to take the doctor's word, considering their arm just had holes drilled in it. But Lars had done a lot of homework on the surgery before he went under the knife—a lot. In fact, it wasn't uncommon to catch Lars reading books on pharmacology or medical journals in the locker room.

The doctor explained the process of recovery—how breaking up all the scar tissue is excruciating and how the body has to go about it slowly to build up its tolerance. Lars looked the doctor in the face and bluntly asked, "Pain is the only thing? There are no other repercussions?"

"The kind of pain I'm talking about is enough of a repercussion."

"So, I could get it back now if I could take the pain?"

The doctor laughed. "Sure, but you don't want to do that."

Lars stood up right then and there, pulled off his sling, placed his arm in the frame of the office door, and jerked his arm straight. He swooned and passed out. When he came to, despite the chastisement of his doctor, he could extend his arm straight.

Of course, this story didn't shock me that much. Before he had Tommy John, he chose to have open-back surgery with no anesthetic. He said that, at the time, he believed experiencing the farthest reaches of pain would serve to expand his ability to appreciate life more fully. It was part of his metaphysical period, in which he also got high and traced his out-of-body experiences in spiral patterns, hoping to capture thoughts created by brain activity usually operating in the subconscious.

You can't see the scar on his back. It's covered by a tattoo of Atlas, the mythological god who carried the world on his own back. The variation depicted on Lars's body was slightly different though because his Atlas let the world fall and splatter all over the ground like an egg and is walking away from it. When I asked Lars what it meant, he said, "Atlas is basically saying, I don't give a fuck about the world, and I'm going to do my own thing."

Lars and I actually lived together for part of a season. A very nice, well-adjusted, Catholic host family with three kids, a cat, and a dog put us up. Lars, despite all my expectations, did not kill any of them. In fact, they loved him. He was a charmer and a gentleman, and never missed a chance to TiVo *Grey's Anatomy*. To Lars, there were no set ways to do things, no rules of operation, no expectations but his own.

Lars stood up and walked to the front of the group. Earp, who simply thought Lars was batshit crazy, was giddy at the thought of what might come out of Lars's mouth.

"Got a good one for us?" Earp asked.

"I like it," Lars replied in a way that conveyed he didn't care if anyone else did.

"Alright, lay it on us."

Dryly and completely void of emotion, Lars looked to us and spoke, "What's the hardest thing about rollerblading?"

"I don't know. What?" Earp asked.

"Telling your parents you're gay."

Chapter Nine

After that, Lars was elected to tell jokes at most of the morning meetings. A few days later, he led the day off with one about an octopus who could play the bagpipes. The punch line was something along the lines of this: "Play 'em? Once I get these fancy pajamas off, I'm gonna fuck 'em!"

We've heard funnier jokes, but the situation Lars told it in made all the difference. A film crew was on location to document the life of another camper, Cooper Brannan. Cooper was a former soldier injured in the War on Terror, when a flashbang grenade exploded in his left hand, costing him a digit. Before he joined the service, he was a pitcher with aspirations of going pro. In what was sure to become the feel-good story of the season, the Padres signed Cooper to a spring-training deal, stirring up a media frenzy.

Everyone from Jim Rome to *Deal or No Deal* was in, asking Coop what it felt like to go from active duty to pro athlete in America's greatest pastime. To Coop's credit, his answers were always humble, respectful, and genuine. He was a media darling, and the cameras seemed to appear at his command. Unfortunately, they did not disappear at his whim, or maybe they would have opted out of videotaping Lars's morning joke.

Rather than toning things down, the first thing Lars did was walk up to the panoramic lens of the film crew and put two middle fingers into view, causing his peers to erupt with laughter. Then, after taking his place in front of the group, he proceeded to stretch the joke into a five-minute, Andrew Dice Clay swearfest, dropping lines like "Holy fucking shit, that octopus is the most fucking amazing musician I've ever seen, he's like Prince." Before he reached his conclusion, the camera crew had to stop recording, as none of the material was usable in Coop's daily in-the-life-of documentary. The entire camp tittered like naughty little kids each time Lars used a swear word, including Earp, who had no one but himself to blame.

Along with Lars's jokes, Coop's film crew became a normal camp occurrence. On the cover of many magazines and television screens, Coop was a sensation, while Lars's humor was a centerpiece for player discussion. Coop, it could be said, represented the side of the game most people wished it to be, which is why it was such good television material. Lars, on the other hand, represented what baseball life was really like, raw and unrefined. I found it odd that both could exist in the presence of one another without canceling each other out.

Evidence of Coop's mass appeal was apparent thanks to the stream of letters from well-wishers and supporters, which came pouring into his locker daily, not to mention the many boxes of complimentary equipment that showed up with his name on it.

Before he was signed on, there were reports of Coop's ability to gas the ball into the low nineties from the left side. Maybe it was this particular spring, maybe it was always this way, but all the hype surrounding his ability to bring lefty heat looked like make-believe because most of the time he labored in the low eighties, scuffling for outs.

To most folks, that didn't matter. His testimony steamrolled right over such trivial things like production, even though it was make or break for everyone else. Coop was the most remarkable story in camp, and it was generally accepted that he'd have a job come the end of it—a fact that sat well with most players, though the reasoning behind it was undeniably questionable, considering the business's normal operating procedure.

Coop had that kind of an image—too good to waste. So good, in fact, that it made the normal business of the game look ugly in comparison. He was such a quality individual, a credit to the service, that there was something cheap about how much attention he garnered. I was actually a little pissed off about it. Not at Coop, he was a class act, but at the industry for lavishing so much product and attention on him hoping to look good by association. People stood to profit from him, as they did from all great athletes, but something about the way they chased after Coop made me feel that no one really cared about Coop as much as they cared about the marketing potential of his story.

Possessing undeniable nobility, Coop would say he felt as if he were playing on behalf of the other wounded and injured, but the companies weren't concerned about them. They were only concerned about one wounded veteran ballplayer who made for fantastic advertising. It made me wonder if all wounded veterans received free shoes and sports equipment or just those who had camera time. I know if it was up to Coop, they would.

On the off chance Coop climbed all the way to the top, it would be a Hollywood event. I'll bet Ken Burns wet his pants at the mere thought of it. I know Coop wanted to earn it, but even if he didn't, the industry would profit from him. A minor league roster spot was a pittance to pay for the kind of attention Coop could generate. It would be stupid not to keep him around even if that meant someone else who loved the game, who grew up wanting to be a baseball player his whole life, who broke the mold to get the chance, would lose his job. The numbers demanded sacrifice, and for every dream come true, there was a price.

For years, I believed that baseball was survival of the fittest, and I didn't care about anyone else's survival except my own. My story was the one that mattered, and as long as it ended with me in the big leagues, I could care less about anyone else's chances. I never stopped thinking this until I started watching Lars and Coop go about their day.

Say what you want about Lars, he's one of the freest guys I've ever seen on a baseball field, completely marching to the beat of his own drum; something I've always admired about him. He saw baseball as an instrument, a means to an end, an expression, and he was never afraid to approach it from a different angle. It almost seemed sacrilegious the way he could speak so nonchalantly about baseball, or maybe his stark, bare beliefs simply showed the myth in my own—maybe.

Then there was Coop. When Coop was enjoying his day at the park, it was impossible not to enjoy it with him. It was easy to pick up a ball, throw it around, chase grounders, and laugh at jokes about octopi, while I doubt many of us could easily pick up a rifle and face what he did. Cooper was getting a second chance at something he almost forfeited his life protecting, an ideal that afforded the very chances we had at our own dreams, on and off the field. Coop was a great man who didn't need baseball to tell him so. Though it was contrary to the rules I knew pro baseball by, I couldn't deny my hope that Coop would get his chance. I felt he earned it for what he'd already done. If my career was scratched from the lineup so he could have a shot at his dream, so be it. Hopefully, that wouldn't be necessary.

Chapter Ten

On field six, it was business as usual. Another day of Pitcher's Fielding Practice, or PFPs. We do roughly four-billion hours of PFPs in spring training to prepare us for the five or six real plays we'll get during the year. Many pitchers are of the opinion this is just busy work. That's because most pitchers are athletic. I'm not. I pitch, and that's about the extent of my athletic prowess. Essentially, PFPs are just four-billion great opportunities for me to embarrass myself.

We all lined behind the field four mound, while a coach, one of the few I did not know, hit grounders back up the middle to us after we went through a fake delivery. Some guys wound up in overexaggerated Japanese-style deliveries, whereas others didn't bother to bend over before heaving their ball of make-believe. When my turn came up, I wound in my own mechanics and delivered a nasty sinking, invisiball, which induced a chopper back my way. The ball took a late hop off the dirt. I missed it, the ugly kind of miss where the fielder pulls his glove up in expectation of a hop that doesn't come, the ball darting between the legs.

"Get back up there Hay. Get you another one," the new coach said.

I made a packing motion with my glove, climbed the summit

of the mound, and reloaded—the delivery, the pitch, a chopper back up the middle. Hayhurst sets, he reaches, he fumbles, and he catches the grounder with his forearm. The ball ricochets off him into no-man's-land. The ghost runner is safe at first on a pitcher's fielding error.

"Maybe they should rename this PFEs, huh, Dirk?" Ox chimed, standing behind me with his arms crossed.

"Yeah, yeah."

"Come on, Hay, you got this!" the coach called.

It's worse when you miss two. The embarrassment starts to add up, and you can feel the expectation of a third miss percolate. You have to catch the next one just to prove you aren't a lost cause— that you can do something Little Leaguers do.

I climbed the mound again, wound, delivered, and induced a slow roller back to the mound. I charged it—too much charge. My glove came down and smothered the ball, but did not suck it up. The ball had stopped rolling, and I reached down with my free hand to make a quick throw before the imaginary runner got to the bag. As I pulled the ball up to fire it, it slipped out of my hand, making a backward lob to third base though I was facing first. I was a train wreck.

"Cocksucking balls!"

"Interesting choice of swear there, Dirkus."

"Save it, Ox."

Out walked the coach. I stood awkwardly as he approached. I had warranted a complete stop of the drill, and I would pay for it in total peer embarrassment. The coach put his hand on me and walked me to the summit of the mound. He stopped, released me, crossed his legs, and leaned on his fungo bat like it was a cane.

"Hay," he began, pulling out his dip can and pinching a wad as he spoke—"have you ever held a titty before?"

The boys behind snickered. Someone repeated, "Huh, huh, titty."

"Excuse me?"

"Have ya ever held a titty before, yes or no?"

"Yeah, I've held one before." I adjusted my hat, and kicked some dirt.

"Well, catching a baseball is a lot like holding a titty," he said, pressing his dip into his cheek line.

"Uh."

"You can't grab at it." He stuck his hand out to imaginary boobie height. "You have to caress it. Be gentle with it, or she won't call you back." He finished his demonstration by moving his hands in a way I'm sure I'll have nightmares about.

"I want all of you to stick your hands out and caress that titty." As instructed, we all put our hands out and, well, started caressing imaginary titties. The whole pack of us, standing on the mound of field four, hands out, sexually harassing the air in front of us.

"Good. That's *real* good. Now, let's try it again." He retreated back to home plate. I put down my imaginary titty and climbed the mound as if I were about to be executed—deep breath, shoulder wiggle, delivery, chopper up the middle.

"CARESS THAT TITTY, HAY!"

I stuck my hands out, and in slow motion came the bouncing, leather mammary. The ball nestled itself lovingly into my mitt; I turned and sent it off to first.

"Attaboy, Hay, she'll call ya back now."

"Great. Can't wait to hear from her," I said on my way to the back of the drill line.

"I don't know if I can do this," Ox whined.

"Why is that?" I asked.

"I'm not used to holding titties this small!"

As the days of spring passed, it became apparent that if something embarrassing was going to happen, it was going to happen on the field with this new coach. He never missed an opportunity to bust my balls, thus inspiring me to dub him with the private nickname of "Coach Castrate." Every time I saw him leaning on a fungo at the field I was headed to, I cursed.

Finally, the perfect storm converged and my two worst on-field elements came together, Coach Castrate and bunting. The Padres are in the National League, so pitchers need to learn how to handle the lumber. Now that I had already been taught to handle baseballs as though they were titties, if I didn't get the bunt down, what would he say I should imagine holding the bat was like?

I wasn't such a bad fielder, really. I just had a bad day that became a worse one when Coach Castrate turned it into an event. I was, however, a terrible hitter no matter what day it was, no matter who was watching.

I was a marked man. Coach Castrate had labeled me as the nonathletic guy, so everything I did was subject to ridicule. When it was my turn to bunt, I marched up to the plate like a man ready to take my medicine. *Screw this can't bunt talk,* I thought. *I'll show this motherfucker who he's messing with.*

My first attempt went over the backstop—the second straight into the plate. I missed the third one altogether. "Jesus Hay, you look like you're trying to take a shit in the woods." Here we go again.

Guys started snickering. I wanted to tell Coash Castrate he could take this bat and shove it. "Here, give me that bat," he said, grabbing it from me and squaring around as if he were some bunting ninja. He had one of the other pitchers feed the pitching machine, and he laid the bunts down like he invented the art. "See, relax, not so stiff. You need to go to the bathroom before we continue?"

"No, I'm fine. I got it." He handed the bat back to me and returned to the pitching machine. I missed four out of the next five, and he called for the next man in line because I was wasting too many balls.

We were supposed to take two turns bunting, but I skipped my spot in line, hiding in the background until we finished. "Okay boys," Coach Castrate said, "we're going to play a little game. We're going to bunt to each side of the field and then a squeeze. If you don't get 'em all down, you have to stand on the plate, tuck your nuts between your legs, bend over, and take a pitch in the ass."

I dropped my head immediately.

"This guy's fucking crazy," Ox said. "I love it!"

"Here, I'll show you what you have to do."

"Is he really gonna—" Then Castrate walked to the plate.

"Here's what you do. Take the helmet and turn it around so the bill protects your neck." He spun the helmet around so he looked like a football player. "Then, make sure you protect your nuts, pull 'em up so they don't get smashed, and bend over." He turned away from the pitcher's mound where the machine was sitting, bent over, scrunched his balls, and tucked his arms in. "Keep your fingers safe, you don't want to hurt one of them either." I hate to say this, but he had very good technique.

"Alright, let one go."

"Are you serious?"

"Yeah, let it go," he called, with his head still tucked down.

One of the pitchers reluctantly took a ball and stuck it the machine. The ball whizzed through the air and thudded into his left ass cheek. He flinched slightly, then stood up, and turned to look at us. "See? Nothing to it."

"Fuck that!" one of the other pitchers declared. "I'm not standing in there and getting cranked with a ball! What the fuck is that going to prove?" Several of the other guys grumbled in agreement, but we were at his mercy.

"Hay! Why don't you start us off?" Of course, why not, I was a safe bet for a baseball enema, so I might as well get it over with. I took my bat and helmet and walked to the plate as if I were on the green mile. The first pitch I took for a ball. The next I punched down the first base line.

"Okay, now one to third."

I stuck the bat out and tried to keep it balanced, imagining what would happen if I missed. What if when I had to take it in the rear, the ball hit me square in the center and got stuck?

The ball bounced off my bat and headed toward third. It teetered on the foul line but remained fair. Two down.

"Squeeze!"

I took the bat and put it on my shoulder like I was going to swing away. I waited for the coach's hand to rise with the ball. When he brought it down to the machine, I squared to bunt. The ball whizzed, I deflected it into the ground fair—three for three.

"Attaboy, Hay. Even a blind squirrel finds a nut now and again."

It didn't matter what he said. I got 'em down. Whether I looked like I was trying to take a shit in the woods or a twenty-year vet, I was off the hook. I was going to enjoy laughing at everyone else for a change!

The coach looked at his stopwatch. "Alright boys, time to rotate. This group's heading for field three."

"What? No, no!" He planned it! That son of a . . .

Chapter Eleven

I may have had my share of embarrassing moments with Coach Castrate, but overall, camp was going well. I was pitching well, collecting outs, and throwing a mile or two harder, thanks to a deal I made with the guys running the radar gun, at the cost of a log of dip and a six-pack. During those days of spring success. I found it easy to believe all was at peace. Good days at the park have a way of ironing out life's wrinkles.

I knew, however, from way more experience than I'd like, things don't go well forever. Whether here in spring or on a team this season, I would struggle again. A moment I sincerely dreaded. If good moments make you carefree, the bad ones suffocate you.

Of course, I couldn't control my results; all I could control was my approach, but sometimes the results control the approach. I had a lot of failures in my career. Even my successes felt like failures, seeing how I had nothing to show for them. When I failed, it felt so colossally taxing, I became afraid of the slightest potential of it happening each time I took the mound. Soon, it was the only thing I expected myself to do.

It's easy to talk about success when failure doesn't mean anything. To me, failure meant a lot. It was something along the lines of self-destruction or imprisonment. It felt like an angry scream from my dad, or an intoxicated fist from my brother. It's what motivated me, punished, me, and branded me. It was my very wicked master. Thus, each success I had this spring was tempered by the looming shadow of my possible meltdown. Sure I was happy about the results so far. I was doing well, but more importantly, I wasn't blowing it.

It doesn't take an all-star to realize this way of thinking was wrong, though, I'll admit, I never really thought about much of what was going on in my mind until this year. I never thought about quitting before this year either. I needed some answers to big questions. Like, why did the Baseball Reaper show up to only my games, and how could I perform at my best if I was always afraid of the worst? What do you do when all the stars in the canopy of your baseball life turn out to be holes?

I think I would like baseball better if it had superheroes in it. Coping with the game and its uncertainties would be so much easier if there were guys captaining teams who could bench-press trucks and freeze things with their breath. I could always look to their fearless example for inspiration and morale. They'd have all the answers, and if they didn't, they could just look majestic until you forgot what you were asking. Unfortunately, baseball has no spandex-clad heroes. It does, however, have the next best thing: players with multiyear contracts. That would have to be enough.

Just after the halfway point of spring training, Trevor Hoffman was scheduled to address the minor league pitching staff. Every year during spring training, a big-league pitcher who's had a good amount of success comes over to talk shop with the minor league pitching horde about what helped them. They talk about what they overcame to get to the golden shores of multifigure contract bigleaguerdom. In previous years, we'd talked with the likes of Rick Suttcliffe, Greg Maddux, and Jake Peavy. This year it was Hoffman's turn, and I was thrilled.

Despite the lack of merchandisable superpowers, Hoffman was one of my heroes in uniform. He was one of the few remaining players who had not fallen victim to the pitfalls of the sport via performance enhancers or media persecution. He was an icon in the game and someone I thought of as above and beyond the rest of us. If anyone had answers to deep questions and fears, surely it was him.

Why I thought so highly of Hoffman is tough to explain. He had staggering success, but lots of players had that, and I didn't care much about them. Money was another by-product of a sports star in his stratosphere, and, again, I wasn't wowed by every player to bling his way onto a magazine cover. Recognition from an early age was a big part, but I never really followed baseball when I was young. I didn't collect cards or memorize stats or dress up in the jersey of my favorite team and learn to cuss at bad plays with my dad. All the Little League teams I played on made fun of my sports neglect, as if my lack of baseball knowledge were an unforgivable sin, but I didn't have time to hassle myself with icon worship. I didn't like watching sports, and when I did, I turned the volume off so as not to be annoyed by announcers incessantly prattling on about how great they once were. I preferred to read comic books.

I encountered Hoffman in the pages of *ESPN The Magazine*. Someone had stuffed a Spider-Man comic book into it on the bookshelf in the dentist's office waiting room. The article was skillfully crafted, making Hoffman sound amazing, larger than life, as if he threw laser-guided fastballs and Jedi mind-trick-caliber change-ups touted as the best in the game. I read how the stadium went super-freak when he entered in the ninth to the rockin' sounds of AC/DC and how it was one of the most electrifying moments in sports. It was kickass stuff I had no idea baseball players could do. I thought they just argued about which wife had the cooler upgrades. In that article, Hoffman was like a superhero.

I was so excited to hear Hoffman speak, Larry wanted to punch me in the head. Ox told me I was borderline gay, and Brent said he wouldn't sit near me because he was afraid I'd embarrass him. It wasn't that other guys weren't excited; it's that I was "Star Trek geek at a convention" excited about it, which tended to freak my friends out. They didn't understand because they didn't see how great my expectations were. If anyone could shine a light into my baseball universe, I knew it would be Hoffman, and I couldn't wait to hear the pearls of wisdom straight from my hero's mouth.

After breakfast, before morning meetings and Lars's joke, the minor league pitching troupe marched over to the major league side of camp's bullpen area. We all sat Indian style on the grassy portion of the big-league pen, turning the mound into a stage: what better place for a pitcher to address a crowd?

Grady started the meeting, offering some forgettable introduction, as if it were needed, and then out came Hoffman to take the stage. Up he strolled, majestically, the first time I had ever seen him take the mound without musical accompaniment. He placed his hands on his hips and, in a very gym teacherly way, said, "Good morning everyone. Thanks for letting me come out here and speak with you today."

I love how really smooth celebrity folks say stuff like "Thank you for letting me," when they could say, "You're lucky I bothered to waste my time with you insignificant peons." Actually, that's about what my first real interaction with the guy went like. He didn't call me a peon, but that didn't stop me from acting like one.

My first bona fide encounter with Hoffman came in my second spring training. He actually approached *me*. Hoffman, or Hoffy, as we folks who are on speaking terms with him call him, came into the lunchroom after what I'm sure was a long day of keeping baseball full of magic and wonder. I'm not ashamed to say I watched him like a little peasant boy gazes on royalty. He grabbed a hot plate of food, a glass of refreshing Gatorade, and a plastic fork. Then he walked over to my table.

I almost spilled my drink in my lap. I thought, *It's him. It's Trevor Hoffman!* He looked at me with that "destined to be bronzed on a plaque" face of his and said, and I'll never forget it, "Hey, can I borrow your salt?"

Nothing came out as I stared at him like a mental patient, choking on my tongue.

He picked up the salt and sprinkled some on his food, despite me. *Look at his salt-sprinkling technique—masterful!* I thought.

He placed the salt back down, and I still couldn't make any words come out. He looked at me again, and in a very uncomfortable way said, "Uh, thanks." Pretty amazing stuff.

Today Hoffman got right to the point, launching into a speech about preparation and routine. About not only how practice makes perfect, but how it's not just practice at the pro level, it's a way of life. Successful athletes control all the variables. They are disciplined with their rest, eating, workouts, and love lives. They set goals and reach them.

Next, Hoffman started talking about how good and bad thoughts influence our ability, how negative thoughts can defeat us before we take the field, and how positive ones can help remove doubt. He said he talked to himself, confessing, "When I have a bad thought, like I think I can't make a pitch or I worry about a negative result, I stop myself, pull the thought out of my head, crumple it up, and throw it away." Then, to demonstrate, he took his hand up to his head, grabbed an imaginary object floating next to his ear, pulled it away from his head, crunched it up, and threw it on the ground. Whoa!

Hoffman finished his speech with a customary message of hope, telling us we could all make it to the bigs someday because stranger things have happened. He said that he, for example, was drafted as a shortstop, and his legendary changeup didn't come along until later in his career. Then, before closing, he put his hands back on his hips and in a very magnanimous way said, "As long as you have uniforms on your backs, you got a chance." I expected him make a dramatic exit, like flying off into the clouds. Instead, he opened up the floor to questions.

Some hands popped up while I mulled over his words. To be honest, his speech disappointed me. It was like Captain Kirk talking about what it's like to work with his producers and not about fighting Klingons or firing photon torpedoes. He didn't even talk about sexing up green chicks. I wanted more. I needed more. He was supposed to tell me the meaning of the baseball-player life and why I wore my secret decoder jersey. Where was all the deep, mind-blowing insight? Most of this stuff was on the wall in my high school guidance office.

Unsatisfied, I started thinking of a question to force depth out of him. I set my vocabulary to stun and threw my hand up. Hoffman's gaze came down on me, "What's your question?"

"I was wondering," I said, "what kind of mantras or psychological routines you operate under? Do you have beliefs that you inculcate yourself with to remain focused and directed as a player?" I thought the question was deep, intelligent, and perceptive. Surely, a man of his greatness was impressed by it. Hoffman stared at me as if I just asked him what testicles were.

"Whoa, whoa, whoa there, buddy. I don't know about all those big words. 'Mantras' and 'inculcating,' whew!" he chided, smiling at the rest of the guys as if to imply *what's with this guy, huh*? Brent's head dropped, Ox snorted. "Why don't you try and keep it down to a level we can all understand. We're just baseball players here, pal."

The minor leaguers surrounding me begun chuckling. Partially because I just went Rambo with a thesaurus and partially because if Trevor had simply snapped his fingers like the Fonz and said, "Laugh now!" everyone would have.

"Are you trying to ask me what kind of things I think about to stay in my element?" he said, offering me a rephrase.

"Uhm . . . Yeah, that's it,"

"Well, what I do . . ." and he went on to list a series of things I didn't hear because I was too busy trying to calculate just how badly I embarrassed myself in front of my peers and a baseball demigod. When Trevor finished his answer, he looked back to me and asked, "Does that answer your question?"

"Oh yes, yes it does, thank you," I lied.

"Any other questions?"

No one else dared raise his hand, not even to ask the quintessential Hoffman must know of, "How do you hold your changeup?" I had officially snuffed out the meeting, and we sat awkwardly looking at the floor while Hoffman towered over us.

"Well those were all very good questions, and I wish you all the best of luck." On that, off he went to sit on his throne of saves.

The assembly broke and I walked like a black sheep to the minor league side's morning meeting. Lars told his joke, we stretched, and camp moved around me while I remained stuck in the dialogue of Hoffman's speech in search of a hidden message.

How could I be so stupid? How could I be so nerdy? Was I destined to look like an idiot in front of the guy? It would probably be the last time I would ever have a chance to talk with him, and I asked him how he inculcates himself. Why didn't I just ask him how he held his changeup? Then we could have spent the rest of the day flinging changeups at each other like mini Hoffmans.

Besides, what did I expect him to say to me that hasn't been said before? Was he going to petition the big-league squad to call up a man with my all-star caliber vocabulary? Was he going to invite me over to his house to sip hot cocoa while we wore matching sweaters with embroidered *H*'s? The purpose of his talk was to offer advice to his fellow employees on how to do their job better, and he did just that. What else would he do?

I guess it was my fault; Hoffman never asked me to put him on a pedestal. He never asked me to grade him under unrealistic expectations. He was just doing his job the best way he knew how, which was pretty damn good whether it was the way I imagined it or not—so much for my moment of heroic inspiration.

Later on in the day, I took the mound in a scrimmage against the Cubs. I was slated for one inning of work, which I wasn't locked in for, not after the morning meeting. I got blasted and found myself surrounded by base runners, pulling bad thoughts out of my head, struggling to escape. When the last out was made, I went into the dugout and plopped on the bench, took off my hat, and hung my head. Ox came over to me, slapped one of his big meat hooks on my shoulder, and asked, "So, what mantras or psychological routines did you inculcate yourself with to get your ass kicked out there today?"

Chapter Twelve

In the last few days of camp, with cuts looming visibly in the distance, my Double-A pitching group gathered and was told the positive, uplifting news that all of us were potentially on the chopping block. Our pitching coordinator informed us that cuts were coming, and we should all take the next few days of opportunity very seriously. "I am not trying to scare anyone," he said. "I am just trying to let all of you know the situation. There are not a lot of jobs to go around this year. Most of the spots we have are already decided on. Some of you guys may be operating under the assumption you have a job locked up, and I am here to tell you that you may be disappointed."

I can't imagine how a person could leave that meeting with a smile on his face. He was trying to brace us, maybe motivate us, but all we heard was, "I am not trying to scare anyone, but I have to tell you, most of you are screwed and you should be terrified; in fact, most of you are dead men pitching."

Every spring training there will be releases, and we know why teams have cuts. The organization brings in players, gives them a chance, and then takes the best. It's how the business works. But understanding it and dealing with it are two very different things. I didn't appreciate the doomsday message, no matter how good the intentions were behind it. All it served to do was compound my already overloaded mind with worries and concerns about the future of my career. Then, after I firmly intended to make the best of whatever shot I'd left, my remaining chances were stripped from me, thanks to a horrific bout of food poisoning.

Starting as soon as I got back to the hotel that night, I spent the rest of the day, as well as the next two, on the toilet—well, mostly the toilet. Later, when my butt started to bleed, I lay in the bathtub with the shower running on me and just crapped straight down the drain so I wouldn't have to endure the pain of wiping. It was the worst bout of sickness I've ever dealt with. Every seven or so minutes a team of horses wearing cleats raced through my intestines and opened fire on the toilet with scattershot.

A few trainers resided with us at the team hotel, stationed there in case of emergencies like mine. They provided me with enough Imodium to pave a driveway, but it had no effect. After chugging the bottle, I informed them my situation wasn't improving, and they said I'd have to hold strong until the next day when I could see the team doctor.

"I have to come into camp and see him?"

"Yes."

"What if I crap my pants in the van before I get to camp?"

"We don't recommend you do that."

"But it's like clockwork, every seven minutes Godzilla attacks my ass and—"

"You're going to have to come in. There's nothing else we can do for you. You'll have to hold it. Sorry."

"How am I going to sleep tonight?"

"It should calm down once it expels everything out of your system. Just make sure you keep drinking water."

"But what if it doesn't calm down?"

"It should. Keep taking your meds; keep drinking water."

I kept drinking fluids like the trainers told me to, but things didn't slow up. The fluid only served to turn solid expulsions into watery ones. When Larry came in later that night, he asked what was wrong with me. I told him I contracted an extremely rare, highly contagious disease and stage one was explosive diarrhea.

"Yeah, I'll bet you did [spit]," Larry said.

I was lying on the mattress in the living room/kitchenette like our last conversation. This time I was wearing only a bath towel. My hair was wet and matted to my head, still wet from my last trip to the shower/toilet. I didn't bother to change back into a full outfit in between trips because I'd only take it off again the next time the horses rounded the track. I used the towel as a kilt and covered my shoulders with a blanket.

Larry was again standing in the doorway, fellow hotel-room-bound players walking by and peeking in. I knew more of them by this point in the camp, some waved, others flicked me off—both can mean hello in the world of minor league baseball.

"No. I'm serious," I said. "In stage two, your wiener swells and gets all lumpy, like a chewed wad of bubble gum dipped in nerds. In stage three, it falls off. Like in those pictures they showed us at the drugs, sex, and conduct meeting." It was one of several man-datory meetings we have in spring training and by far the most memorable. Because Professional Baseball is one of those job titles that attracts women of a certain make, ones we commonly refer to as beef or cleat chasers, the opportunity to get into some sexu-ally related trouble is much higher. You don't know where some of these eager ladies have been. Since men are visually stimulated, the speaker used some of the nastiest visuals imaginable. If you weren't sick before you entered the lecture, you would be once you left. Hell, you might join a monastery.

"Good thing you don't use it for anything [spit]," Larry said.

"That may be true, but I'd still like to keep it around for senti-mental reasons. We've had a lot of good times together."

"Jesus-age, man, this place smells like a sewer." Larry let the door shut as he walked around the room trying to find a spot that didn't reek. There wasn't one.

"You're one to talk. I endure this from you on a regular basis."

"Mine smells more like jerky; yours is straight asshole."

"I can't help it, I got food poisoning or a virus or a curse or something. I might crap a plague of locusts next, at the rate I'm going."

"Well what am I going to do? What if I gotta shit too? [spit]"

"I don't think there's even any toilet paper left."

"I'll just go down to the one in the lobby then, I guess."

"I hope you blow up that toilet like you do here. Don't flush it. Leave it for some poor sap to stumble on. You're good at that."

"At least I'm consistent [spit]."

My stomach started to rumble. "Here we go again; it's like clockwork man." I got up and scampered into the bathroom with my legs pressed together, slamming the door behind me. If you were standing outside, you would have heard the toilet seat of my throne come up, me sit down, and then the sound of air-compressed water, followed by splashdown. I wanted to use the shower, but I didn't want Larry to know he was bathing in my repurposed toilet.

Larry stood outside the door. It's funny. I can't stand the sound of people going to the bathroom, but when I'm around the boys, it's so commonplace that it doesn't register. At the training complex, the bathroom houses seven stalls. After breakfast, all the stalls will be full of minor league asses. It's more like a library than anything because everyone who comes in to make a deposit brings his favorite reading material, crossword, or puzzle. Some people read Harry Potter, others *USA Today*. Public bowel movements are so common in this line of work, it's considered bad etiquette if you don't offer the paper you were reading to the set of panted ankles in the stall next to yours when you finish.

"So what do you really think you got? [spit]" asked Larry, who was apparently leaning on the bathroom door.

"I have no idea, bro, but it's terrible. I wish I could just drink Drano and flush it all out."

"What are the chances of me getting it?"

"Again, no idea, but I stopped using your toothbrush just in case. Ern . . . hold on . . . more on the way." I went again. Larry laughed from the other side of the door. Something about bowel movements will be funny to men until the end of time.

"So, what are you thinking about cuts after today's feel-good message?" Larry asked.

"You mean, who do I think is going to get cut, or how do I feel about them in general?"

"Who do you think is going to get cut? [spit]"

"I don't know. I've been throwing well, but after being bounced around all season last year, I got a strange feeling that I'm expendable."

"Yeah, I hear you there. I'm getting worried myself."

"You? You throw in the low-to-mid nineties with a nasty hammer. How could you be worried?"

"Grady is systematically getting rid of guys who have track records of injury. I don't think he likes me, the surgeries and all. Besides, they got me out of indi ball, and don't got shit invested in me [spit]."

"I don't buy that. They've developed you for the last two years and promoted you to Double-A; they have to like you. They love hard throwers. At least Earp does."

"I don't think his opinions count for too much anymore."

"Well, then I guess it was nice playing with you. We can go play on the same church-league softball team when we get chopped."

"I don't think you're going to get chopped, and I'm not going to go play church softball—you can't drink in church league [spit]."

We could have spent all day telling the other how they weren't going to get axed. Even if we thought the other would be released, we'd rather boldface lie about it than say it. No baseball player will ever tell another baseball player his future is over. If someone believed the object of your heart's ambition was unattainable, would you want to hear that person say it?

It's the hardest for middle-of-the-pack players to feel safe. They're lukewarm and in the gray, unsure if it's their time to get spit out or not. If you know you're on your way out, you can prepare accordingly. Call your uncle in the oil well company, get an internship with a bank, or finish your degree. You can hop out of one profession and get tied up in another one before the reality of what happened sets in and you find yourself back in Grandma's basement, consumed with your failure.

Everyone frets about cut day, either for himself or for a good buddy who is trying his damnedest to hang on. It can be a very depressing time. The lockers are quieter, coaches less jovial. We all know what it means. For many, being released means the end of a dream, or a fantasy, or a lie, depending on how they made their way to the pros.

I didn't say much after Larry said he wouldn't play church league. I suppose I could've kept telling him about how I was sure I was going to get released, fishing the barrel for his reassuring compliments. I didn't want to talk about it anymore because I knew no matter what we decided, we weren't going to affect the outcome.

I just didn't want to be jerked around. It may sound crazy, but it'd be such a relief to know I'd no chance at all. None. Then I could say I did all I could; I could close the book and walk away from it with no regrets. Instead, I'm supposed to live by the mantra, "If you have a jersey on your back . . ." Is that a chance I want? Don't keep me around as an innings mopper or a babysitter. Don't lie to me; don't postpone my life with false promises. Is that too much to ask?

"I have to tell you Larry, you're kinda weirding me out lurking outside the door while I'm throwing mud in here."

"My bad. I was just thinking and you know how rare that is."

"Well, don't think too hard. We're baseball players after all, just ask Hoffman."

"By the way, what in the hell does 'inculcate' mean? [spit]"

"It means to instill an attitude or a belief by persistent instruction."

"Like brainwashing yourself?"

"Yeah, I guess you could call it that too. Inculcate is a nicer way of saying it."

"Shit, I thought it meant you got something pregnant. Like, I hope the Domos don't inculcate my sister [spit]."

"If she hasn't gotten pregnant yet, chances are she never will."

"You gonna be able to play tomorrow, or will you still be inculcating the toilet?"

"I don't know. I see the doctor in the morning and I hope to the Lord above he can make this stop because it's killing me." *"And maybe my career,"* I thought. Of all the ways I imagined I'd go out of this game, explaining to my grandkids that I crapped myself out of a job was not the one I expected.

Chapter Thirteen

The Imodium I downed didn't kick in when I was with Larry, but during the next few days it came on in full, creating a force field around my ass through which I couldn't squeeze even the tiniest of nuggets. By the time I was feeling better, it was cut day, and my first sick-free morning was met with the nauseating thought of what would happen to me when I arrived at camp.

I had done all I could. I had played my hardest, dug for answers the best way I knew, and adjusted radar reads diplomatically to give me a little extra edge. If I didn't make a team, then baseball just wasn't in the cards. At least I could walk away knowing I did the best I could. I would be okay with that. I think.

When Larry and I pulled into the complex, a group of players stood by the entrance in their street clothes, packed Padres bags on the ground next to them. They all had their cell phones to their ears. Some talked loudly and in angry tones, other in diffused, forlorn tones. Their time with the Padres had come to a close. At least they got to keep the bags.

"Anyone you know?" I asked, hoping Larry could identify the bodies.

"No. I think they were younger guys. I saw that one with the sunglasses on his head in the treatment room a lot though. That makes me feel *real* good, lemme tell ya."

"You sure you're ready for this?"

"Shit, it is what it is." We exited the van and headed in.

No roster work groups were up on the cork scheduling board. No names on the early work sheet, no clues of any kind. The atmosphere of the locker room was like a funeral, somber and stark. No one joked around; most of the guys just sat at their lockers with heads down in respect for the fallen.

Everything is done in person. Bruce Wick, the equipment manager and Lord Clubbie of the minor league side, plays the harbinger of death. He is commissioned with the duty of telling the players who are soon to be unemployed that their presence is requested in the back office by Grady or Earp for execution. Players who really want to know, find him.

The locker next to mine was cleaned out, several others as well. Come day's end, would mine be empty too? A pile of abandoned baseball equipment was forming next to the trash bin. Someone would take it for themselves before the end of the day, but not until cuts were over. It would seem too much like grave robbing.

Many players had not yet changed into their workout uniforms. I suppose there was no point in changing if you were going to be out of a job. Undeterred, I sat down on my dressing stool and started to dress. I got my jersey pants on, then started slipping my Ringor sports shirt over my head. My vision was obscured briefly while the fabric went over my eyes; when I got it past my face and my sight was restored, there was Bruce, the Clubbie of Death, standing in front of me.

"Son of a bitch," I said.

"You're alright," Bruce said. I sighed. He probably wanted to reprimand me about not staining my jock so bad. It wasn't my fault, I'd been sick.

"Have you seen Larry?"

I thought about not answering. It didn't matter; they'd find him eventually.

"Did you check the training room?"

"Yeah, he's not there."

"Did you check the lunchroom?"

"Not there either."

"Well, then he's probably taking a dump. Check the bathroom. Though I suggest you wait for your own good."

Bruce left.

Larry was gone, just like that. I didn't pursue Larry. There was no way to stop what was in motion. So after changing, I hit the cafeteria, finding a seat with Brent and Frenchy. After a few moments of silence, Brent asked in a whisper, "Did you hear they released Varner?"

"Varner? *Varner?* That's ridiculous. He was doing great. He's had nothing but success. Why?"

"I don't know. I think it's because he had that positive drug test."

"Yeah, but you know he wasn't doing anything. I mean, look at the kid. He's not exactly the model of fitness," I said. Varner was a stocky reliever, known for his in-season diet of Doritos and Mountain Dew. He was a member of the notorious "Bad Body Bullpen," a group of very successful relievers who had a "little more" to love.

Varner got popped for banned substances last year, though he looked no different. In fact, he may have put on weight. "He probably took some shady product that lied about its ingredients. It happens more than people think."

"Doesn't matter. It's about the image that comes with it. People think steroids, which might as well be pedophile as soon as it's tagged to your name. No one thinks honest mistake," Frenchy said.

"I suppose, but wow, I did not see that one coming. And, if you didn't know, they just released Larry too."

"Larry, huh? Well, I hate to say it, but that one makes sense to me," Brent said.

"Yeah, me too." I exhaled deeply. "Even Larry felt like it was coming. Still, it sucks. He was my roommate."

"Sorry, bro."

"What can you do? I mean, it's part of the game. . . ." I attempted to rationalize it to myself, but it didn't feel any better.

"He was too injury prone."

"I know, and they seem to be weeding out guys who have injuries."

"Makes me wonder what kind of injuries you're allowed to have." Brent had torn a muscle in his foot last year and missed a large chunk of time.

"Well, judging on how the guys with any type of arm trouble are dropping like flies around here, I'd say the one kind of injury you can't have has to do with the arm."

"Unless you're a big money pick. If they have a lot invested in you, then you get some grace."

"It's funny, but it's a lot like who has the big stack at a poker table, isn't it?" I asked.

Frenchy chimed in, "I think they are going to cut more guys tonight too."

"Really?" I thought I'd dodged the bullet.

"Yeah, I heard some guys talking about how they can't cut everyone in the same day because of the way it would mess up the on-field rotations." That's true, they'd need bodies to fill positions, if even for just one more day.

"You guys know everything, regular pipelines of information. Have you bugged the coaches' locker room?"

"Think about it. It makes sense." Unfortunately, it did. I was supposed to pitch today.

"Can you imagine knowing you're going to stick around for one day just so you can take up a field spot while someone else gets work in?" Brent asked.

"I'd be pissed. I'd want to know I wasn't wanted as soon as they decided on it," Frenchy affirmed.

I said nothing.

There was no sure way to tell why anyone got released. Some things played bigger parts in the process than others, but any of us could go at any time. Though some players are safer than others, this wasn't like *Survivor Peoria*. There's no immunity, no factions to unite with. Everyone with a jersey is a commodity, and if the right (or wrong) set of variables presented themselves, we could disappear.

The two lefties and I conjectured over probabilities. We did it because it made us feel safe. If we could figure out why a guy got canned, we could rationalize how we weren't like him. And as sad as it sounds, along with every pang of remorse, there was a sigh of relief.

When I left the cafeteria, yelling was coming from the back office, the executioner's room. From what I could hear, the player inside had been released and was venting his dissatisfaction. Not everyone goes down without a fight. A competitor is a competitor. If he doesn't like an umpire's call, he's probably not going to like the call of management declaring him out of a job. Seeing as he'd already been tossed, he might as well get his money's worth.

Heated voices raged from within. The door remained closed so the drama didn't spill into the clubhouse, though several guys lingered around the door trying to catch wind of what was going down. Then the door of the office flung open and out walked Lars.

His face was flushed and his eyes were full of the same intensity he had when he took the mound in late innings. He made his way to his locker, kicked the chair out of the way, grabbed his bag, and began slamming stuff into it. The locker room fell silent, the players dispersed, watching him from a safe distance. I felt as if I were miles away, watching across an impassable chasm. The mighty Lars, his jokes, his antics, the character he brought, gone—the end of an era.

He, like Larry, was one of the players who made my baseball life interesting, bearable even. The friends you make in this grind are what make it survivable. Yet, such friendships are dangerous when days like today come around and those bonds are ripped out of your life. After years of battling in the trenches of the minors, making the best of it with the boys you're fighting alongside, they vanish in a matter of minutes.

Outside, Larry sat on the concrete lip of the sidewalk bordering the parking lot. He had his cell phone out, spinning it over in his hands. Whom do you call first when your career ends? Your wife? Your parents? Your agent? Larry sat there, talking to no one. Maybe he had already called them, or maybe he was still waiting for it to make sense to him before he tried explaining it to someone else.

I sat down next to him on the dusty concrete. The sun's glare beamed off the expensive cars. The world went about its business in the distance, a world Larry was now a part of again.

"How you holding up?" I asked.

"I'm okay," he said. "I thought it might happen."

"Yeah. You know what you're gonna do from here? Have you talked to Adam?"

"Not yet. But I'll get a job playing independent ball somewhere or catch on someplace else."

A lot of guys say, "I'll catch on someplace else." There's no guarantee that'll happen, but it's a positive way to look at things. The only thing I could say was, "Yeah, I'm sure someone will snag you. I know the manager of the Washington Wild Things, if you think that would help."

"I got a few connections of my own."

"What are you going to do in the meantime?"

"Relax. Spend some time with the fam until that agent of ours finds me a job."

"You thinking about independent ball in any place particular?"

"Varner and I are going to try for the same team together."

"You two on a team . . . Wow! I don't know if that league knows what it's in for. Two chunky, Blue Collar Comedy extras tearing up indie ball."

"Bad Body Bullpen, brother!" Larry said, giving me a slap on the shoulder. He laughed for a bit, before slipping back into silence as we both came to terms with the fact he was leaving and so would all of our interaction.

"Well, I better call Adam and let him know what's going on."

"Yeah. Well, look man, if you need anything, call me, okay?"

"Same to you man. It was good playing with you. Git-er-done out there."

"I'll do my best. You be good now."

"Me? Always," he said and then winked. We exchanged man hugs, and he got on his phone. I walked back to my career.

More people got cut that day than any other cut day I had been a part of in my four spring trainings. It was a real butchering—hard to watch. The stretch lines were noticeably thinner and social circles were sparse. There was no morning joke. When Grady spoke at the morning meeting, it was easier to gather in because most of the space formerly taken up by extra players was vacant.

Grady informed us that the updated rosters would be set before the end of the day and that there were a few cuts still remaining. The green light for us to coast was definitely not on. Frenchy nudged me during that part.

Grady told us this was one of the hardest days in his career and it's never enjoyable releasing players. He said that he released a lot of excellent men today. I'm glad he said that part. I'm glad he took a moment to acknowledge them as men, not just cattle. Then, however, he said something that will never leave me. "Gentlemen, in just a short while, you'll be heading off to your respective towns and teams. Remember, you are gods to the people in these towns. You are their entertainers. Conduct yourself accordingly. Be professionals and represent yourselves and the organization well." Was that what this was really all about? Being a god of entertainment?

When I left camp in the afternoon, I was still on the Double-A roster. Some cuts came at the end of the day—people who played in the games like the lefties predicted. I was not one of them. I had made it. I had survived another spring training, something I did not truly grasp until that evening when I sat in my hotel room alone. The maids had come while I was out and erased any trace Larry left behind.

I sat in the dark at the tiny kitchenette table, television off, curtains pulled shut. I thought about various mantras of the sports world—how winning is about beating out the other guy and only the strong survive. I thought about being a god of entertainment. I thought about the people who would worship me. Finally, I thought about the guys who lost out to me in this spring's battle for roster spots, and about all those years together in the trenches, only to be shot down by friendly fire. When I got into the game, I never thought I'd be friends with the guys I'd have to beat to keep my dream going. Winning doesn't feel like winning when it happens this way.

Coaches tell Little Leaguers "heart" is the most important

thing a player possesses, yet when money mixes into the equation, heart slides to the bottom of the list. Heart has this do-gooder, patriotic nature to it, like George Washington had a lot of it and so did Gandhi. What about Lars, pushing through agony to get his arm back in shape, and how bad he wanted to make it, no matter how much pain he had to endure? I guess sometimes heart doesn't look as warm and cuddly as we expect it to. Sometimes it looks like a tattooed maniac who listens to Rammstein. And sometimes, it doesn't matter how much of it you have. On days like this one, a person could swear the meaning of life is as simple as making a roster.

I thought for a long time about the game, about now I was back in it and about how I got the chance I worked for all off-season—a chance to be someone again, someone with a title and a purpose. I was back on track to be a Double-A player, maybe prospect again. I wouldn't have to bend the truth about my career, and maybe, just maybe, I could make it after all.

After two hours of sitting in silence, the sudden ring of my hotel room phone was deafening. I stood up and grabbed the receiver.

"Dirk?" the voice of one of the trainers asked.

"Yeah, buddy, how's it going?"

"Hey, uh, Earp wanted me to call you and tell you not to pack for the Double-A van tomorrow."

"What?"

"Yeah, he said not to bring your stuff to the field."

"What do you mean *don't bring my stuff to the field*? I'm on the Double-A roster, we leave tomorrow."

"I don't know what's going on with that. He just asked me to call you and tell you this."

I sat down. "Do I at least have a job?"

"I can't answer that."

"If you know, you should at least tell me for God's sake!" I could feel my heart start racing. The volume of my voice was beginning to spike.

"I mean I don't know, and I don't. He said you can call. Well, he's out now, but you can talk with him in the morning."

"I have to wait till morning for this? You've got to be kidding me!"

"I'm just the messenger man. I'm sorry."

I was teetering on the edge of screaming long, coarse barrages of expletives, but I knew it was not his fault. "Fine," I gritted out. "Fine."

He continued speaking but I did not hear him. I was no longer in the conversation. I was tumbling down from my own pedestal. I couldn't catch my breath as I fell, like falling and suffocating at the same time. "Sorr—."

I hung up. I was standing, holding the receiver and the set in my hand, though I don't remember picking it up. I began a hectic search around the room. For what, I don't know. Maybe I expected to find an answer, but there wasn't any. A minute ago the room was serene, calm, a safe haven for me and my thoughts. Now it was a prison, and I was trapped with my racing mind scratching feverishly against the walls. I hurled the set at the wall, the corded receiver following after. Next, I grabbed the kitchenette table and flipped it over along with all its contents. An end table followed and then a lamp. Then I sat down, put my head in my hands, and tried to stop the spinning.

Chapter Fourteen

I called my parents first. I don't know why. I don't know what I expected to hear them say to me, but it was the first number I came to in my contacts list when I started searching for people I could vent to. They didn't answer. The phone rang and rang, but no one picked up, not even the answering machine with my mother's shrill voice declaring, "If you're a telemarketer, you can hang up now!" That's funny, because my mom is a telemarketer.

The next person on my hit list was my agent, and unlike my parents, he could actually influence the situation. A good agent is patient. He has to be. If he isn't, he won't stay an agent for very long, not with the amount of demanding phone calls he'll get every time a player gets his feelings hurt.

I remember how many times I called my agent my first year. I thought he was my publicist, legal counsel, and mother all rolled into one. Anytime I got a bad write-up, I wanted him to sue the reporter, spin the bad number so it looked good, and tell me I was a big boy now. I expected a lot, and to my agent's credit, he never once told me I was a demanding prima donna. So yes, all agents are liars.

Agents can specialize in different areas. Some are great lawyers, talkers, bargainers, arguers, or accountants, but the one thing they've in common is they're all great babysitters. It's not easy to deal with the massive and fragile egos of athletes who are simultaneously self-impressed to the point of narcissism and yet fearful to the point of paranoia. Receiving calls in the middle of the night from a player who's convinced management hates him because he's too good not to have been promoted by now is a specialty all to itself.

When I called my agent, it was about 11:00 P.M. his time. He answered because right now was that odd season when he gets lots of calls to inform him certain players under his representation were looking for new jobs. In fact, Larry and Varner had already called him. When Adam picked up, he greeted me with what had become his standard hello, "Shizzle! What's up man?"

He called me Shizzle because for a while we thought it would be fun to pretend I was a first rounder with a Snoop Dogg-type entourage. Alright, I thought it would be fun to pretend it. I forced him into it, and it stuck. So far from our natural personalities, it was funny for us to add izzles to the end of our dialogue. Now as I look upon the reasons for calling my breaking ball my curvebizzle, I feel extremely stupid.

"Hey Adam, we got a problem."

"Alright, lay it on me," he said. One quality I loved about the guy.

"I might not have a job come tomorrow."

"You might not because you're worried, or you might not because you've been told something."

"The latter."

"Give me the scoop."

I recited how it all went down.

"That's all he said?"

"Yeah, just like that. If I wanted to call in and ask for more information, I could, but I thought that might be a bad idea since

I would probably start yelling at anyone who answered, so I'm calling you for advice."

"Good decision on your part."

"What do you think I should do?"

"I don't think you should call."

"Okay, but what else is there I can do?"

"Nothing."

"I was afraid you would say that. Sitting here thinking about it is killing me."

"Sure, I'll bet it is."

"What do you think it means?"

"It could mean a few things, but since they don't want you to bring your bags in for Double-A, I don't think they'll send you there."

"Damn it." I moaned, and sat down. When I walked into camp today, I was okay with everything ending if it had to. But when I left, I did so with the belief I had earned my keep on the roster I set out to make. Now what had I earned?

"If I don't go to Double-A, should I ask for my release? Do I get out of this organization and try to catch on with someone else? I pitched well against the Braves last year; maybe I could catch on there? Maybe they'd give me a better shake; I mean, I earned Double-A, right?"

Adam didn't answer immediately, which meant he was trying to find a way to phrase something I wouldn't enjoy hearing as positively as he could.

"Just tell me," I said.

He took a breath. Cleared his throat. "Your chances of getting on another team right now aren't that great. It's not that you aren't talented, but it's just the time of year. Teams are setting their rosters. They've looked at a month's worth of tryouts and let go of most of them just like the Padres have. Also, you've got to understand you're an older guy with a mixed bag of results. You got experience at the higher levels, but the numbers aren't impressive. The reality of it is, the Padres see something they like about you, which is why they've kept hold of you. You may have the benefit of the doubt with them you wouldn't get someplace else. It may not be what you want to hear considering recent events, but they're still your best chance for a future in this game. It just might not be Double-A, even if you've earned it."

I held the cell phone to my ear in silence. I get quiet when I'm angry. Walking over to the hotel room window, I pulled the curtains and looked out. In the hotel's hot tub were a group of players soaking. They were probably talking about the day's cuts, where they were going, how they thought they would do on their respective teams. They probably didn't just get a call telling them they might now be out of a job—those bastards.

Adam spoke up, trying his best to make sure I didn't get defeated. "It's baseball, brother. One of these days, when you're in the bigs, you'll look back at this and laugh."

I hated when he talked to me like that, when he brought up being comfortable in the bigs, as if it was just a matter of time before I was there sipping from drinks with umbrellas in them while the good life washed over my toes. It was just a matter of time for guys who signed for millions to get there, not guys like me who've beat around the bush leagues and signed as seniors in college. I was a realist, and the big leagues were further away than ever.

Regardless of how inward focused and sure a player is, there'll always be wavering moments of doubt. Sometimes, when the game's going my way, when batters fall like autumn leaves and I can wring strikeouts out of my jersey like so much excess water, I permit myself to believe I can make it. Most of the time, however, when I'm in between excellence and catastrophe, I just hope I can. But in times like this, when I watch the window of opportunity slip shut and can feel the cold end of my career coming, I feel as if I'll never make it and kick myself for ever thinking I could.

Not much was left to believe in now. The reality of the situation was the Padres probably liked me more than any other team, and their "liking" me may only mean they deliberated before releasing me on the final day of camp rather than pulling the plug when they axed everyone else. I probably wasn't going to make the Double-A team, which meant I'd head back to High-A Lake Elsinore if I got to keep my job at all. It was now the best scenario. Adam was a good agent, but he wasn't going to turn this turd of a situation into a first rounder for me.

"Do you think they'll send me back to High-A?"

"They could."

"Oh God . . ."

"If that's where they stick you, Dirk, then that's the best chance you'll have."

"I seriously need to quit." But I couldn't. I wasn't a quitter—a curse of mine.

"Quit? Quit pouting maybe. It could be worse. You could be like Larry and Varner or that crazy dude with the tattoo."

"You mean Lars."

"Yep, you could be like him. You've still got a chance—I'll bet they'd trade places with you in a heartbeat."

"I'm not them, Adam. It's not apples to apples here. I don't know what they were playing for, but I can tell you what I'm not playing for. I don't want to waste another year of my life kicking around the California League with no idea what the fuck I'm— Hold on a sec."

My phone beeped at me, it was my mother on the other line. She was calling me back. I let it beep, deciding to call her back when I was done with Adam. I put the phone back to my ear.

"I want a better quality of life to come along at some point. Is that wrong? I'm not a quitter, and I think that may be just stupid of me. I think if I was smart, I'd get out of this now. I know this is a dream and there's an argument to be made for walking away from it, but it's not a fairy tale. I don't open up the fucking wardrobe and frolic into Narnia every time the umpire says play ball."

"I've never heard anyone put it that way."

"You know what I mean."

"I understand what you're talking about, and I'm not going to tell you you're wrong. There aren't any guarantees, and there will always be some dumbass fan who freaks out about you pissing away the magical experience of baseball. I would never tell you it's not a hard life, but this is part of it. You make the best with the chance you got. I know you aren't a quitter, so, even though you're angry, we both know you aren't going to give up this chance."

"I'm so tired of hearing that word! Chance, chance, chance!" I transferred ears. "It's okay to chase it when you have some promise, but you can't honestly tell me my chances just improved with this news?"

"No. No they didn't, but you still, as much as you are sick of the word, have a chance, is what I'm saying."

"Maybe."

"You do."

"Is it a chance I want?"

"You look at things differently than most players. I mean, you just used Narnia and fuck in the same sentence. I think you need to take some time and think about all this, and if you are as serious about walking away as you think, then I'll support you. I'll make some phone calls and see if I can get some more information. Just don't do anything you'll regret in the meantime."

I looked around the hotel room. All the furniture was flipped over, strewn through the place with a lampshade speared by a table leg.

"Don't worry. I won't."

When I got off the phone, a message popped up to inform me I had a voice mail from my mother. I dialed my voice mail box, and when the message began, my mom's exasperated voice said, "Hey babe, if you want to get a hold of us, don't call the house phone. Your brother came home drunk a few nights back and started doing his usual." She said it as if he brought home another bad grade, as if she were accustomed to it now, more disappointed than angry. "He started in on your father, and your dad got so upset with him I thought he was going to have a heart attack. Dad threatened to call the cops on him, so your brother ripped the phone off the wall and smashed it." I looked at the broken phone in my room. "I had to call the cops on my cell. We haven't seen your brother in a few days—probably hiding over at your grandmother's, who, by the way, has called us three times to tell us she doesn't want you back because you eat her out of house and home and take her stuff. Anyway, the caller ID still works, but the handset is busted. I can't get your dad out of the house to get a new one. I don't know what you wanted, so if you need us, just call me on my cell, okay? Alright, pitch good. Bye." Her voice was so casual, so everyday, it was as if she were describing her trip to the grocery store. The message played through. The robotic voice of my inbox informed me what to press to delete it. I closed my phone and set it down.

In the bathroom, I scooped up some water from the sink and splashed myself in the face. I let it trickle down my neck and soak into my shirt, not bothering to stop it. The hair on the side of my head matted to my face, and beads of water hung on my nose. I passed a hand over myself to flick off the excess. Then, flushed and broken, I stared at my disheveled reflection in the mirror. I looked in at Dirk, the baseball player. He stared back at me in his pristine uniform, hat on, glove at his side.

"You lied to me," I accused.

"You lied to yourself," came the calm response.

"Don't give me that! I've done what it takes to get us here."

"You've inculcated yourself."

"Very funny, smart-ass."

"You're uptight because you're afraid."

"Afraid?" I laughed. "Afraid of what?"

"Afraid of the day you'd have to take this uniform off."

"I'm not afraid. That's ridiculous! I was ready to quit before I came here."

"No," he said gently, "you were ready for Dad to say you could quit, but he didn't."

"That's not true. I can do it anytime I want," I said like a defiant child. I knew the truth though, and my words weren't convincing.

"I don't blame you, really. You've been hiding behind that jersey for years now. It's what you know."

"Hiding! Who's hiding? I've always been out in the open."

"Out in the open that you play baseball, sure. But you're afraid you won't be important without it."

"Fear has nothing to do with it! I've earned the right to be a respected athlete. I've paid my dues. There are only two kinds of people in this world: somebodies and nobodies. Baseball has made me somebody!"

"Really?" A skeptical look followed the question.

"Yes! I'm one of the special few who gets to do this!"

"Do you feel special right now?"

" . . . "

"You don't know who you are, and you're terrified of losing this." He tugged the uniform.

"It's my gift! Baseball is my gift, and I'm fighting to keep it."

"Baseball is also your curse, and the fight to keep it is killing you."

"Wrong—it's the only thing that's keeping me going. I have nothing else."

"You have more than you think."

"I don't believe you."

"That's your biggest problem."

The next day, I took the early van to the complex. I didn't talk to anyone, not Frenchy, or Ox, or Brent. No one knew what was going on, except maybe the maids who would have a hell of a time cleaning up the mess I made of the place. I cut through the crowd on a direct line for the back office. I didn't bother to look for Bruce; I went right to the source.

I came to the executioner's office and walked in without knocking. Sitting at his desk, Earp turned away from stapled sheets full of stats and names and looked at me. The stark expression I wore did all the talking.

"I'm sorry. You had a good spring, and I fought for you. You're not gonna like this, but it's a numbers game." He offered me a job in Lake Elsinore, Single-A ball—if I wanted it.

Chapter Fifteen

On buses like this, there are certain seats that can be removed and modular tables put in their place. These particular seats offer a few more inches of legroom as a side effect of their dual-purpose architecture. It's hardly perceptible by those who don't spend weeks of their life aboard buses, but I know it's the best seat in the house, and every bit of leg comfort counts.

I placed my backpack down on the seat closest to the window, emptied my pockets of my cell phone and wallet, feeding them to one of my pack's many outside pouches. Then I sat next to the pack in the seat closest to the aisle, stretched my legs out and kicked my feet up onto the armrest of the seat in front of me, and waited. The bus wasn't going to move for another half hour, and I was the first person on it.

Prime seating was the reason I arrived so early. The only good reason I had. Even now, the urge to get up and get off this bus was still hard to resist. I could be on a plane right now. The Padres owed me my last year of college via our contract, and I would finally have time to get that degree in communications studies, which, I admit, was something almost as useless as the five fruitless years in the minors were shaping up to be. If I got up right now, I could go home—home, yeah, right. That was the reason I got on this bus.

Sanchy, a Spanish catching prospect and this year's starting catcher for Lake Elsinore, boarded after me. He sat his pack down, unloaded a few travel items, and seated himself.

Catcher is the only position that has to worry about mound-side manner. A good catcher is one who can handle a pitcher well even if it means treating him as if he were the second coming when he's on the mound or handing him crayons because he's too stupid to read a coloring book. Catchers have to have a way with encouraging words. Sanchy dug into his pack and produced the book *Ingles Para Dummies*—so much for that idea.

Two more players, gangly pitcher types, galloped onto the bus. They squeezed Sanchy's shoulders in place of hello then proceeded farther into the bus. Chatting as they came toward me, the lead looked back to his partner and said, "So then he says, 'No, it's not gay, he was sucking *my* dick.' Can you believe that?"

I knew the speaker from playing with him last year in Lake Elsinore. Rosco, an easygoing right-handed reliever, was my former road roommate—I chose him because he was affable, well tempered, and didn't snore. The guy behind him was not a new face, but someone I didn't know. I saw a lot of him during the spring because he was part of a band of guys always horsing around near my locker. They were hilarious to watch, even though I didn't know what was going on, like right now, for example. Their in-jokes reminded me that I was on the outside of the loop, and worried about making a good first impression. The pair made their way back toward my seat and parked. Rosco looked at me and said, "Dirky."

"Rosco," I responded. The other gentleman reached out his hand and introduced himself as Pickles.

"He's got a big one," Rosco said, commenting on Pickles.

"Umm, that's great," I said, shaking Pickles' hand and then wiping my own on my leg. By the time the bus was done filling, I wouldn't know most of the people on it. All my friends were off to San Antonio, and the few people I did know on this team, like Brent and Frenchy, had found other rides. They worked out arrangements to drive with other players. Lake Elsinore is the only minor league team location that players can drive to in the Padres organization. All the other affiliate cities were flights. The busing service was provided for those who didn't have cars. Maybe I could have found a ride, but since my roster change was on such short notice, I was out of luck for an open seat.

Just as well. The bus would have ten people on board, if that. It would be relatively quiet and relaxed. I could throw my headphones on while we drove and listen to Bono or Dylan or some other great lyricist to help me make sense of what I'm doing with my life from the sanctity of the bus's rear.

Next to board the bus was a broad-shouldered, aloof-looking guy who seemed so mellow and pleased, you could mistake him for stoned. Behind him sprung an animated character sporting a polo shirt with its collar messed up, wrinkled khaki shorts, and flip-flops. As relaxed as the first gentleman was, the second one seemed just as tightly wound.

A horn honked outside the bus, and the excitable guy pressed his head against the bus window, immediately flicking off the car driving by. "Yeah, fuck you, guys!" he screamed.

Pickles greeted our excitable new friend with, "What's the matter now, Slappy?"

"False friends is what. Don't worry Pickles, you don't need to know," said Slappy who instantly stopped the conversation by starting another, telling Sanchy, "Attaboy Sanchy! English—mucho bueno!"

"What's got Slap-nuts all wound up now?" Rosco asked.

"Slappy is pissed because he thinks the other guys set him up.

He says they lied to him about giving him a ride just to break his heart," the stoned-looking fellow said. He was like Slappy's missing half, cool and collected, almost lethargic in comparison.

"Pshhh. . . . Fuck. *No Maddog.* Why would you say broken hearted? I mean, . . . look I'm just saying . . ." Slappy spoke in rapid, spasmodic fire—recovery breath, finger point, continue. "I'm just saying, you don't tell people you're going to give them a ride, then say, 'Oh no, wait, we would rather take this guy with us, even though we told you we'd take you.'"

"What are you saying, Slap? You don't want to ride with us?" Rosco said.

"Yeah, what's wrong with us? Not good enough?" Pickles echoed.

"What? No. *Come on.* Actually"—finger point—"that's exactly how I felt!" He was an emotional bell curve. "But you guys don't really feel that way, which is why I don't feel bad about telling you, 'cause you're understanding. You're real friends, not like those false ones out there." Slappy looked out the window with a hopeful face as if those he christened assholes might still return to pick him up. "You know I love you. You guys are my boys."

"We do have big ones," Rosco said.

"Big ones!" Pickles repeated in a singsong voice.

"I know you got big ones. Guys with big ones don't tell a person you're going to give them a ride, then"—he put his hands up to his head and made quotations while switching to a mocking voice—"*suddenly forget you offered one.* You just don't do that to a friend, right?"

"They did it on purpose Slap. Those bastards," Maddog said, stirring the pot while smiling at Slappy like a big, contented dog.

"I know, right? Those fuckers!" He looked out the window again.

"What's Slappy bitching about now?" Tiny Mexicali asked, having gotten on while the conversation was in motion. Tiny hopped around the system quite a bit last year, and I knew him from spending overlapping days on teams. He spent the bulk of his time with the crew already on board the USS *Lake Elsinore* and entered the conversation with ease. He was a big guy, who seemed to thrive on slamming Slappy.

"Slappy says there's a conspiracy to screw him out of a ride to Lake Elsinore," Rosco said.

"No, no, no, I didn't say conspiracy, I said—"

"You would say that Slap. Jesus, you're such a baby." Tiny wasted no time, coming on to the scene like a sledgehammer.

"Me? *Oh,* okay. You were the guy crying about how you're friends weren't really friends because they didn't offer you a ride at all."

"Yeah, but I'm not throwing a fit about it now, am I?"

"I'm not throwing a . . . who is throwing a . . . what? You wouldn't even know . . . fucking Maddog," Slappy moaned, jerking around at Maddog who sat placidly as if nothing were wrong.

"Look at you, you're a mess. Grow up Slappy," Tiny continued hammering, passing out a mischievous grin to the rest of the audience, their cue to join in.

"Whatever, you fat Aztec Eskimo. You just don't have any friends," Slappy countered. Group laughter bloomed from the remark, even from Tiny, who actually did look a tad Aztec and Eskimo.

"Whoa, that's just mean spirited, Slappy." Tiny feigned real pain, then started to squeeze his love handles, just to check.

"Wow, Slap, wow. You're destroying this team before game one," Rosco said, hissing the words. "You're a cancer."

"Me? I'm destroying . . . what? No, no, no." His finger shot up again. "The cancers are the false friends who promise rides but then show how fake they are by forgetting."

"Those bastards," Maddog strummed.

"I know, right? Fuck them!" Slappy turned and nodded at Maddog who looked exactly the same.

"They don't have big ones, that's for damn sure."

"Heck no, they don't." Pickles and Rosco high-fived.

"Still bro, calling me fat and a racial slur? That's harsh. I've got a fragile ego, I don't know if I can pitch at one hundred percent knowing my relievers feel that way about me. I can't help the way God made me."

"Well, sorry about your luck. Should have thought about those sensitive feelings before you started dishing out what you can't take, fatty."

"But I'm not fat, I'm big boned. No, seriously guys, I am. I have big bone density. I swear dude, a doctor told me that."

There was a pause in the conversation while everyone assessed whether Tiny was kidding. He continued squeezing his sides, indicating he was not.

"See what false friends do? Tiny's fat now because I didn't get a ride, which is okay, me being here that is, because I'm with real friends now, who would never lie to me."

"Those bastards."

"I know, right?"

"Screw that Slap-nuts, I wouldn't give you a ride. Six hours in a car with you would make me drive off a fucking cliff." This from yet another new voice that belonged to a muscular-looking guy who just boarded. He wore a designer brand T-shirt, jeans, and sunglasses like Magnum P.I. and stood with one leg up on one of the bus's front seats, staring at the pack of us like a parent watching kids get their good clothes dirty. "Sanchy! English! Attaboy!" he finished.

"Easy for you to say, Seth, you're on the bus like me," Slappy retorted.

"Even if I could drive, I wouldn't give you a ride because you're a fucking douche bag."

Slappy laughed hard, like a stiff wind bent him over backward as he bellowed. "That's such a position player thing to say. So predictable. You've been waiting all this time to call me a douche bag, haven't you? Did you stay up all night to think of that?"

"I don't have to wait to call you a douche bag, douche bag."

Let's be clear, Slappy wasn't the target. He was the lead singer of this band, even though he was getting beat on like a drum. It was all play fighting as everyone had a smile on his face. I learned a long time ago that the boys on a baseball team chewed on the people they liked, almost like how lion cubs wrestled and chewed on each other, but no one got hurt or cried to mommy. Playful, vulgar, personal at times, but no one took offense. Indeed, it was a form of team chemistry, everyone adding his own personal contribution. Well, almost everyone.

"Why's Slappy a douche bag?" a new player asked. Everyone turned to see who had spoken. He deflated upon eye contact. The party stopper stood in the bus aisle with an unassuming smile like Forrest Gump, except with a massive underbite and the face of Michael Phelps. It was as if everyone was listening to a joke about a minority and that particular minority just walked in.

"Uh."

"Yeah . . ."

"Oh, you know . . ."

"I was just saying that false friends are the reason for most of the world's evils."

"Those bastards."

"It's why Tiny is fat," Slappy continued.

"Big boned, bro."

"It's why Seth's a douche bag." Seth, who had taken a seat toward the front of the bus, didn't turn around, instead nonchalantly threw up his middle finger in response.

"And why this team's already got cancer before we even leave Phoenix."

The newcomer stood with the same slack look on his face, searching for answers where there were never meant to be any.

Rosco and Pickles looked out the window. Seth put on his headphones. Maddog looked laid back in his seat with a spectator's grin, and Slappy sat down as if everything made perfect sense upon his explanation. There was a stretch of silence while the new fish tried to make sense of it all. Someone coughed; Sanchy tried to pronounce a new phrase in English.

"Yeah, false friends are bad, huh? Totally." the new fish said.

"Yeah."

"Mmmm, hmmm."

". . ."

Crickets. Conversation killed.

"Have you guys ever seen the movie *Layer Cake*?" the new face asked. Everyone moaned, as if this topic had been broached several times before. "What? It's a good movie."

"No Daigle, we haven't seen it for fuck's sake."

"Well it's good. We should watch it on this bus trip."

"We are not watching fucking *Layer Cake*."

"I'm telling you, it's not what you think. It's a rich, complex tale of—"

"I don't care, I don't care how rich it is! We are not watching it!"

"Fine, sheesh, you guys don't have to get bent out of shape over it. It was just a suggestion." On that, Daigle, who may have been the nicest, most well-meaning one in the group, turned around and made his way back toward the middle of the bus like a whipped puppy, curling up somewhere between Seth and the crew in the back near me.

"Some guys just don't know when to quit, huh?" the group of lion cubs mumbled.

"So where were we?"

"I have a question," Pickles said. "If a guy sucks *your* dick, does that make you gay?"

"Absolutely."

"That's what I thought."

I followed Maddog's example, reclined my chair, and kicked my feet up with a grin on my face. Not only was this free entertainment, but it looked as if it could go on all day. And to think, I was worried about making a good first impression.

Chapter Sixteen

"This is just great," Slappy said. "We got Hayhurst with Triple-A time, seventeen fucking prospects and high-round picks and superstars on this team—I'm never going to pitch!"

It didn't seem as if Slappy was the kind of guy who received many compliments. "Relax Slap-nuts," Rosco said, sitting on his knees facing back toward me, with his head popped over the seat back of his chair like a prairie dog. "They'll need someone like you around to fill in innings between when the studs throw."

"I think that's my job, actually," I said, inducing a polite, if not merciful chuckle.

The bus was settled, and we were rolling now. Having made each other's acquaintances, sorted out the histories of our respective careers, and made an orientation ruling on oral sex, we did our best to deduce who would be in what role this season: starters, relievers, closer, and all the guys in between. Seth and Sanchy stayed up front. Daigle refrained from participation. The rest of the clan settled around me in the back and talked shop.

I was the oldest of the group. Having some higher-level time, I was treated as if I knew more about the game than I actually did. If anything, at this point, I knew less than ever.

"Seriously, what is your job?" Tiny asked. "Are you starting?"

"I don't know. They didn't tell me," I said.

"I'll bet you're starting. I'll bet the rotation is you, me, Frenchy, Brent, Daigle, Buschmann—oh, wait, that's six guys."

"I don't think I'm starting. I think I'm long relief."

"No, that's Pickles." Pickles smiled, and mouthed the words *big one*.

"Well, then I'm the bullpen coach. Hell, I don't know. All I can say is I'm not starting."

"You started in Triple-A though, right?" Tiny asked.

I was honestly sick of hearing about what I did in Triple-A. "I did, but it wasn't all that spectacu—"

"Holy shit, you started in Triple-A and now you're down here in the bullpen. Wow, that really blows, huh?" Slappy blurted.

"Jesus Slappy—" Rosco put his hand to his forehead.

"What? I didn't mean that as a knock against Hayhurst. I'm just saying. That blows."

"No offense taken." I had nothing left to offend.

"See? We're cool."

"So, you think they are just sending you here to get you some innings?" Rosco asked.

"They didn't say. The only thing I can tell you is, I'm not a priority."

"I'll bet you were pretty pissed when they told you that, huh?"

"Well, I wasn't thrilled about it, but . . ." I let the answer slip away.

"So what are you going to do?" Tiny pressed.

I looked out the window. The desert rolled by. The sun was starting to set, painting the skyline in oranges and purples. How many days of my life have I spent on buses like this? How much longer until the sun sets on my career?

"Not much I can do, bro. Keep pitching is all. As long as you got a jersey, you got a chance," I robotically regurgitated.

Tiny scratched his head. "Well, if they would have told that stuff to me, I would have . . ." Off he went, doing what all players do in situations where they vicariously live the life of a player they believed was screwed. They do what I told myself I was going to do a million times before I went into that office. They talk big about how they'd tell the brass to shove it up their collective asses, get their licks in, and be big men who don't take shit from anyone. When I think back to how I humbly accepted the demotion, even though, inside me, I was screaming the same ideas Tiny was grandstanding right now.

"I still can't believe you went from starting in Triple-A to no role in the pen here," Slappy mumbled.

"Look, Triple-A is just more of the same, okay. The hitters are a little better because they're older and a few have big-league time. I got my ass kicked up there because I spent too much time obsessing over how I was in Triple-A to do my job. I pitched terrible. If you can pitch, if you can execute, you can do well at any level because it's all the same game. I was so afraid of blowing it that that's exactly what I did. Don't let anyone tell you it's something it isn't or tell you you're something you're not. You guys are all more talented than I am, and if you do your job, you could be up there before the year is out." My words caught me off guard. I'd never been that honest before. It was just too much work to be dishonest about it anymore. Funny, being honest actually sounded strong. It made me realize how fearful and fragile it sounds when all a person does is cover up the truth or talk about how good they are. I don't think I could've spoken that way even a week before.

No one had time to digest the words as Slappy interrupted with, "Hey, you guys want in on this?" and produced a bottle of vodka from some mysterious location. Maddog countered with a bottle of Sprite.

That wasn't supposed to be on the bus, but then again, there were no coaches on board for this trip. What the management didn't know wouldn't hurt them. Hell, even when they did know, as long as they didn't see it, they didn't say anything. This generation of players were definitely not the first generation to booze their way through a long bus trip.

This bus was heading toward the Lake Elsinore Hotel and Casino, so if you were a player doing the math on whether this was a safe trip to drink on, it was relatively risk free. Once we got off the bus, we'd be checking into a hotel, not driving around under the influence. The coaches wouldn't be there when we got out, and since this was a minor league squad, there wouldn't be a horde of fans awaiting our arrival. If you had any concern about the image we would present to the hotel operators—wait until you see the place.

"I'll jump on that," Rosco said. He guzzled the water remaining is his bottle and handed it over to Slappy, who used it to mix up some time-travel tonic. Pickles handed his over next.

"How strong do you like it, Pickles?"

"Strong enough to put hair on my chest."

Slappy played bartender, and mixed up stiff ones for Pickles, Tiny, Maddog, Seth, and himself.

"You want to hit this Hay?"

"No, I'm good, thanks."

"You sure?"

"Yeah, I'm sure, more for you."

"I like where your head is at Hay!"

One hour and several refills later, we were out of vodka and Sprite. Slappy was passed out. Maddog watched the scenery pass by on the highway—his head hitting the seat back as he followed it. Rosco drunk dialed folks in his cell phone contacts. Pickles was glued to *Layer Cake*, watching it over the shoulder of Daigle, who had it playing on his laptop. Tiny was talking to me, or at me, rather, forcing me to practice in drunk psychiatry.

"Yeah bro, and then she was like, *I just wanna be friends.* How can we be friends after that man? Am I supposed to forget it, I mean, we have it on film, bro." I'd give you the details, but it would be $2.99 for the first minute and $1.99 for each additional. Suffice to say, it was a situation in which all I could offer was, "Women, what can you do?"

"I know man, I fucking know. Women!" He took another slug of his drink to emphasize his point, then slapped a heavy, big-boned arm around me. "What about you, bro? Let it out man, I'm here for you. You know you can trust me."

I smiled at Tiny. He was right, I could totally trust him because in his current state there was no way he would remember anything I said.

"I don't know, Tiny. I don't know what I'm feeling."

"Dude, I can totally relate to that."

"Yeah, well, I'm a little angry and I'm a little sad, but mostly I just feel lost."

"Yeah. Lost. Like you woke up naked and there was a camera and you don't know how you got there."

"Um . . . not like that, exactly."

"My bad, dude, my bad, I'm drunk." He made a motion as if he were zipping his lips.

"It's okay. It's just,"—I took another long look out the window—"I've been telling myself for the longest time this game had answers. It was going to give me worth as a person. That a jersey would make me somebody. I was going to make something of myself in this sport, and everyone would treat me like a superstar." Tiny exaggeratedly bobbed his head up and down as I spoke. "I can't even make it out of A-ball!" I tossed my hands up and let them fall.

"I guess it's my own fault. I believed it all. I believed that if I won enough, I would be changed into something larger than life. Like I could fix the bad things in my life if I was super successful. I could fix the way I looked at myself. I could fix my family. I could fix everything. But baseball results don't fix anything. . . ."

"You know what I think," I declared, "I think if we spend years of our lives playing this game and the only thing we have to show for it when we are done is a beat-up jersey and a string of numbers next to our name, then it was a hell of a waste of time. There has got to be more to this than just living and dying for the opportunity to wear the uniform. If that's all there is, then, I hate to say it, but professional baseball is a waste.

"You know, the best part of my baseball career didn't even have anything to do with baseball. I met a homeless guy in a shelter this off-season and gave him the shoes off my feet. He almost wept, dude, wept over a pair of shoes. I didn't have to be a superstar to do that; I just had to be me. In fact, I tried to be a superstar first, and it was as if I just separated us further. I've never seen a person react that way to anything I've ever done in baseball. God, it just makes me wonder if I'm going about this right. . . ."

Tiny looked at me real hard, it seemed as if the conversation sobered him. His eyes looked down and then back up to me, a deep thought forming on his brow, "Do you think I should get her some shoes, bro?"

I stared at him for a second or two. "Yes Tiny, that's exactly what I'm saying."

Chapter Seventeen

We spent the next few nights at the Lake Elsinore Hotel and Casino, ironically, only an hour north of San Diego itself. Casinos are one of those things that have flashy, movie-quality associations attached to them. When your brain hears the word, it gets giddy, and the mind's eye conjures forth a movie reel of flashy lights and showgirls. The Lake Elsinore Hotel and Casino is pretty much the opposite of that fanciful imagery in just about every way.

It's as if someone took a truck stop, a bad truck stop, with mysterious stains on the bathroom floors, racks of sticky-paged magazines, and shady travelers, then bred that scene with a dilapidated bingo hall. The place is full of sun-dried mummies wearing BluBlockers and Hawaiian print shirts. They fight with comic convention fan boys toting fanny packs and shifty Asian tourists for table minimums, propelled by a never-ending stream of mentholated cigarettes and white Russians.

In the hotel and casino, there's a bar the baseball community refers to as the Star Wars Cantina. It was christened such because you never know what kind of alien life you'll discover within it—women with sagging, pruny faces balanced by plastic, buoyant chests who will do things for poker chips that would make a sailor blush; broken-down old men who have drunk themselves out-ofbounds of space and time; and with every Lake Elsinore home series, the visiting baseball club.

The Lake Elsinore Hotel and Casino is the Lake Elsinore Storm's official hotel, as well as the official accommodations of the visiting team. It leaves its stink in the clothes of many a Cal League player. I've stayed in it my fair share of nights, and I know how bad it is. When the new-to-the-Lake faces started circulating how shockingly awful their living arrangements are, it came as no surprise to me. I already knew the covers beneath the comforter had pictures of airbrushed women riding white tigers à la Ronnie James Dio. I knew that if you turned a black light on in the room, it would look as if Jackson Pollock had painted on your bed. I knew the cinder block walls have bullet holes in them. I knew the hotel restaurant's food is made by someone who seems to shed pubic hair. Yes, I even knew that is what blood looks like when it dries. The Bellagio, it ain't. But home it is, unless you get a host family pronto.

The host family business is an interesting one. Essentially, a local family agrees to shoulder the burden of an extra person, a baseball-playing person, during the length of the season. They provide a spare room, a few meals, and transportation if they have it. It's a lot to ask, but a host family is an absolute necessity as living in Southern California isn't cheap.

The Adopt-a-Player campaign starts before the team arrives in hopes willing families can be lined up for a seamless transition. However grateful we baseball players are to the families who adopt us, we also know not all host families are created equal.

Beggars can't be choosers, so there's a certain degree of luck involved when getting paired up with your new family. Some families are the perfect model citizens, Mr. and Mrs. John Q. Host family with their white picket fence and adorable little children with cherub faces who can't wait to be just like their new older brother. Some families are wealthy and treat you like the draft pick you always wanted to be. Some host families aren't even families at all; some are just one person: a well-toned Cougar looking for an after-hours power hitter to keep her company between filming.

Depending on the makeup of the player, all these choices are desirable. However, they only represent one side of the coin. On the flip side, there is the family who has a pack of misbehaved trolls for children with parents who don't believe in discipline. The reason your PlayStation has peanut butter leaking from the optical drive can be chalked up to "youthful curiosity." You may live with a super fan who wants to play coach, manager, and parent. He'll live vicariously through you and evaluate, criticize, judge, blog, and call the organization about you. Or you may end up with a miserable old spinster who loves cats and hates men. She'll give you a sleeping bag next to the litter box. She'll turn off the air-conditioning in the hot months, yell at you when you don't polish the spoon you used, curse you for coming home after sunset, and accuse you of going through her things when she's away.

Players aren't saints either, and it takes a special family to agree to house one. If you're a devout Catholic family, getting a Mormon player can make things a tad awkward. If you're parents of little children, getting that Bostonian player who uses "fuck" for greetings, good-byes, pronouns, adjectives, verbs, and prayer might be more than you bargained for. If you're the proud parent of daughters close to the legal limit, it doesn't matter who you get, you're asking for trouble.

For the most part, players get paired with families somewhere in between the best-and worst-case scenarios. Just normal folks lending a helping hand. I had the good fortune of getting paired with good hosts every year I was at the Lake, including this year. I landed a big-hearted family with an extra car. They had a pool, a spare room, and all-you-can-eat groceries. To balance things out, they also had a dog who hated me. A little Jack Russell terrier who thought I was pure evil. It would growl at me whenever it saw me, lurk around corners giving me the stink eye, and crap in my shoes. I got even with it by waiting for it to fall asleep on the family's plus-sized beanbag, at which time I would leap on the bag launching the dog like a mortar shell across the living room and into the wall. Jack Russells are surprisingly aerodynamic.

The first few days with a newly formed club serve as orientation for the players. For most of the players, it's a new routine in a new town. We'll be playing at night, with games ending at 10 P.M. instead of us going to bed at that hour as we did for the last forty days of spring training. In order to get acclimated to the time differences, practices are scheduled late in the day, under field lighting. Our bodies won't adjust in the few days we have before the games start their inexorable march to September, but it's a start.

This is also the time that jersey numbers are fought over, lockers are chosen, uniform pants are altered, and hats, bats and gloves are broken in. Franchise front-office faces are linked to names while hands are shaken and pictures are taken. Video clips for the big display board in the outfield are recorded. Come-out music for batters to walk to the plate and pitchers to take the hill are selected.

My number that year was 35. I didn't pick it, I just took what fit. Some of the guys fight over more prized digits. Numbers 21, 22, and 23 are always hot commodities. The 7 or numbers with 7s at the end are also highly sought. Double digits are precious as well. Certain digits endear themselves to different players for different reasons. A player may have had a great college career in a number, and he hopes to keep the streak alive by wearing it in the pros. Maybe a relative wore a certain number, and it's family tradition to keep it. It could be the number of a former baseball hero, and it gives you the goose bumps every time you put it on now that you're a pro too. They're all great reasons; it's a shame there's only one of each number.

A pair of guys ended up gambling over a digit. They turned to the precision-crafted, divinely empowered, age-old, time-tested decider of rock-paper-scissors. Rock won in the decisive third round, capturing the honor to wear number 23. Scissors was left with 28. I have also seen numbers bargained for using the baseball equipment commodities market. Dip, chew, extra batting gloves, bats, and mitts have been used to leverage jersey numbers.

Come-out songs, are selected in a much more metaphysical way. Guys will skulk around with their headphones on, iPods cranked, trying to gauge the "power" of favored songs. Then they'll turn to their teammates. "Listen to this. Which one do you think sounds more badass?" The head phones will get passed, the music replayed, the headphones passed back. "I don't know; they're both good." Very few players have one song they favor over all others, and it usually comes down to the wire.

Country boys will choose country songs—tunes about their homeland, their heritage, and their pickup truck. The prima donna with the flashy car and the jet-setter wardrobe will select a hip-hop ballad declaring what a stunner Pimp, or Baller he is. The hard-edged guy with the short temper and addiction to Red Bull will require a rock song that makes him feel like Bruce Banner on the verge of becoming the Incredible Hulk. All these choices are safe, but the ones that make for the best are those that stray from the beaten path. Some guys may like the path they're on just fine, but personally, I believe a little originality makes a player and his tune memorable. This year I decided that if I didn't pitch well, at least I would be remembered for my song. I picked "Give It to Me Baby" by Rick James.

I enjoyed my few days before the start of the season, planning out player appearances, talking with front-office people, and getting to know my host family and their dog. There was too much to do to think about roles, futures, and demotions. I was angry of course, but I pressed it deep down inside, where it bubbled and stewed. Whenever I let it creep up, the antics of Slappy and the boys kept me distracted. I had nearly forgotten that I had been banished back to A-ball. At least until the night of the 2007 *Meet the Storm* Diamond Club dinner party, that is.

Chapter Eighteen

Four of us sat in a row, perched on the Diamond Club's bar stools like bachelors in a dating show. The audience was composed of host families, season ticket holders, fellow teammates, coaches, and front-office staff. The lighting was dim, not too dim, just enough to give the occasion an air of class. Something not easily done since the players being met wore suitcase-creased collared shirts and tastefully frayed blue jeans.

Behind the Diamond Club's bar, tall windows stretched up to the setting California skyline. Oranges and sapphires blurred together at the pointed, glassy peak. Not only did the club make its home down the left field line of the Storm's stadium, it also resembled its jewel namesake in construction with its angled glass prismatic.

Candles flickered on tables, and canned heat burned under trays of catered food. Next to the trays were homemade desserts furnished by the host families—cookies, cakes, and pies. Some were store-bought in a pinch, others painstakingly labored over by loving hands. Tupperware bins filled with ice held bottles of Sierra Mist, Dr Pepper, and spring water. A bartender dispensed adult refreshment—free to the players, a benefit that became a liability every year.

The club's radioman, an excitable, energetic fellow with a goatee and a silver tongue paced about in front of us with a microphone. The first time I met him was in 2004. I was called up from Low-A toward the end of an all-star caliber season to get a taste of the Cal League. I did terribly. The team was selfish, the casino was a nightmare, and my pitching abysmal. It was my first time shouldering expectation, and I did not shoulder it well.

You'll talk to anyone when you're doing badly. I quickly exhausted my teammates with my woes. What were they going to say? They all had their own careers to worry about. After my last outing of the year, a particularly bad one, I found myself outside the hotel room of the team's radioman. When he opened the door, the first thing he did was offer me a beer, something he was rather notorious for. It was kind of him, but I refused in favor of his ear. He listened as I exhausted myself trying to figure out the dilemma of my career in High-A. When I was done, he told me something very simple. This level was like a classroom. Each level was. Our job as players was to learn in each classroom and get As. It was okay if we didn't yet make the grade immediately; the important thing was, we try to learn as best as we can. Next time we're tested, we'll do better, he said. It was about the most poetic thing a man in his boxer shorts, white undershirt, and dress socks could say to another man while polishing off a Bud Light.

Unfortunately, instead of taking it for the insight on life that it was, I insisted on harvesting the sour message that I had gotten an F. In fact, I got an F four years running. I'm sure he didn't remember that conversation while he acted as the night's MC. But I did.

"Tell us about your hometown, Dirk," he said, lifting the tip of the microphone into speaking range.

"I was born in Canton, Ohio, home of the Football Hall of Fame." This is the third time I've told him this little factoid, complete with the Hall of Fame reference. I don't care for football, but the town is rather unremarkable in all other aspects. We have a few chain restaurants, manufacturing on the decline, and potholes.

"Where did you go to college?"

"I went to Kent State University in Kent, Ohio." Another repeat.

"Did you graduate?"

"Not yet."

"What will the degree be when you finish?"

"Communications studies."

"Thinking about going into radio when you finish?" he asked, in a coy manner.

"I don't know if I have the personality for it," I mumbled.

"Now, we both know that's not true, you're quite the talker."

The radioman spun around and faced the audience. He smiled, recalling a particular memory, then turned back to me. "For those of you who don't know Dirk, he has been here before. This is his fourth year with us, and he's become a bit of a fan favorite . . ." My mouth curved up at the enthusiasm in his tone, but my eyes betrayed me, falling downward. My head followed. *Fan favorite? The only reason I'm a fan favorite is because I never leave!*

"Dirk is in contention for a Storm Record," he continued. "He's only . . ."

Who cares? Contention for most something of some stat that didn't even remotely matter to me. Some pile of minor league numbers I'd gladly exchange for being a step up or a single second of big-league time. He talked happily though, enthusiastically, as if I won on a game show.

"Dirk, I have to take a moment here and go back in time with you. I want to go back to a game in 2005. Do you remember that championship game?"

"Yes, I do." Of course, I did. How could I forget that giant mental splinter?

He replayed the tale of the most infamous game of my life. The six dominant innings I pitched. The horrible feeling when the bullpen blew the game. Of course, he said it all more cheerily than I would have. "That was one of the best games I've ever seen pitched, certainly one of the best Storm games ever played."

"I appreciate that."

"Why don't you tell us what that felt like, pitching in a game like that?" He brought the microphone up to my lips to collect my answer. Those sitting around perked up for my insightful monologue.

Sure, I could tell you what it's like: it's as if your soul gets ripped out of you. It's like someone stomps on your neck and then giggles. It's as if, oh, I don't know, you're getting told you had a good spring, but you're going back to A-ball.

"Best moment of my career," I said.

The radioman was so well meaning. Nothing he said was meant to hurt, and still I felt as if I was being flogged in public. It's no fun lying to make yourself look good, but worse still is keeping up a lie so others can believe in you. I wanted to escape, but the microphone wasn't going anywhere, unfortunately, and neither was I.

"It's good to have you back Dirk, though we doubt you'll be here very long. What are your thoughts on this upcoming season?"

This is the part where the player says he's going to do great, where he's sure the team will win, and where he'll pitch the hell out of it. I didn't want to lie, and so I didn't want to answer. I didn't even want to speak. The anger and the disappointment would surely come out if I opened my mouth. I wished Maddog or Slappy would do something stupid and distract the audience so I could sneak out. I wished for Armageddon, as I did minutes before the championship game we just blissfully discussed.

I dropped my head. The radioman shifted awkwardly. I'm sure the crowd thought I was choosing the right words, but I wasn't thinking about that season. I was thinking about my life, and how I got up on this stage, and how I had had enough lying about the situation.

I lost faith in the game, lost faith in myself, and felt chained to something I didn't care about anymore. How it was all a sham. I was tired of being a stat, a bad one, and I didn't want to be remembered for what I almost did. You sell your soul to this game, and it gives you nothing to go on but the promise of chance. We chase it like donkeys after a carrot until we are put out to pasture or ascend to what? Gods of entertainment? Who cares what happens this season?

This is a wicked business, hiding behind soft candlelight and homemade desserts. I was tired of being a commodity and tired of lining up and thanking people for the opportunity of almost making it. I was tired of getting dragged up in front of people and having bad things spun clean by nice-speaking people. If I was going to be lost in the folds of some minor league town, then I go out on my terms. This rage and disgust was coming out, and I didn't care what happened. I was already a loser, how much worse could it get? Send me back to my junkyard of broken dreams, I will find another way if I must. I was a competitor scorned, and believe me, I had a few things to say about it.

All the emotions of my private battle with the game swirled up to my tongue. The radioman lifted the microphone to my face, and I felt the fire coming up inside. When the heat came to my mouth, it melted away the Diamond Club walls and burnt the roof down. The whole place disappeared like smoke, and before I could puff out a word, I choked on something like an epiphany or a parable.

I was on a ball field, atop a mound, with fans and players and families standing behind me. Across from me, in the batters box, the Baseball Reaper came up to hit. This was it, where it all would end. I swore I would beat him. I would not stand in fear of him any longer. I dug in on the mound, wound up, and threw my best fastball in for strike one. The crowd behind me cheered, and I lapped up their praise. The Reaper, however, stood motionless. No emotions to be seen underneath his dark mysterious hood as I showboated.

I wound again—a fastball again. I felt my arm would snap as I gave it everything. The ball shot from my hand like fire and down the middle it went, popping into the glove for strike two. The Reaper did not move, his cloak blowing lazily in the wind, with the bat still motionless on his bony shoulder. The ball returned, but the praise and support were gone. Somewhere in the distance, some prospect of unknown origin stood surrounded by the people who once watched me. They had moved on. I was alone, forgotten, and suddenly cold.

The Baseball Reaper did not forget. I owed him another pitch. Once I started this challenge, there was no backing out. Silent, ominous, and sixty feet away, he stood piercing me with his gaze. The reaction came up inside me again, the fire that raged at the game and all its lies. Who cares if the rest of the world was here to see it or if I was alone? I would beat him, or I would watch my career go down in flames trying—it didn't matter anymore. This was now a competition of will, something beyond muscles, velocity, or baseball talent. All I could control was my approach, and so I wound up with the will to win, unafraid of the worst.

The ball went into flight, rolling off my fingers the way it did so many times before. It spun over and over as it made its way to the mitt. The reaper stood motionless, waiting for the ball to come to him as though he was waiting for the demise of my career.

The ball whipped by him, slamming into the glove for strike three. He did not move. Everything froze. I stood staring at the Baseball Reaper—no emotions, no fear, no joy, no fans, no cheering, no lights, no reporters, nothing but him and me. The reaper dropped the bat, reached up to his cowl with his bony fingers, and pulled back the fabric that hid his face. It was me underneath. It was always me.

The radioman's microphone lingered near my mouth. "So Dirk, your thoughts?" he asked again.

"I feel very optimistic," I said, and for the first time in a very long time, I meant it.

Chapter Nineteen

I didn't get to ride on the fire truck, which sucked. I mean, this was my fourth year at the place, the least they could let me do was ride on the fucking fire truck. Instead, mostly position players came rolling out on the polished red engine. I walked out of the dugout and stood next to it, but you could tell all the fans thought the guys who rode in were much more interesting than me.

Opening night at home is always one of the best experiences in baseball. Though we started the year on a seven-day road series, the season doesn't have the same kick-off feel to it as it does the first night you walk out to a packed house of your own fans. Most stadiums won't see this many fans again until a fireworks promotion or a championship series, but it still makes you feel like a rock star even if most of the crowd just happens to be here because it's dollar beer night.

The bullpen in Lake Elsinore sits down the left field line. It's cut out of the left side of the stadium, in the left field corner just below the outdoor decks of the Diamond Club. There is a metal bench in the pen, but no one sits on it. Instead, the players use plastic lawn chairs, common seating arrangements for bullpens around the league. When there aren't enough chairs, players have been known to steal the soft, bar-stool-style seating from the Diamond Club.

Both the Diamond Club and the Lake Elsinore bullpen are good places to watch a game from, though each has its advantages. The bullpen, for example, gets you away from the oppressive eyes of management who will insist that we care about what's going on on the field and stop our talks about boobs, guns, or boobs with guns. The Diamond Club, on the other hand, serves beer. Though we have gotten beer served to the bullpen before, it's difficult to spend time in the Diamond Club during a game without the coaching staff getting upset.

Before our merry band of relievers took to the pen, Pickles jumped up onto the lip of the grass and shouted in his best superhero voice, "Bullpen, assemble!" Supposedly, we relievers were to leap to our feet and rush to his side like the Super Friends, maybe even combined into one large reliever like Voltron. Instead, I got up from the dugout bench like an old man getting out of his rocking chair, Slappy put a dip in, and Maddog accidentally dropped his glove on someone's spit out gum.

As we made our way to the pen, fans splashed against the stadium's fencing, begging us for autographs. We signed everything from hats and programs to ticket stubs and sandwich wrappers. It always boggles my mind how fans will fight all over themselves at a chance to get one of our names scribbled on their souvenirs. If only they knew what we were under these jerseys. Just hours before the game, the team debated the question of when a protein shake should be consumed—before or after sex? During, we decided, if you have a hand free.

After signatures came the sound of something I truly despised—the constant petitioning for the game's more revered souvenir.

"Can I have a ball?" legions of children squawked.

"No. Sorry."

"Why not?"

"We can't give these out."

"Why not? You have a whole bag full of them."

"I'm sorry, I'm not allowed. Our coaches will get mad at us. I can only give out foul balls."

"Well, if you get another foul ball hit down here, can I have it?"

"Yeah, sure."

"Can I have a ball?"

"No. Sorry."

"Why not?"

"You were standing right behind the other kid when I told him no. Weren't you listening?"

"Can I have it if I listen?"

"No kid, you can't have a ball. I can't give these out."

"Why not?"

"Because our coaches will get mad at us."

"They don't have to know."

"They'll find out. Sorry I can't give you a ball."

Some of the other guys on the team handled it differently—like Slappy, for example.

"Can I have a ball?"

"Sure, they're ten bucks at the gift shop."

"Why can't you give me one?"

"It's un-American to give it out for free."

"You're mean."

"You're annoying. Go sit down."

Then there was the Spanish rejection.

"Can I have a ball?"

"Que?"

"Um, can I have a ball?"

"Que? No habla Ingles."

"But you were just talking to that other guy in English."

"Que?"

And, my personal favorite.

"Can I have a ball?"

"No."

"I'll give you twenty bucks for one."

"SOLD! Show me the money kid."

"I don't have it; let me go ask my parents."

"Well hurry up because I don't know how much longer I can guarantee this price."

"Dude, you're not seriously going to sell that kid a ball are you?"

"Why not? I need the money more than he does. I can't afford to come to these games on what I make."

The pen's seating arrangement puts us close enough to the edge of the stands to warrant constant petitioning for baseballs throughout the contest. If you ever come down to the pen to ask for a ball from a player and he ignores you, it's probably because he knows what you want, can't give it to you, and is sick of explaining it. We began rejecting requests one after another until we were sick of rejecting fans and just ignored them altogether.

"You know, there has got to be a better way to deal with this," I said.

"What do you mean, like make a big sign that says 'no free baseballs'?"

"No, I mean, we have this high-demand item. Every kid wants a baseball. It's a simple economic issue—supply and demand. We could make this profitable. Back in my communications studies days my professors always said collaboration was the best way to solve an issue. Well, this is America, we are capitalists, they're rich little snots, and there has got to be a way this works out to our benefit and theirs."

"I am totally cool with selling balls to kids, but I'll bet we get into trouble for it," Slappy said.

"What if we made a game out of it?" I said.

"Oh yeah, I've heard of this before. Like make them pay for a chance to win a ball," Rosco said.

"Yeah, I've heard of other teams doing something like tossing a quarter in a cup."

"It's called quarter toss. I've heard of it too. Oh shit, we totally have to do it! I heard some team made enough money to buy a ping pong table for their clubhouse doing this," Slappy said.

We took one of the plastic cups next to the bullpen's watercooler and filled the bottom of it with a little bit of dirt so it wouldn't tip over when struck. Then, we counted by paces from the railing of the seats to a spot in the pen, about eight feet. We placed the cup down. That was as elaborate as it got.

"So who's going to be our salesman?"

"Slappy, that's all you, baby."

"Yeah, sure, that's fine. I'll keep all the money we make, though."

"No, come on, this is reliever money. It's bullpen cash. We can use it to pay fines in Kangaroo Court on—"

"To buy dip!"

"Or a night out."

"Let's not get ahead of ourselves, we haven't even made our first quarter yet."

"So, before I start selling this, what are the rules?"

"If you toss a quarter in the cup, you get a ball. If you miss, we keep the quarter—simple."

"Fuckin' all right then." Slappy turned to the audience. He didn't see kids; he saw dollar signs. "Step right up for quarter toss. Everyone's a winner! Only costs you a quarter to win a baseball. Step right up!"

"Wow, he was made for this," I said to Maddog as we watched Slappy go.

"Can I have a ball?" our first customer asked.

"No, but you can *win* one," Slappy beamed.

"What do you mean, win one?"

"Well . . ." Slappy explained the rules. He pointed out the cup and to our bag of balls. The kid's face turned skeptical, but Slappy assured him in a "just get in the car and I'll give you candy" kind of way. The kid produced a quarter and set his feet at the edge of the stadium's railing, teetering over, dangling into the pen. He tossed his quarter, which twirled through the air and landed with a dull thud in the dirt near the cup—a miss. We were one quarter richer.

"Darn it!" the kid said. His hand shot into his pocket.

"If you have another quarter, you can try again, as many times as you got quarters for. I believe in you!" Slappy was a regular carnie.

The kid tossed and missed again. Fifty cents richer. Another miss followed shortly, 75 cents. Then another. One dollar.

"Oh, you were *so* close. I thought for sure you had it that time," the consummate tempter hissed.

More kids came down. They lined up, taking turns tossing for a chance at a ball. As they missed, Slappy played devil's advocate and assured them it was only a quarter, or a dollar, or five measly bucks. So many children began to congregate that the stadium's ushers had to shoo them back to their seats.

"Hey you're killing our business here!" we protested.

"I'm sorry boys, we can't have them blocking the view of paying ticket holders."

The kids all took seats near the bullpen. But when the ushers left, we encouraged them to toss again.

"Wow, this is amazing," we remarked.

"I know, and profitable. Why didn't we think of this sooner?"

"What if they drain one?" Pickles asked.

"We'll just give them one of the scuffed-up balls."

"Slappy, what's our total up to now?"

Once Slappy had four quarters, he started changing in dollars. Once he got five dollars, he started changing fives. "About $17.50," Slappy replied, as he sifted through the wad of dollars and quarters in his pocket. We had only been playing for about thirty minutes.

"I love opening night!"

One little boy came up and confidently declared he wanted a dollar's worth of quarters. Slappy happily obliged him. The new boy set his feet, stuck his tongue out like Kobe Bryant, and shot his first quarter with both hands, free throw style. The silver circle tumbled through the air and landed in the center of the cup.

"Yea baby! Yeah! Give me that baseball!"

"Alright, that's how it's done right there," Slappy declared, announcing to everyone in earshot as if it was the perfect advertisement. We knew someone would eventually get one. We fished out a beat-up ball and handed it over to the boy. He didn't care that it wasn't a new ball, a pearl as we called them. He happily took it, passing it around and high-fiving his friend.

"Okay, let me take my next shot." He still had three quarters left. Slappy obliged. The odds of him sinking another were slim to none. Giving out one ball was good for business in a way.

The boy lined up his next shot, put his hands in the air, and let the quarter loose. It landed in the center of the cup. "Wow, this kid is amazing. Great job kid!"

"That's right, that's right, this game is easy! Bring your quarters, everyone's a winner!"

We fished him out another ball. He handed it to one of his friends as if it were a large, stuffed dog he won for knocking down milk bottles, then set himself up for his next shot. A quick glance at the inventory of balls revealed that we didn't have that many scuffed balls, in fact, we had no scuffed balls left. It was early in the season, and we hadn't beat too many balls up yet. If he drained another one, we'd have to pass him a pearl. I did the math in my head. If this kid made his next shot, we'd be giving out balls at the rate of one ball every six dollars. They cost ten in the gift shop.

The boy set his feet and steadied himself. The quarter tumbled through the air and came up short. We all breathed a little easier. The boy fell back as if he were shot, and all his friends groaned at the near miss. He recovered, set his feet again, and let his last quarter fly. It landed in the center of the cup.

"That's great, good for you, bud," Slappy said through gritted teeth. He handed over a perfectly round, rubbed up, game ready, pearl from our bag. The boy took it, chest bumped his compadres, and reached his hand into his pocket to produce another dollar.

"Sorry kid. Game's over," Slappy said. Maddog picked up the cup and threw it in the trash. Rosco shut the ball bag.

"But you have a whole bag right there."

"Sorry. I can't give any more out."

"But why—"

"Here kid, take this as a 'cancelation' prize," Maddog said offering the kids Bazooka Joe bubble gum.

"I don't want no gum."

"Tough," Maddog said, pushing gum into the kid's hands. "Here you go, now you kids go sit down."

"But—"

"Usher! These kids are bothering us." The usher came down at our call and shooed the children back to their seats. The boy who won three baseballs told us that we sucked.

"We are going to have to start finding ways to build our inventory if we plan to keep doing this."

"Let's all just steal them from batting practice. Those balls are all chewed up—no one will miss them."

"I just have one question," I said, looking at Maddog.

"What's that?"

"Did you call it a cancelation prize, Maddog?"

"Yeah, you know, a prize you get when you don't get something you want."

"It's consolation, buddy. A consolation prize."

"A constellation prize?"

"So-lation. Consolation."

"I like cancelation better."

Around the fifth inning change, Stubbs Wimperton, the team's soft-throwing left-handed relief specialist who relied on a steady diet of smoke and mirrors to get outs, came walking down to the pen. Fans cawed at Stubbs to take a detour over to them for signatures and souvenirs, but he ignored their requests in favor of stirring his coffee as he plodded along. Not the largest, most masculine build compared to his teammates, Stubbs was about five feet six inches with a receding hairline. He had a waddle to him like a penguin, and an excitable little giggle that followed his words. However, expertly landscaped facial hair and features like Kevin Spacey more than made up for his lack of manly size when it came to impressing females in the audience, something he was a natural at. As he passed the last section of seating, he gazed into the stands and saw something that held his eyes until he reached the pen.

Slappy counted quarters, Maddog folded a gum wrapper into a dart, and I flicked sunflower seeds aimlessly while the others guys conversed.

"Did you guys see that girl in the stands?" Stubbs asked.

"There's like a million girls in the stands, Stubbs."

Stubbs rolled his eyes. "Well I know, he-he, but did you see the one right next to us?" He pointed at her. We all turned in our chairs to pick out the chick in the stands. She was wearing a tight white shirt and jeans, and was surrounded by middle-aged kids.

"I wonder if she's a teacher."

"Why would you wonder that?"

"Because of all the kids around her."

"Maybe she's the big sister?"

"No, she looks like a teacher to me, he-he."

"I didn't know they had a specific make to them."

"Are you going to talk to her?"

"How? What am I going to do? Yell at her in the middle of the crowd?"

"Send her a ball-o-gram." Meaning, write the message on a baseball and toss it to her.

Stubbs sat for a second to consider the option. "Do we have baseballs we can spare?"

"We don't have any more scuffed ones, but we can use a good one for this worthy operation," Rosco said.

"We'll write it off as an entertainment expense," Slappy said fumbling with his fistful of change.

Stubbs fished out a ball from the bullpen ammo bag, then asked one of the waitresses in the Diamond Club beer garden for a pen. Taking the pen to the ball, Stubbs wrote, Teacher or student? on it. Then he walked over to the base of the stadium seating containing the girl in white.

Stubbs pointed at his lady. She looked confused. He pointed again, this time showing the ball, making pantomime motions of his intent to throw it to her. Other fans started begging for the ball like dogs panting at the dinner table. Stubbs explicitly expressed whom it was for and tossed it to the girl. She caught it, then looked at the ball. She looked back at Stubbs, who slyly mouthed, "Write me back." It was the baseball equivalent of passing notes with *Do you like me? Check yes or no.*

"Do you think she'll write back?"

"I don't know. I think she might, but she looked confused," Stubbs said.

"She'd better write. That was a good baseball," Slappy said.

"If I would have taken it over, she'd write back for sure. I don't know about you though, Stubbs. You might have scared her off," Rosco said.

"He does have a big one," Pickles echoed.

"Fuck you, guys. Ladies love my style. I'm cuddly, he-he."

"And can fit in most overhead bins."

"Screw you."

This lady must have dug Stubbs' style, because five minutes later, the ball came back. The lady in white walked over and returned the ball-o-gram to sender. Stubbs caught her toss, rolled it around until he could find the reply message, which simply said, "Teacher."

"See! I told you she looked like a teacher! He-he."

"That doesn't mean anything Stubbs. She could have written that to imply she wasn't a kid. Or even that's she's a freaky kind of girl, you know, like she'll teach you a thing or two big boy."

"Hey, hey, hey! Now we're getting someplace. You gotta find out Stubbs," Slappy said, grabbing Stubbs' shoulders. "Dealing with little jerk-off kids all day, dreaming of meeting a professional athlete at night. She needs an outlet! You gotta find out!"

"Okay, okay!" Stubbs said, wrenching free of Slappy's grip. Stubbs set to writing his next letter on the remaining ball space. "Want to come over to my place and play after school?"

"Wow, that's a bold move! What if she's not old enough? That statement to an underage girl is incriminating as hell."

"Well, she couldn't say she was a teacher if she wasn't old enough."

"No, no, no. She could totally say that. Girls lie about shit all the time," Slappy insisted.

"You were the one that wanted me to write her back, Slappy."

"I still do."

"Are we going to see you on *How to Catch a Predator* someday, Slappy?" I asked.

"What? No! Come on. I'm just saying she could lie. Look, if she writes back she's definitely freaky." He rubbed his hands together.

"But if she's not of age, then it doesn't matter."

"It does matter if she's not of age. You could get in trouble, Stubbs."

"Only one way to find out," Maddog said. We all looked at Stubbs, who held the ball. It was his decision.

"Oh what the hell!" Stubbs got up and made his way to the stands. He delivered the ball and walked back. None of us spoke as we waited. Five minutes later the ball was returned to us with the following words: "What happens if I've got detention? I've been a very naughty girl."

"Ohhh shit!" the pen roared.

"Wow, he-he."

"You gotta find out how old she is man."

"She looks older to me. Definitely over eighteen, like young twenties, for sure."

"I don't think it matters at this point."

"Yeah, what kind of underage girl writes this kind of stuff down?"

Stubbs wrote out the request and made the pilgrimage to the stands for a third time. Again, the ball came back, this time with the following: "Old enough to teach, but young enough to tease. Amy, twenty-five years old, 951-*** ****.

"Wow, who would have thought it would be that easy?"

"Never underestimate the power of a man in uniform, boys," Rosco said.

"Are you going to call her?"

"Heck, yes, I am, he-he."

"Oh, we gotta know how that goes down."

"I wonder what her students think right now?" Pickles said.

"I'll bet they all wish they could be you, Stubbs!"

"I'll bet they don't—most of them are taller than you."

"Screw you, guys!"

Chapter Twenty

I walked through the clubhouse doors around 2:00 in the afternoon. I put my backpack down and checked the itinerary on the dry erase board. It read Pitchers' Stretch at 3:15, Position Players at 4. There was a note under the Kangaroo Court list that said Offenders, Pay Your Fucking Fines!

Pickles was standing naked in front of the big screen with a pair of sunglasses on. He was rocking out to "Free Bird" on Guitar Hero. He tells everyone he plays better naked—you get used to it. As long as he doesn't use his "extra mic" in the song, we're fine. Several of the other guys were perched around the place, watching Pickles go, like at a real rock concert. He's fun to watch play, not because he's naked, but because he really gets into the music, windmilling the guitar and drop-kicking furniture when he hits climactic notes.

I picked my way around the awestruck spectators and dumped my stuff into my locker. You may think it's strange, grown men sitting around watching a naked man play digital guitar. Maybe it is, but you get used to that too.

I changed, threw on some sandals, and made my way back to join the crowd. I was going to sit on the floor in an open area, but before I could, Slappy grabbed my shoulder and told me not to.

"Why not?" I asked.

"Tiny threw up there, last night."

"What do you mean, last night? When? We were at the Diamond Club." The front office keeps the club open for the boys every dollar beer night.

"No, after the Diamond Club. Tiny was so drunk that he didn't want to go home to his host family, so he came back here and crashed on the couch. He rolled over and threw up on the floor there." Slappy pointed at the damp spot I was about to sit in. Tiny must have taken liberal advantage of the free brews for players rule.

"He went to the bathroom and threw up there a few times too, then passed out, and slept on the floor in there."

"He slept on the bathroom floor?" I said, mouth open and hand stuck to forehead. I looked into the bathroom where the floor was wet from some mysterious leak. At least I hoped it was a leak.

"Yeah. It was fucking hilarious. You should have seen it," Slappy roared.

"Come to think of it, the place does smell a little worse than usual. Did you take pictures?"

"Yeah, but he doesn't know it yet, so don't tell."

"Oh, that's going to be great blackmail."

Pickles was just getting into the "Free Bird" guitar solo. We watched him rock, destroying the expert setting as if he wrote the song. He played it through its completion, maxed out all the points, and then tossed the guitar down as if he were bored. He faked a yawn and walked away. Some of the guys applauded.

"You done, Pickles?" Seth asked.

"Yeah, I'd play more, but I can't get more perfect than perfect," he said, strutting around.

"Good. Now put some fucking clothes on; I'm sick of looking at your naked ass."

"I'm not naked." Pickles tipped his shades so he could just see over the rims. "I got sunglasses on!" He then bounded over to his locker and started putting on real clothes.

Frenchy and Brent selected two-player mode now that the master was done. Frenchy picked up the extra guitar, but Brent just stared at Pickles, not wanting to touch it because "the master" had rubbed his junk all over it. "You need to clean your guitar off when you're done, Pickles. It's got wiener sweat on it."

"I know. It's how I mark my territory," Pickles said, jerking up a pair of sliders.

"That's sick," the irritated Brent complained. Staring at Pickles' guitar, Brent slumped his shoulders and went into the training room to get a pair of rubber gloves and some sanitary wipes.

While he was gone, Seth stole the remote and changed the channel to something other than video games. No one griped much. Guitar Hero is live in concert every day in our clubhouse, so a break is always welcome.

Seth changed the channel to some elimination date show on MTV, and again the boys were transfixed. Tiny walked in shortly thereafter. Slappy clapped his hands together and greeted him with, "Well, well, well. Look who it is. How you feeling today, broken arrow?"

"I've felt better," Tiny said. He walked to his locker and sat down on his dressing stool. His face was like a bad watercolor portrait. He made changing into his uniform look like a workout.

"I'm surprised you don't have some incurable rash growing on your face from sleeping in the bathroom last night," I said.

"I suppose Slappy told you everything." Slappy just put his hands up as if to say, "What did you expect?"

"Yeah, man, I can't believe you heaved on the clubhouse floor," I continued. "This is my fourth year here, and I don't remember anyone puking in the clubhouse."

"I did?" Tiny asked. He was in mid change, about to put on his shorts, but stopped to check out the place I was pointing to.

"I don't remember that one. I remember puking in the bathroom, but not there on the floor. Remind me to tip Ephrian for cleaning it up."

"Oh, don't worry," Slappy said, grinning maliciously. "I don't think you'll have any trouble forgetting this stunt. Not if I have anything to do with it."

"You're one to talk Slap-nuts," Tiny said. "You made out with one of the front-office chicks last night. You fucking savage. You took her into the kitchen and sucked her face for like an hour!" Tiny thought he had some dirt on Slappy, but you could never have dirt on Slappy because he didn't care. He once slept with a chick who was so hammered on cranberry and vodka that she puked on him in the elevator before he got her back to his hotel room. He took off his shirt and they did their thing. The next day when she was sober, he made her buy him a new shirt. Then he never called her again. Standard Slappy operating procedure.

"Yeah, I did make out with her," Slappy said, nodding his head with pride. "And then, get this, and then, Buschmann took her home! I hope he realized I got her warmed up for him! *God*, girls are such sluts. They try and make you think they're not, but they are!" he said, oblivious to anything that may have made him look bad.

"You didn't tell me that part Slap," I said. "Which girl was it?"

"I don't know. The only fucking one that looked decent out of the pack."

"You must have been really drunk—they were all bad look-ing."

"I was. That's normally how I end up with most of the chicks I get with." Slappy was completely unashamed.

Tiny shook his head as he pulled up his long, uniform socks. "No shame at all. Zero. What a savage."

"Why am I a savage? She's the one that made out with me, then left with Buschmann. She's worse than I am. I'm telling you, girls, all of them—sluts." Slappy was so passionate about certain things that he made you question your own position, even as you realized he was completely nuts. He had just enough truth in every argument to make him impossible to dismiss outright.

Almost on cue, the girls on the elimination dating show were taking turns kissing some guy to convince him not to eliminate them. Slappy busted up laughing when he saw it. "I told you! I rest my case. Girls are way worse than guys."

"Impossible," Seth said. He wriggled his way out of his comfortable spot on the couch and turned to face Slappy. He'd been listening the entire time, just waiting for a chance to chime in. In the clubhouse, you can hear what everyone is saying, so you're in every conversation whether you want to be or not. Most minor league clubhouses are so small, you can hear everyone's goings-on, unless they are specifically trying to keep it private. Players will add their two cents to any conversation at any time.

"Guys run on pure hormones. It's what the porn industry is built around. I can't believe girls could possibly be worse than guys," Seth continued.

"See, that's where you're wrong." Slappy was getting wound up now that he had someone to debate with.

"Great, now you got him going," Tiny said. He'd finished putting on his uniform and was now walking over to the Gatorade machine with a dollar. He needed some electrolytes after the night he had. In the upper levels, Gatorades are free. Here, however, you've got to spend a buck if you want one. Tiny put his dollar in the machine and it ate it.

"Piece of shit!" he yelled, punching the thieving machine. He didn't love tap it either; he beat the hell out of it. That machine ate more dollars than it vended, and we broke it several times in retribution.

Slappy paid no attention to Tiny's siege on the vending machine. He was focused intently, listing his reasons on why girls were worse than guys. Unfortunately, the "man on vending machine" violence distracted me, so I only caught the end of it.

"And if you do the math, the average girl holds about fifty penises in her lifetime."

"Fifty penises? Fifty? You're out of your mind. Maybe twenty, but no chance fifty," Seth countered.

"I can't believe you are arguing about this. You should know better, Seth," Maddog said, sitting on a beanbag chair with a huge dip in it. He had been silent the whole time too, save for when he'd spit into his empty Gatorade bottle. He loved watching Slappy go.

"Sometimes his bullshit is just so ridiculous you have to straighten him out," Seth said.

"It's not bullshit. It's math. It's numbers, and numbers don't lie. I'm working with empirical fucking evidence here!" Slappy said.

Guys were coming in and changing throughout the conversation. Because the crowd for the debate reshaped so frequently, it was often paused and reexplained so that newcomers who wondered why in the hell Slappy was talking about fifty penises could catch up. Maddog, Brent, Frenchy, Pickles, and I all sat in a row watching it unfold. Seth, Tiny, Stubbs, and Frenchy argued for the under. Slappy, Pickles, and Lunchbox claimed the over. Yordanny tried to steal the show with stupid stories of his own, but was ignored. Blanks and some other position players just walked away, tired of hearing Slappy argue about something as stupid as the average penis-handling level of American females. I don't know where the rest of the guys were, but they were missing out.

It ended ultimately in a stalemate. Slappy said most sexually active chicks touch about three to six wangs in high school, at least one a month in college, around a dozen when they got out of college, and, with the current divorce rates in America, at least two in their marriage years. Seth said it was less because the kind of chicks Slappy was used to were desperate to begin with. He also said Slappy's math didn't account for nuns or lesbians. Slappy countered with porn stars, but the peanut gallery agreed "sexual professionals" shouldn't be included in the sample. All in all, it was a fascinating discussion, utilizing the full brainpower of the average minor league team. It was concluded just in time for batting practice that girls today are probably more slutty than we think, and if needed, we could prove that fact to anyone complete with supporting graphs, charts, and migration patterns, if necessary.

After batting practice, we retreated from the hot desert sun to enjoy a snack and a break before the start of the day's game. The clubbie put out a spread, the guys beat upon the vending machine until everyone got a Gatorade, and text messages were returned.

Pickles picked up his axe and went to turn on Guitar Hero, but I stopped him. There were more important things to be done during this break. There was Kangaroo Court. Today was the first paycheck of the season.

Kangaroo Court is a team-created legal institution made up of peers and elected judges. It's how the team regulates all the stupid and unprofessional things that happen during a season, using a system of fines and mock legal proceedings to embarrass transgressors.

There are no real laws and no set fines, and the whole thing is one big social normalizer. When we believe someone has broken an unwritten law of the Kangaroo Court, aka did something stupid, we write down the stupid act, suggest a fine, list a witness, and put the written offense in the Kangaroo Court Fine Box (an appropriately marked shoe box) located in the middle of the clubhouse.

During court, a chosen player empties the fine box and reads the offenses to a panel of peer-elected judges, typically composed of a pitcher and a fielder and one other player to break ties. The act is weighed for its stupidity, comedic value, and relevance. It is then fined accordingly. If an accusation brought before the court does not cover all the requirements, with special emphasis on making the team laugh, the judges can vote down the stupid act, in which case the person who wrote the offense must pay the fine for wasting the court's time. This ensures that players make their fines as entertaining as possible, the real point of why we have court.

The accused can contest a fine, in which case the court will hear his plea. If he does an excellent job of refuting the accusation, meaning he makes everyone laugh and embarrasses the person who wrote the charge. The judges may overrule the case, effectively reversing the fine. The judges may still fine both parties even if the whole case is funny, just because they can and because the collected money goes toward a party during the All-Star break.

The court recognizes that not every player is a natural, comedic speaker. This is why lawyers can be purchased. If the party in question cannot afford a lawyer, the court will appoint one for him. The accused has the right to remain silent as all misspoken admissions to drunken stupidity can and will be used against him in the Kangaroo Court of Law. In the Kangaroo Justice System, the players are represented by two separate, yet equally important groups: the players who investigate crime, and the vindictive pack of minor league degenerates who prosecute the offenders. These are their stories.

Last year's group of players, now the Double-A team, had such great chemistry that Kangaroo Court became a prime-time event. Full-out legal battles with reenactments and key-witness testimony were brought in. Though usually held the same day paychecks were dispensed, we began making up excuses to have "emergency sessions" of Kangaroo Court.

Last year, a player on the team by the name of White Choco-late, named because he was the blackest white guy any of us had ever met, got caught with porn at his host family's house. If the offense had been written as simply as I just described, he may not have gotten fined. Instead, those crafty court masters who made last year's legal proceedings so much fun exhausted every avenue of humor they could.

When the emergency sessions were held, the prosecutors, who also happened to be roommates of the accused, asked White Chocolate to his face if he was doing anything perverse in his host family's office. He said no.

"Did you look up porn on your host family's computer?"

"I haven't done anything you guys haven't done."

"Answer the question, please. Yes or no. Did you look up porn on the host family's computer?"

"Yes."

"What did you do after you looked up the porn?"

"I went back to my room."

"Did you try to do anything else on the computer?"

No answer.

"Did you do anything else on the computer, and need we re-mind you, you are under oath."

"No."

"Did you turn off the computer and exit the room."

"Yes."

"You didn't masturbate in the room before you left."

"Hell no! Come on dude!"

"Did you print anything while you were on the computer?"

"No."

"No?"

"NO!"

"Your honors, it's true when White Chocolate says he did not print anything off the computer. The fact of the matter is, he tried and the computer would not print." The prosecutor turned and gestured to all in a very theatrical manner. "Sometimes computers and printers don't connect like they should. Chalk it up to Windows. Sometimes the printer receives the instructions to print and saves it in its memory until the computer is restarted and whatever signals were crossed work themselves out.

"As it would happen, just today, we, along with our host mother, went into the office to look something up on the Internet for her." Chocolate's head sunk. "When the computer turned on, the printer began printing items stored in its memory. At this time, we would like to submit the following evidence to the court."

The roommates' lawyers handed seven printed photos of nude, extra dark chocolate women. Each in an exotic pose: spreading, bending, begging. The lawyers laid the pictures down before the courtroom to the roaring laughter of everyone present. Judges fell on each other laughing. People in the court rolled onto the floor. White Chocolate turned to red chocolate.

"Chocolate, are you serious?" a judge asked.

"It wasn't me," he offered.

"Yeah, right. Who else lives there and is obsessed with black women?"

At this point, one of the guys on the team who was black came over to inspect the photos and declared, "I know you like black ladies and all, but damn, Chocolate! At least you could have looked up some good-looking ones. This here is some fucked-up shit!"

"Your honors, I would like the court to know we were present as each photo printed painfully slowly in front of our host mother. She was so embarrassed, we had to escort her from the room. We would like the court to take her pain and suffering into consideration when it rules."

"Do you have anything to say for yourself White Chocolate?"

"What can I say? I like black women. I didn't know it would print out like that though. It's not my fault."

"You really must have been horny," one of the judges said. "You printed it out seven times."

"Five," another judge corrected. "This one is crawling, that one is doing splits—the other one with the lollipop is a repeat."

"Got a thing for lollipops, Chocolate?"

"How does the court rule?" a prosecutor asked, pleased with the production.

We convened to discuss the issue. It was an open-and-shut case for our cybercrimes division.

"Chocolate, here is your fine. A buck for each picture you printed out and three bucks for embarrassing yourself and your roommates in front of your host mother. You owe your host mom an apology when you see her again, and you owe your roommates dinner for dragging them into this."

"I didn't drag them into this. They were the ones who made a big deal."

"Chocolate, seriously?" an incredulous roommate of his asked. "You tried to print out hard-core porn in front of our host mom. Why would you even print it out?"

"Well, I wasn't going to do my thing in her office," he said, making a lewd gesture.

"Why would you even look it up on her computer?"

"Because, bro, I'm a man. I got needs." More laughter came from the crowd.

"Chocolate, just don't say anything. If you keep talking I'm sure the fine will get worse."

The first case of today's court, the first court of the season, was against Slappy. Go figure.

The official court reader, Maddog, pulled the complaint from the box and spoke, "Okay, this fine is on Slappy."

"Guilty!" Slappy yelled, jokingly. The courtroom, which was our locker room with three judging players sitting to one side of it, chuckled.

"Slappy stands accused," Maddog continued, "of making out with girl at the Diamond Club and then losing her to another guy."

"What? No, no, no—that's not something I should be fined for."

"Hold on Slappy, we have rules here. How do you plead?"

"Not guilty, of course."

"It says on the complaint that the team witnessed this."

"I'm saying not guilty because I made out with her. Maybe that's all I wanted to do."

"But she was ugly, dude. Ugly and fat."

"That's not what I'm being charged for, though. I'm being charged for losing her."

Seth was on his feet and ready to prosecute. "That's the whole point, Slap. You don't just make out with ugly chicks because you like kissing them. You have to go all the way. And that's only because it's part of busting a slump or something. I mean, unless you like fat, ugly chicks, the only purpose they serve is health related."

"That's true, Slap. Fat chicks should be used for medicinal purposes only."

"It was the beginning of the year, bro. I was just getting warmed up. I'm not in mid season form yet," Slappy countered.

"That's no excuse for you to lose her to another guy," Seth said, pushing the issue.

"Why am I the one getting fined? Buschmann should be getting fined, since he stole her. He went out of his way to take an ugly chick from me! That's real desperation, stealing a fat chick from a teammate! I'd like to cite the law of Bros before Hos here!"

"I don't think it applies in this case," a judge said.

"This is a mockery of justice!" Slappy wailed.

Brent's hand when up. "If it pleases the court, I think Buschmann should get a credit under his name for stealing Slappy's girl."

"That's bullshit!" Slappy wailed.

"And that's one dollar, Slap. No swearing in Kangaroo Court— we're professionals here." Maddog wrote down a dollar fine for Slap.

"Fine, that's *bullcrap*," Slappy rephrased. "What kind of team-mate steals another player's chick, regardless of how nasty she is?"

"Personally," Frenchy said, "I think she had a chance to up-grade from a bad body reliever to a starter and she took it."

"Maybe we should give her a credit too," Brent said.

"That is a veteran move."

"She's got a big one," Rosco said.

"I think the court has heard enough to render a decision."

Slappy was fined three dollars, one for illegal use of a potential slump buster, one for losing said slump buster to another player, and one for swearing.

"Next fine." This was for Lunchbox. "For making the com-ment, 'It's a good thing dolphins don't have hands or they'd prob-ably take over the world.'"

"Did you really say that, Box?" a judge asked.

Lunchbox stared at the court with a dull face of wonder. "What? I was just saying that they're smart, I think, like the smartest mammals on earth, right? If they had hands, like us, I'll bet they could challenge us." Blank expressions as the entire locker room stared back at Lunchbox. "You guys don't think so? Like, they'd be dangerous if they had fingers and thumbs?"

"Box, you might want to think about appointing a lawyer. Would anyone like to represent Lunchbox?"

Seth shook his head. "I'm not even going to touch that one."

"What? If they had fingers, they could use guns."

"Where are dolphins going to get guns, Lunchbox?"

"Submarines."

Lunchbox was fined one dollar. Someone helped him count it out.

Chapter Twenty-one

The boys showed up at the park early because of the scheduled bus trip. We were on commuter time. Our destination was High Desert, with service to Modesto following the game. This marked the first day of a four-game road trip.

We changed into our uniforms at the park, halfway at least, not bothering to tuck tops in or put hats on—certainly no spikes. There was no reason to look game ready since we were just going to hop on a bus for the next two hours. Suitcases were packed for the overnight portions; Padres-issued equipment bags were stocked for the day. We, a gang of half-dressed baseball bums, lugged our cases and bags to the curb of the stadium's parking lot and waited for the arrival of the team bus.

When the bus huffed and puffed into the parking lot, all the future occupants sprang to attention and began forming a line at the presumed point where the bus, or rather the door of the bus, would stop. Everyone jockeyed, shoulder to shoulder, nudging and bumping each other almost in front of the bus itself for a chance at prime seating. As soon as the bus rolled its last inch and its pneumatic brakes exhaled, signaling a full stop, the doors folded open and the gang burst into it like zombies in a cheap horror flick. I got on last. There was no reason for me to rush.

Part of being the oldest guy on the team with higher-level time is I get whatever seat I want, regardless if someone else has it or not. It's baseball tradition that older guys get the pick of the seating litter, and always has been. I'm not sure where the tradition originated, but it is what it is, and I for one was not going to challenge it.

I walked up the steps to the bus aisle proper and stared down it like Death looking for his next victim. The occupants who had already gotten comfortable held their breath as I made my way down the aisle. Some players pretended to look away, as if I didn't exist. The age hierarchy of priority seating was law, and it was mine to enforce however I saw fit. I came to a stop in front of the seat I usually take, the one with the few extra inches of precious legroom. It was occupied by Matt Bush.

Bush was the 2004 first pick overall. He was made a millionaire three times over by the draft and wasn't even twenty yet. However, not even a month into his professional career, he fell out of favor for some stupid stuff he did off the field involving underage drinking and anger. He wasn't performing as the Padres hoped he would, thus his exploits off the field were his most notable career achievements. Partially the business, partially his own fault, he was under tremendous scrutiny and pressure. I felt sorry for him, actually. Just not sorry enough to let him have the good seat—not this year.

"Beat it, Bush," I said, like a king throwing the jester from his thrown.

"Come on man, are you serious?" In his defense, no one, regardless of the round they were drafted in, would be happy about this.

"Hell yes, I'm serious. I'm the oldest guy in the Cal League. Now gimme my damn seat!"

Bush rolled his eyes, then retreated to another location. He was definitely irritated, but he didn't bite me or anything. It felt good to push a first rounder around.

As the time of departure drew near, those players who came late were punished by having to double up with other players for the trip. In order to make their seats seem less inviting, the players already seated spread out as if they had spontaneously gained weight. Some were stretching uncomfortably over the seats, arranging their backpacks, iPods, and magazines in ways that screamed "no room for rent." Some even pretended to be asleep, hiding under their dark sunglasses.

"I can see your eyes, dude. Just let me sit down and quit faking it."

"For fuck's sake, why don't you just show up on time!"

"It doesn't matter if I did—there aren't enough seats for everyone to get his own. Someone was going to double up, so deal with it."

"Well it didn't have to be me! God . . . I hope you get beaned tonight."

I believe this reaction is why things like seat hierarchies are created.

When everyone is on board, the bus is supposed to go forward—supposed to. Occasionally, some things will occur that alter the normal series of events. Things like breakdowns or late players. Or things like what happened today when the bus driver got on the mic and began talking to us—

Baseball players are not nice, tame animals. Especially not in packs, when they feel safe to bark and snarl and spit thanks to their superior numbers. When the bus driver turned around, the first thing we all noticed was that he was cross-eyed, severely cross-eyed, noticeable even to me sitting in the back. The next thing we noticed, by the excitable way he breathed and groped the bus's built-in tour-guide microphone, was that he was a baseball fan.

"Uh, hello everyone. I really hope you guys win today. I'll be cheering you on from the bus. If you play hard, I know you'll all be winners. Do it for your love of the game and stay positive—"

"Get off the mic!"

"Drive the bus!"

"Turn around."

"Stop looking at me that way!"

He looked at our team's manager, who pretended he was asleep.

"Uh." The bus driver tried to figure out what was happening. He forced out some nervous laughter, wringing off the microphone chord. "You guys are all winners and—"

"Are you a coach or a bus driver?"

"Why are we still here?"

"We pay you to drive."

"Sit down, Ralph."

"Turn the air-conditioning on, Steve."

"Let's fucking go, Barry."

"Have a seat, Don."

"Quit staring at me, Ronald."

The rattling off of names was done in an attempt to guess the name of the bus driver. It was almost a game to see who could guess his name first, each guess with its own complimentary insult.

"My name's Tim, and I'll be—"

"GET OFF THE MIC, TIM!"

Overwhelmed, poor Tim consented. The manager still feigned sleep, but there had to be a smile on his face. Tim put the mic down, and we started applauding him. He didn't know it, but he was just initiated into the fold. If he did a good job, the guys on the team would treat him like royalty. If he did a bad job, well, he may as well drive this bus off a cliff. We wish we could all be winners, but let's be honest, the "everyone's a winner" talk lost its meaning back when fathers stopped buying ice-cream cones after the games for their red-blooded American boys. This is a lifestyle now, not a feel-good exercise. If you are going to work closely to a team, do yourself a favor and check your clueless speeches at the door.

As the bus crept up into the mountains on its way to High Desert, a master plan was hatched. It was partially my fault, since I was the one who brought it up.

"Do you remember what Skip did last year?" Brent asked, sitting up a few rows from me.

Skip did a lot of things, to a lot of women, in a lot of towns. It was hard to pinpoint exactly which incident Brent was referencing. "Which girl?" I asked.

"No, not that. I meant the sign he made for the bus trips."

Oh yes, that. Skip thought it would be a good idea, a boon for team chemistry and all that, if he solicited those passing us on the highway for free entertainment. He drew up a sign, written on a white trainer's towel that read Please Show Us Your Boobs. Cheers!

It wasn't so much that the idea was invented. In fact it was actually rather odd the idea hadn't come up sooner. I think every minor league team has done it. I'm confident major league teams would do it if they didn't fly places. Rather, the irony was that so many women obliged.

Car after car of ladies would do double takes at the white towel flown by lustful faces pressed against window glass. Several women would laugh and shake their heads, but a certain sect acted as if it were an audition. They'd steady the wheels with their knees; then they'd flash the bus for a second or two before blushing and laughing hysterically at their inner naughtiness. Once we encountered a very willing caravan full of sorority girls, and on yet another trip, we had so many ladies flash, a couple guys drew up additional numbered signs and acted as judges. Out of decency, we never offered a score below an eight.

"Yeah, I remember," I yelled back.

"Remember what?" Slappy asked. Brent and I looked at each other. A mischievous smile curled across Brent's face. I put my hand on my head.

I explained the story to Slappy, and his reaction was immediate. "Do we have a towel?"

"You are such a savage, Slappy."

"Yeah, like you don't want me to do it, Tiny."

"People are going to think we're perverts."

"It's Southern California—they're probably perverts too."

I actually tried to talk Slappy out of the idea. It usually ended with a strict scolding from the team manager. But there was no stopping Slappy now that the idea was out in the open—a new crop of players, a new manager, a new highway full of talent. History looked as if it would repeat itself.

Slappy sniffed out a towel, then commandeered a Magic Marker. He wrote out the message while four or five players leered over his shoulder, anxiously observing the inscription of each letter like school kids about to pull a senior prank. As soon as the advertisement was complete, Slappy chose the side of the bus with the most traffic lanes and ran the towel up like the Jolly Roger while his pirates played lookout.

The first car with potential had a cute blonde at the wheel. Some of the players started banging on the window glass, even yelling, as if the girl could hear them—it was probably for the best that she couldn't. She casually looked over, then did a double take. She mouthed the words of the sign, daringly keeping her eyes on the road. The pirates continued to hoot and bang.

"Is she going to?"

"How the hell do I know? I'm not her."

"I think she's going to."

"I hope so, she's cute. She looks foreign."

"Foreign chicks are so hot."

The cute, foreign, blonde started talking aloud again.

"Who's she talking to?"

"I don't know. Maybe there is another chick in there we can't see. Two, hot, naughty foreign chicks!"

The passenger's seat folded up, propelling the formerly sleeping form of a male counterpart. He was not happy, and his finger went up to prove it. He was not foreign either as the words he began angrily mouthing were easy to lip-read by such well-trained swearword translators as us.

Of course, this wouldn't stand with the Lake Elsinore Pirates. We fired back with dozens of choice fingers. The car we were laying sexual siege to countered, defending itself with two middle fingers and a barrage of angry words we couldn't hear. Nor could the vessel hear us screaming back, though I'm sure they got the gist.

The battle raged until someone on our side put his ass on the window. The car sped away at the sight of it, and the cheeks left a wide smudge on the glass. We were left pants down and boobless, cursing at the one that got away.

Life on the concrete seas is harsh. To survive, you must focus on the next prize, the next car of hot foreign boobies. "Hey guys, we got another one," came a call from starboard. The boys tucked their fingers in, smoothed their hair back, and pulled their pants up. Faces returned to the glass, except the part with the smudge.

A small car, with tinted windows cracked oh so slightly, rolled up beside us. From the crack in the car's window, long, wavy lady hair that framed a face mysteriously hidden by large sunglasses could be seen.

The banging and hooting started again. You'd think we were

smart enough to know she couldn't hear us. Or could she? Eyes hidden behind sunglasses coolly turned to peek through the crack in the window. She was looking at us—looking hard, more than looking. The sunglasses lingered longer than a person driving a car should let a gaze remain. She was good.

"Oh, she is totally going to."

"She's a vet. Look at that car control."

The window went down a hair, low enough to see her smile and nothing more. The boys started clapping at her, giving her the thumbs-up, and cheering. Slappy shook the sign like a bull-fighter.

She gave a thumbs-up back, stirring the bus into a frenzy. Next, she put up one finger as if to say "Just a minute boys" and the dark, tinted windows went up.

"Oh my God, this girl is awesome!"

"She's a professional. I'll bet she lives for buses like ours!"

A moment later came the yell, "We've got action!"

All eyes went starboard. The window came down all the way, with full exposure.

It's obvious we needed the sign since there was no way for us to scream out through the window glass, though that didn't seem to stop us from trying. There was no way for the ladies to hear our hoots and cat calling—no way to vocalize our request for high-velocity boobies. A sign on a towel and pantomime was all we had. It made things interesting, even challenging. However, while we were happily up to the task of getting girls to oblige our requests, no one ever stopped to think about how to get them to stop.

Her face was cute, at least the portion that wasn't hidden behind tinted glass, which turned out to be a very small portion. The rest of her looked like melted candle wax—white, pasty, melted candle wax with two large, drooping pizza dough boobs and pepperoni nipples on an acne-speckled chest.

Dry heaving, coughing, and moaning, the pirates fell back in their seats, hitting the deck as if fat, fleshy, pendulous cannonballs had struck the bus.

"That's the most disgusting thing I have ever seen."

"I think I'm gay now. I think I just turned gay because of that."

"Take the sign down! Take it down before she does anything else!"

Someone's ass went back up against the glass, but she didn't leave as the other one did.

Slappy wadded up the towel and threw it at me. "Great idea, Hayhurst. My penis hates you!"

Chapter Twenty-two

The area around the High Desert stadium is not among the most picturesque locations in baseball. There is a beautiful view of snowcapped mountains during certain times of the year, but the immediate view is far from captivating. It looks like a former testing ground for atomic bombs—flat, barren, windswept land with a burned out feel to it. There isn't much development near the stadium either, giving it a remote feel sitting lonesome off a bumpy stretch of road on the outskirts of Victorville, California.

The place depresses me. Something about long stretches of flat, cold, windy deserts just feels sad. Then there is the high altitude. They don't call the place High Desert for nothing. The stadium is the minor league equivalent to Coors Field. Couple the elevation with the wind, and it's easy to understand why the park hosts so many games in the ten-run range. The unceasing high-altitude jet streams act like a tractor beam, simply sucking fly balls over the fence. If you aren't depressed when you get there, you will be after you watch your ERA increase in altitude.

At night the temperature drops substantially. The park's bullpen, which is nothing more than a single slat of wood forming a bench only four relievers can sit on at a time, offers no shelter from the elements when the sun sets. The wind picks up and the cold air cuts through our spandex outfits as if we weren't wearing anything at all.

Though not the oldest in the league, the park is not a very comfortable experience for the away club. The locker room is nearly the size of a semitruck trailer. Lockers line the sides of it, with folding tables in the center. The confines are so tight, when pregame food is put out, players have to sit wedged inside their locker cavities to make room for others to get through. Poorly ventilated, fly stripping hangs over the meals, coated with the dead insects like a decaying chandelier.

There's no training room. The trainer's table and equipment are also crammed into the locker room, as are all the coaches, the manager, and his desk. There is a soda machine, which would only make sense, and the manger's desk sits next to the toilets and showers to make room for it. Sure, his shoulder is getting brushed against by naked guys who just took a dump, but on the bright side, he's only an arm's reach away from a Dr Pepper.

When the bus pulled into the parking lot and the boys began to filter out I languished at the end. I watched the guys exit noticing how the wind grabbed their coats when they stepped out. The unseen force, a constant at this park, smeared their hair and pulled it across their faces. It was gusting, straight out toward the outfield.

Getting off this bus was a gut check for me. I couldn't believe I was here, again. It's amazing how nice parks make you feel proud of your career, whereas garbage ones make you wish it was over. I got off, grabbed my equipment, and fought the gale into the locker room. I picked a locker away from the high-traffic areas ensuring that I spent as little time forced in my locker as possible. Apparently, there were not enough seats to go around today. Some of the plastic chairs were broken to begin with, the backs snapped off or kicked through, no doubt the aftermath of a pitcher releasing his frustrations. Some were destroyed altogether, accounting for the lack of supply. I changed standing up.

At game time, I found myself sitting in the makeshift away-team bullpen with Pickles, Rosco, Slappy, and Maddog. The temperature had dropped significantly, forcing us to layer up, going as far as to scavenge batting gloves to use as winter gloves. We sat down the right field line, huddled in a pack like Eskimos.

"We need something to take our minds off this weather. This is miserable."

"Yeah, we need to get a good conversation going here. Anyone got any good shit to talk about?" Rosco asked.

I thought for a second about some of the things I would talk about in the past dead times like this. I once read this book of superstring theory, black holes, and quantum mechanics—seriously. I thought I needed a crash course in something smart to test how many brain cells baseball had killed.

I thought about bringing up some of the wild topics it covered. Stuff like time travel, alternate dimensions, and gravity wells. But Slappy, a black hole of a different variety, was the first to speak. "Okay, I've got one. What if you meet a girl, like the hottest girl you've ever met—like a Jessica Simpson, but hotter. And she's all over you, right?"

"This happens to me all the time," Maddog said, rubbing his knuckles on his jersey.

"Well, women are only human, Maddog."

"Anyways, she's all over you, and she takes you home and you're messing around." Slappy started making messing around movements, which I won't describe right now.

"Right, right. I'm pickin' up what you're puttin' down," Rosco said.

"She stops before it gets too serious, and tells you she needs to go freshen up. She goes into the bathroom, strips down butt naked, comes back out, and *boom*—she's got a penis."

"What do you mean boom? Like it just appears there?"

"No, she's had it the whole time."

"Like she owns one, like a toy?"

"No, it's hers. It's on her."

"So she's a dude, like a superhot, Jessica Simpsonesque tranny?"

"No, she's a hermaphrodite. She's both."

"She's both?"

"Yeah. She's packing both."

"So she's the hottest chick that's also a man I've ever made out with."

"Ever? Do you do this frequently?" I asked.

"Come on dude, I'm being theoretical."

"Of course, of course. Who am I to stand in the way of science?"

"Yes," Slappy continued, "she's a hermo, and she's ready to go the rest of the way with you. My question is, Do you still do her even though she's got a penis?"

The boys did not respond immediately. Rather, as if they were in math class and asked to solve for x, their faces shifted to deep thought. "Wow, good question."

Did I hear that right? Good question? Not, Where do you come up with this stuff? Or what the hell is wrong with you? Or you need to pick higher-quality websites. Or do you think you could just plain stay off the Internet altogether?

"Are we really having this conversation right now?" I asked. "I mean, is this a real-world situation we need to plan for?"

"I'm just trying to spark some conversation."

"You never know what kind of beef Slappy will bring home," Maddog said.

"Why is it always me that gets ridiculed?" protested Slappy. Everyone turned and stared at him. "Okay, I *know* why it's always me, actually, but it's not like I'm the only one here. You slept with a married chick in rookie ball, Maddog."

"I was drunk so it didn't count," Maddog replied, giving a wry smile.

"No, no, no, it counts—you can't just say it—"

"Wait," Rosco interrupted. "How drunk am I when I'm with this chick?"

Slappy looked at Maddog. "You can't be so drunk *it doesn't count*," Slappy mocked.

"Yeah, because that would just make this situation *too* ridiculous," I said, rolling my eyes.

"Let's say you have to be stone sober." The council on hermaphrodite sexual relations all grunted, effectively ratifying the amendment, and the conversation continued.

"I don't know if I could do it if I'm stone sober."

"So it's a no for you, then?"

"Not necessarily." Rosco went back to the drawing board in his mind. "Hotter than Jessica Simpson, but has a dong . . . Hmmmm . . ."

"What if you don't think Jessica Simpson is that hot?" Pickles offered.

"How can you not think Jessica Simpson is hot?" bellowed the council, producing a reaction of instant outrage, which made me wonder how we could be totally on board with a subject like man on man-woman relations but be livid when the hotness of a certain blond-haired pop star is brought into question?

"She's hot, but I just don't think she's the hottest."

"Well, then pick your fantasy girl and add a wiener. It's a simple equation."

"So it could be Angelina Jolie?"

"With a wiener."

"Okay, good," Pickles said, smiling contentedly.

"How big is the penis?" Rosco resumed.

"In regards to—?"

"Well is it bigger than mine?"

"No, yours is definitely bigger."

"Okay, so I'm still the king of the bedroom. That's good to

know." Pickles and Rosco exchanged high fives, declaring, "Big ones!"

"Yeah, she's got a very feminine penis," Slappy continued.

"Could you explain that for me? Could you explain *feminine penis?*" I asked.

"Sure," Slappy said. "It's small and cute."

"Cute?"

"Yeah, and it's been accessorized."

"Accessorized?"

"Yeah, like the tip has lipstick on it, and there are two little earrings on the balls and stuff. Maybe she's got a little pink sweater for it or something."

At this point, all I could do was stare at Slappy.

"What?" Slappy stared back, innocently.

"Do I have to see it while I'm doing her?" Rosco asked.

Slappy disengaged from the accessorized penis talk. "No, you don't have to see it. You might feel it, but you don't have to see it."

"If we are under covers and I'm behind her, I should be okay, right?"

"I think so."

Rosco nodded his head. "Okay, alright, I'm in."

"Hey hey, alright!" The council passed out high fives at the decision, passing the bill. Later, the council also ruled all women with penises should declare their arms before taking a man home because it's discourteous. Honesty is the best policy, after all.

"Okay, I've got another one. If you were abducted by the Taliban and they told you they would kill you if you didn't, which guy on the team would you have sex with."

"You've got to be kidding me," I exhaled.

"What? It's life or death. This could really happen, man. Terrorists are some serious shit!"

"They'd go to all the trouble of kidnapping a team just so they could make them—Why am I even arguing this?" I turned my head down to the dugout, checking out of the conversation and catching up on the game. The backup catcher, Lisk, was jogging down toward us. His equipment was on, skullcap on his head with a mitt in one hand and a mask in the other. Behind his running form, standing on the lip of the dugout steps, was Webby waving at the pen. A quick glance to the field revealed runs driven in with a few more on base awaiting a ride home. Brent was in a jam.

In the lower levels, most bullpens don't have phones. This one was lucky to have a mound. Unable to call down instructions, the pitching coaches use hand signals symbolizing each respective pitcher. Mine was the A-frame shape Webby was currently signing to the pen.

"Sorry to leave your life-changing conversation boys, but it looks like I have to go to work." I tore off my clothes like Superman and bounded to the mound.

Slappy and Pickles hopped up as well. They didn't have to warm up, but assumed the roles of bodyguards while I warmed with Lisk. The bullpen was set up so that the catcher's back was to the field when he warmed a reliever. A hitter could line a ball foul and strike him while he caught. Slappy jogged down and stood next to Lisk, defending his back side. Pickles stayed by me.

Though Brent was pumping in strikes, doing his best to grind out the start, the batters were finding holes. He wasn't getting knocked out of the yard, rather, being bled out slowly, single after single. I wanted to believe he'd make it through the inning, but the bases were loaded now and the hook would come soon if he didn't get lucky and roll a pair.

I warmed as fast as I could without mindlessly firing, but the cold makes it harder to get the touch of the ball and your arm feels like a blunt club, not the precision instrument you're used to. I'd be Brent's replacement, probably inheriting a few base runners when I came in if he didn't find a way out first. If I was going to help him out of this mess, I needed to be precise, I needed to be hot and ready.

Another single was rapped out to center, two runners scored. When the dust settled, Webby was standing on the lip of the dugout. Looking down toward the pen, he took his hat off, the universal sign for *Is he ready?*

"You ready?" Slappy asked.

Of course I'm not ready, it's freezing and I've throw ten pitches!

"Yeah, I'm good," I replied.

Slappy took his hat off to signal back. Our manager called time and went out to retrieve Brent.

There's a surge of adrenaline a reliever feels before he enters a game. A quick jog to a pile of dirt under the lights, and the cold, barren, windswept desert is now your battlefield. You versus the guy with a stick, both trying to carve out a living. Numbers will be accumulated, stats added, careers evaluated in that merciless piecemeal fashion baseball is famous for. All of it, humming along in the background whether you're loose and ready or not.

The first batter singled off me and two more of Brent's runs scored. While it may be frustrating to give up my own runs, I absolutely hate giving up other pitchers' runs—especially those of friends. I covered my face with my mitt and fired off nine or ten F-bombs in response to the single. I got the next hitter to pop out, but the damage was done. I hand delivered Brent's runs. Some friend I was.

The team ran me out for the sixth, and I promptly punched out the first hitter I faced. The second hitter, the leadoff man, earned another single. I found myself facing the meat of the order with a runner on, one out, and the two hole stepping in.

It's natural to watch a batter enter the box, because a lot can be learned from observing his setup. Stance, hands, weight, plate proximity—each gives a clue to the type of hitter you're facing. In the case of this hitter, it was none of the above. He was peeking at the signs. Not blatantly gawking, but his eyes were definitely wandering back to Sanchy's hands as he telegraphed pitches.

I stepped off. *Maybe it was a fluke?* I thought, pacing about the mound. I licked my hand, smacked the rosin bag, and reset myself on the rubber. This time I watched the batter and paid no attention to Sanchy at all.

The batter's head shifted slightly and his eyes bounced back. He was looking at Sanchy's hand, alright, *That motherf—*. I stepped off again. Sanchy popped up and called a time-out. He jogged out to the mound to meet me.

"Uh, is you okay?"

"He's peeking at your signs, Sanchy."

"He pee-king?"

"He's looking at your hands." I said it slower, pantomiming with my hands as I talked.

"Oh, he see my hands!" Sanchy looked back angrily at the batter, but I grabbed his shoulder and pulled him around to me. "You want hit that fucking guy?" he asked, making a fist and pounding his glove. I smiled. He didn't speak the best English but didn't need to.

"No," I said. This wasn't the time.

If there's any reason a pitcher can hit a batter, it's for stealing signs. But then he's on base. Next thing I know, I'm watching the three-hole hitter lift a fly into the High Desert jet stream. What was a fun bonding experience with Sanchy is now a bloated ERA. "Go back there and set up outside."

"Fastbol?"

"Yeah, just set up away. Let him see the sign too."

"What, why jou wanna—"

"Let him see it."

"Let's go boys," the umpire said. He had walked out to the mound now, anxious to keep the game moving.

"Sorry Blue, we're good," I said. I nodded at Sanchy, who still looked confused.

Sanchy jogged back to the plate and squatted, the umpire followed. I reset on the mound and the batter stepped in. I watched the batter's eyes as Sanchy put the sign down. He peeked again, just like before. I nodded to Sanchy, accepting his sign, though I never had any intention of throwing what he called, even though I told him to call it.

Leg back, hands up, rock, pivot, step, just like back at Mazz's place. *Alright asshole, you wanna peek, it's gonna cost ya.* I drove down the mound and snapped my best into flight. The batter squared up, full swing, locked in for the down-and-away fastball. What he got was a hands-high four seamer, inside from the start. A high fastball is too juicy to lay off, but the ones on your hands are like the poison apple. It continued riding in, even as the batter realized it was too late to stop his stroke. White leather bored into the handle of the bat, detonating it on impact. The bat blew up in the hitter's hands, spraying kindling all over the infield while the ball spun to second, flipped to short, and fired to first—double play.

As the peeker jogged back to the dugout, Sanchy handed him what was left of his bat and said, "No more fucking pee-king!"

You tell 'em Sanchy. You tell 'em.

Chapter Twenty-three

We lost, showered, and packed up. Before we boarded the bus for Modesto, our clubbie served us our final meal in High Desert. It's called a getaway meal, named because it's the meal we skip town while eating. In A-ball, players typically don't eat after the games like Double- and Triple-A players do. And we wouldn't have been fed were it not for the six-hour trip ahead of us.

Tonight's meal was barbecue. Pulled pork or chicken sandwiches with baked beans—we got to choose. I opted for the pulled pork—mistake. My sandwich looked like someone fed a grenade to a pig. What did I expect?—the food was just leftovers served from the stadium's concessions. Minor league stadium food isn't exactly five-star cuisine. Hell, I've had better barbecue from vending machines.

Bad sandwiches were only a short-term issue. Baked beans was the real problem. A bus trip meal simply cannot contain a time bomb like baked beans. It's only a matter of hours before stomachs start to explode, and the bus takes on the scent of a barnyard. Inevitably, someone will drop trow in the bus's poorly ventilated bathroom. That brown torpedo will remain for the next four days of our trip, marinating while we drive, baking when we play. The trip home will be eight hours in a portable septic tank, with the aroma continuously recycled through the bus's air system.

What can I do? Try explaining the ramifications of poor bus meals to a group of hungry minor leaguers who rarely get a post-game feed. This was a feast! Cold pig flesh and a scoop of turd pills—the team mauled it like lions on a zebra carcass, snapping and clawing when another player got too close.

We left around 11 P.M. The team, fed and sedated, reclined in their seats while the clubbie inserted a movie into the bus's on-board DVD player.

Nowadays, buses equipped with DVD players and at least six televisions to watch the media on make team trips smoother. The sets are staggered throughout the bus, hanging down from the ceiling above the seat backs. Most players take proximity to a screen into consideration when choosing their seats.

The movies played on team trips can be a welcome distraction or an unceasing annoyance depending on how many times you've seen the flick. Usually, during the first trips of the season, the same popular bus-trip movie staples are watched. I can bet, with almost one hundred percent accuracy, the movies most teams watch during this time frame in baseball are *Dumb and Dumber*, *Old School*, *Wedding Crashers* (the unrated edition so more boobies can be seen), *The 40-Year-Old Virgin*, *Gladiator*, and *300*. Sometimes they watch them more than once in the same season, and sometimes more than once on the same trip.

Dumb and Dumber ate up an hour or so of tonight's trip, distracting us as the bus made its way north. The next movie was *Gladiator*, a good action flick to change things up. The third movie was one I had never seen before, *Midnight Express*.

It was early in the morning when *Midnight Express* came on. Most of the team was out of it, trying to sleep in the uncomfortable coach bus seats as we went. The movie was older, produced in the later 1970s, with substandard production values compared to the previous two we viewed.

With no promise of perky female nudity, or at least some mindless explosions, none of us had the desire to trade sleep for its viewing. Several of the players' heads drooped, succumbing to sleep. Headphones went in or over ears; pillows separated craniums from glass-panel bus windows. Things were quiet, peaceful, stinky.

Twenty minutes could not have gone by before the bus came to a complete stop. Instinctively, all players woke up, operating under the assumption we had come to either a rest area or the new town's hotel. The streaking sounds of horns blaring in our freshly woken ears as cars blew past the bus told us something was amiss. No signs or lights marked the outside areas. We were stopped in the middle of the highway.

At the helm of the bus, the cross-eyed bus driver was whimpering to our trainer. The manager's voice chimed in and then the radioman. I couldn't make out what was going on, but news soon trickled back as the grapevine of players passed it along, bus seat to bus seat.

"We're lost," came the headlines.

"What? How? It's this guy's job to know where we're going."

"Have you seen his eyes? I'm surprised we made it this far."

"Easy, it could happen to anyone; cut him some slack," I said, trying to act mature.

"Oh yeah, how many times have you been lost on a bus trip before?

"Maybe we just missed our off-ramp. Do we know how far lost we are?"

The question went down the vine, and soon the answer was brought back. Each time this answer traded mouth to ear, it left the person who heard it angry. Finally, it made it back to me.

"We are like an hour and a half in the wrong direction."

"WHAT! That stupid son of a bitch! It's his job to know where we're going!"

The bus's engine turned over and we started going again, though no one knew where. Information circulated. Ideas were generated. Road times calculated. The bus got off the highway at an exit near a hotel. We hoped we might stop and figure things out in the morning instead of spending all night on the bus. Fingers were crossed, breath was held, and souls were inevitably crushed as the bus sped past the possibility of a comfortable bed and back onto the highway.

Anger, magnified by lack of sleep and the promise of three extra hours on a vehicle that smelled like a horse stall, made sleep-deprived personalities volatile. At the rate we were going, we wouldn't make it to Modesto until 7 A.M.

Meanwhile, *Midnight Express* chugged along on the screens above us, with footage of men scrambling about a Turkish prison. We had missed most of the plot and had no idea why they were imprisoned to begin with. We watched anyway, like zombies with no will to live and too irritated to slumber.

No one spoke. The wrong words would set off this powder keg of bush leaguers. As far as we were concerned, this bus was our Turkish prison, purgatory with coach seating. Our last glimmer of hope rested with this grainy, seventies flick. It was now this movie's responsibility to enrapture us and distract our tortured souls from our present dilemma.

Then as if there was no doubt we might be on the midnight express to hell, the movie ambushed us with a shower scene portraying two male prisoners bathing each other, followed by a passionate make-out session. Time and space stood still as the images washed over us. Then, the spark hit powder and a scream split the night, "WHAT THE FUCK ARE WE WATCHING?"

Chaos ensued. Bottles were thrown at the television screens. Shouts of anarchy, outrage, and frustration mixed with swear words.

"Who picked this fucking movie?"

"Why does it smell so fucking bad in here?"

"Whose fucking hand is on my thigh?"

Oddly, all I could think about was the conversation I missed in the pen, the one about which guy on the team you'd have intercourse with if abducted by terrorists.

The bus came to another stop. The prisoners continued to bathe. You could hear frustrated conversation at the bus's helm and see sexual frustration on the screen above. The radioman was obviously pissed off now, and we could hear his anger, though not the specifics of it. The prisoners were obviously confused, though we did not understand the specifics of it. The nuts and bolts of the situation trickled back through the bus. Water trickled off nuts and bolts above us.

"We are lost again."

"Oh my God! Are you kidding me?" It was beyond frustrating; it was now completely ridiculous—absurd even. It was late, the bus smelled like a Turkish prison, and we just saw two dudes go at it—neither one a hot hermaphrodite.

Our anger subsided only when fatigue overcame frustration. The bus turned around and started going in a new direction. The movie finished, and no one dared put anything else in. It was almost five in the morning, and everyone was thoroughly miserable. Exhausted, uncomfortable, we slumped back and wished for any sleep we could get.

The next time the bus stopped, the sun was up. We were at the hotel in Modesto. Somehow, some way, I shambled through the check-in process and made it to my room where I passed out. An hour later, I was woken up by power tools. The room next to mine was being renovated.

Chapter Twenty-four

No batting practice and a late stretch time—the manager was giving us a break for our enduring the sentence we served to get to Modesto. Even with the relaxed schedule, it felt like a blink from departing High Desert to the time I found myself sitting in another bullpen.

Modesto's stadium was newer. The facilities were good for A-ball: breathing room in the clubhouse, no fly strips, separate rooms for the coaching staff. The stadium itself was situated next to a golf course surrounded by green trees and grassy fairways, a far cry from the barren flats and nosebleed-inducing altitude of High Desert. Though the bullpen was nothing more than a row of chairs stretching down the side of the left field fence, at least there were enough chairs for all of us.

Getting up for a game on no sleep requires copious amounts of caffeine. Some of the guys were nursing their second Red Bulls, others suckled strings of coffee cups. Our eyes were bloodshot and our faces washed out. We looked like animated corpses. Having thrown the previous night, I would have tonight off unless we got into a real mess. I refrained from energy drinks in favor of a nap, inconspicuously nodding off, my hat angled down to hide my closed lids from fans and coaches alike.

"Come on, Hayhurst," Slappy said. "If we have to stay awake, you have to stay awake."

"Why?"

"We're a team."

"You can think of something better than that," I said, pulling my hat back down. "Good night."

About the time I reached the weightless point of half sleep, one of the guys screamed *heads up*, jerking me awake. I tumbled out of my seat and hit the ground as a line shot came screaming into the pen. The ball struck the fencing behind where my head was, bounced off, nicked a chair, and spun in the dirt of the pen.

"Jesus . . . I almost died," I said, watching the ball twirl to a stop.

"You angered the baseball gods by not staying awake," Slappy said.

"Yeah, right. I don't believe in baseball gods." An old heretical wives' tale of supposedly mystical beings who watch over games and act as the ultimate judges of on-field karma—which I don't believe in either. The baseball gods will humble players who get too confident, exalt players who've struggled, and embarrass players who think they're cooler than they are. Essentially, all the unexplainable, ironic, and coincidental stuff that happens in this game can be blamed on the baseball gods if you try hard enough. Most of their god-worthy events are a combination of stupidity, averages, and ego, but it's more fun to say some higher power did it.

"Don't let them hear you say that," Slap cautioned.

"Or what? What are they going to do? Trap me on a rancid tour bus and subject me to gay shower scenes? Send me back to A-ball? Hit me in the nuts with a line drive?"

Another line drive came whizzing into the bullpen. I sidestepped it as it hit the dirt and one hopped into the fencing. "Hit fair, I'm trying to sleep, goddamn it!" I screamed at the hitter. Turning back to the pen, all the guys had moved back from me.

"You've angered the baseball gods, Dirk," Slappy said, pointing at me as if he were some type of witch doctor speaking on the behalf of his volcano god.

"Maybe I should sacrifice you to appease them?"

"You better do something," he countered.

"I'm not sitting by him. I'm going to end up dead," Pickles said, genuinely concerned and picking up his seat to relocate.

"Like what?" I asked.

"Sleep with a fat chick, a slump buster."

"Like the chick that shut you down at the Diamond Club?"

"Ha. Ha." He gave me the finger.

"Sorry, I can't right now. I don't think the coaches will let me leave the game for that." I righted my chair and sat down again.

"Besides, it won't work," Rosco said, matter of fact. "It only works for slumps, hence the name slump buster. Also, Hayhurst is pitching well right now, so—"

"He won't be anymore, not now that he's pissed off the gods."

"I'll take my chances," I said.

"Well, you could play with a hangover," Slappy said, still intent on the issue.

"That won't work either, since he's not a starter," Rosco said.

"Why do these baseball gods require me to sleep with fat chicks or play wasted? Why not donate to charity or something?"

"Obviously, because they're *baseball gods,*" came the harmonious response.

"Well, I don't drink, and I'm waiting for marriage. The baseball gods are out of luck," I said, flippantly. "I'm just going to have to wear it I guess, right?" I turned to face the field, but the silence behind me turned me back around. The bullpen was staring at me as if I walked into a party I wasn't invited to and the record skipped.

"Wait—you're a virgin, Hayhurst?"

"Yes. Why?"

"As in, you've never had sex?"

"That would be the requirement of virginity."

"Holy shit!" Pickles blurted.

"You've played five years of pro ball and never had sex . . . wow. Are you gay?" Slappy asked.

"Come on!" I protested. "Just cuz I'm waiting for marriage, doesn't mean I'm gay."

"Do you even look at porn?"

"I've seen porn before."

"Like what kind? Like the hard-core stuff or just the soft, cuddly, no money shot kind."

I paused to sift through what I was just asked. "How did I get into this? How did we go from baseball gods to what brand of porn I look at?"

"It's important, uh . . . *for the baseball gods.*"

"I doubt that."

"Are you religious or something?" Slappy asked.

"Baseball god religious or real religion religious?"

"Real religion religious."

"Yes."

"But you've looked at porn before?"

I shrugged. "I'm only human. I'm definitely not the best example of—"

"And you don't drink."

"No. I don't."

"Are you a Mormon?"

"No, I'm not Mormon!"

"Well then why don't you drink?"

" . . . "

"Do you think there's something wrong with people who drink?" All the guys currently on the team drank.

"No, I don't think it's evil, if that's what you're asking."

"Well, what's your reasoning?" Curious looks turned to suspicious ones.

I shook my head and took a long look into the outfield. "The reason I'm waiting for marriage is because it's something I believe in, and it's spiritual for me." I'd told this little tidbit with the foreknowledge the boys didn't much care for my personal reasons as much as they wanted to know I didn't think they were sinful bastards. Baseball players in our age group are a lot like the regular nonbaseball-playing-type guys; both like women and pursue sexual relations with them as often as possible. It wasn't easy for me to hold out for as long as I had, and it made me the brunt of a lot of jokes, especially since the movie *The 40-Year-Old Virgin* came out.

Your sex life is private if you want it to be, and I could always cite religion to make the skeptical questioning stop. The drinking thing, however, was a male-bonding ritual. Tossing back a brew with the crew was part of donning the uniform, and guys would frequently remind me that even Jesus put down a glass of wine now and then. The fact is, a lot of guys, baseball or otherwise, don't feel comfortable around a guy who won't throw one back occasionally. Baseball players and drinking go hand in hand.

"The reason I don't drink is because my brother is an alcoholic. He's practically ruined my family's life with his drinking." The words hung for a second. "I hate him for it. As long as he drinks, I won't. That's my reason, and I don't care what you think about it."

There was a moment of silence as the guys thought about the words.

"So you're saying you like whips-and-chain-style porn, then?"

"You just never stop, do you?"

"It's a simple question!"

We all laughed at Slappy's persistence, which broke the tension. I smiled and turned back to the group. "Actually, I like the soft, cuddly, librarian kind."

"That's what I thought! Totally suits you!" Slappy shouted. We all laughed again, especially Rosco, who kept on laughing long after the others. He laughed so hard and so long, it became obvious he was no longer laughing with us, but at something else.

"What the hell crawled in your pants?" giggled up Stubbs.

"Oh man, no offense, Hay, but you being a virgin reminded me of this retarded kid I know."

"Why is it people think if they say 'no offense' before a line, they feel they have the freedom to go ahead and be offensive?"

"He was a virgin too, but, well, it's just funny because if you could have met the guy." He started laughing to himself again. "Oh boy, that guy," he labored for breath as he cracked himself up. "This one time he crapped his pants and . . . the grape jelly . . . the tear gas," then came more laughing. We stared in wonder. When he finally caught his breath, he looked at us soberly, wiped his tears of laughter away, and said, "Anyway, the point is, you're a virgin and he's not. Amazing really."

"Christ Rosco, are you going to explain this story or just laugh at yourself." Slappy was obviously interested.

"He probably met some other nice person with a handicap and they—" I began rationalizing but was interrupted.

"No dude, she was hot."

"Well, hot for him, I'm sure," I said dismissively.

"No, hot for anybody." At this, I stopped trying and buckled down.

"Spit it out, Rosco," Slap said.

"Okay. His name was Carl, and he was a handicapped batboy we had on the team."

"What kind of handicap?"

"I'm not a doctor. I don't know if it was autism or what Rain

Man had. Whatever. He was higher functioning, but not quite normal, you know?"

"So like Slappy?" Maddog asked. Slappy offered the finger to Maddog.

"Sorta. This kid's problems were diagnosable." Slappy offered the finger to Rosco.

"So Carl was our batboy. Actually, he wasn't really a boy, he was more like a batperson. He was older. Older than me at least, but he still acted like a kid."

"So he was a batman," Stubbs said, giggling.

"Sure," Rosco said. "But he was a good guy, meant well, like everyone's little brother repeating what he saw us do or say. We'd hack on each other, so he'd hack on us, and it was fine, funny even. But he'd miss some of the finer points of how guys would bust each other's balls. Sometimes, he'd go too far. Like telling a guy who just blew a save, 'Nice job blowing the game, dumbass.'

"He didn't know any better. So when he messed up, instead of getting pissed, most of the guys would just tell him to fuck off or something."

"Wait, you told a retarded kid to fuck off?" I asked.

"I never told him that," Rosco said. "But that's mostly because we never talked. He didn't think I was cool and ignored me most of the time."

"So a retarded kid thought you weren't cool."

"Man," Rosco said, correcting him.

"Sorry, a retarded man thought you weren't cool."

"Correct."

"Okay, so he was like everyone else in that respect."

"Pretty much."

"Got it. Continue."

"Anyway," Rosco said, "when the stadium hired a cute new concession stand girl, Carl was the first to talk to her."

"Oh shit! He nailed the concession stand girl! Awesome! What did she look like?" This was Slappy, of course.

"Relax Slap, let me tell the story. Carl followed the new girl around like a lost puppy, but he didn't nail her." Slappy deflated. "The girl was nice to him, but the kind of nice that doesn't necessarily mean I like you back. You must be used to that, huh, Dirk?"

"Religious preference, dude, just tell your story."

Rosco continued. "We all knew what was going on, but no one said anything, letting Carl make his own mistakes. Of course, the pretty, new girl liked the players more than Carl, but we all played dumb for Carl's sake.

"Then, in the middle of a losing streak, Carl did that thing where he said something dumb at the wrong time to the wrong player, and instead of 'fuck off' he was told, 'Oh yea Carl, well I took your girl home last night and fucked her brains out. She says she hates you!'"

"Oh boy. How did Carl take that?" Pickles asked.

"He snapped. He charged the guy like a wild animal, flailing and punching and kicking. It was actually pretty noble, him defending his lady. Unfortunately, it ended with him getting stuffed headfirst in a trash can."

"Oh my God, that's horrible!"

"Yeah, it wasn't our best moment," Rosco said, shaking his head. "Carl took it bad too. Not the trash can thing, that had been done before, but the woman thing. We'd seen him upset, but this was like DEFCON 1. He didn't talk to us for a while, didn't even tell anyone to screw themselves like usual. Instead, he started writing up some kind of letter, like a last will and testament. He left it on the table of the clubhouse where the team could read it. It said something about how he was so sad he would die without ever knowing the love of a woman. It was pretty deep stuff."

"What did you guys do?" I asked.

"Well, uh . . ." Rosco scratched the back of his head, clearly a little embarrassed. "We did the only logical thing a minor league baseball team could do to fix the problem. We bought him a hooker."

"You what?"

"Oh, don't act so shocked. You said you'd have sex with a three hundred pound dude if the Taliban put a gun in your face."

"First off, that's because I'd have a gun in my face, and second, if I was sleeping with him, none of the other dudes would mess with me cuz he'd be my bitch. It was the smartest scenario." The rest of the guys agreed. "I rest my case."

"Whatever makes you sleep at night. Anyway, the hooker wasn't really a hooker, she was a call girl. She was higher class. We had to book her and stuff. At least that's what I heard. Our dirtbag clubbie with supposed mafia connections said he would set up the whole thing for us, and we just needed to raise the cash. Before I knew it, the idea had legs, and guys were pitching in money for the Get Carl Laid Fund.

"We ended up raising a decent amount," Rosco said, rather surprised. "We passed the cash onto the clubbie, and he took care of the details."

"Does this clubbie still work in the minors?" Slappy asked. We ignored him.

"The lady they booked turned out to be a real professional with a specialty in role playing. So, the guys scripted out how they wanted the whole thing to go down. They brought her to a game, got her tickets, and told her to hit on Carl the whole night as if she were in love. She was great, had Carl fumbling with his bat on and off the field.

"After the game, she hung around and asked Carl out for a little postgame show. Carl didn't have a place of his own, still living with his parents, and he didn't know what to do. The clubbie thought of that. He arranged it so the two lovebirds could head back to his place."

"Why didn't you get him a hotel room?"

"We were on a budget." Understanding nods all around. The minors were still the minors.

"The girl took care of the rest," Rosco continued. "She walked him through the entire process and rung his bell many times over.

"The next day in the locker room, the guys came in early to discuss Carl's night. When Carl came in, we met him with cheers and applause. Some guys got up and shook his hand, slapping him on the back. I'm surprised cigars weren't handed out. Then we asked him the question everyone was dying to know, 'So, how was it, buddy? Was she everything you wanted?' To which he replied, as cool as ice: 'Oh, she was okay, but the one the guys bought me last year was better.'"

"No way—" the boys around Rosco said, mouths open, staring in disbelief.

"Exactly. I could have dropped dead right then and there," Rosco said.

"Wow! You guys got took by a retarded kid," Pickles blurted.

"Man," Rosco corrected.

"Good, I'm glad you got took. Serves you guys right," I said, my arms crossed like a nun.

"Why are you so offended? I thought you'd be inspired! There's hope for you!"

"Hope that you guys will pitch in and buy me a hooker?"

"I just had a great idea guys!" Slappy declared. He got up, walked behind me, and placed his hands on my shoulders. "I know a great cause we could use our quarter toss money for!"

Chapter Twenty-five

The bus home from Modesto was very much like the bus to it. We arrived early, near the crack of dawn, with a game looming hours away. I went home to my borrowed bed, slept late, went to stretch, and spent another night in the bullpen. The following day brought another game, then another, and another, and so on. Soon the days and nights began to blur together. Sometimes I pitched.

When I did take the mound, I did great. I didn't change my style and it wasn't always amazing, but I was successful. I was confident. I didn't worry about what happened once I let go of the ball. I didn't see the Baseball Reaper anymore, and I didn't fight myself. I was pitching the best I ever had in my four tours of the Cal League—far too well for any defeatist thoughts. The team was great, funny, entertaining. My host family was fantastic. I began to feel like a superhero again, as if I could do great things through my success.

On the top of that list of deeds was swooping into my parents' house. During this visit I imagined they would all be happy to see me. No one would be fighting or drinking or crying. We'd all talk about baseball and about how great it was that I was in the big leagues. I'd turn out my pockets, flush with cash, and we'd go out and get a new car and a new house and a new life. It was a good dream. Hell, I'd even buy grandma a new washing machine.

One night, on an off day, I lay in bed thinking about that beautiful vision and the time line I was on to make it come true. I needed to move forward, and I began to wonder if I would or if I was too stale a product in the eyes of the Brass to escape from A-ball. Then, my cell phone rang. The Lake Elsinore trainer was calling.

"Hey Will, how's it going?" I asked.

"Hey Dirk, I've got some news for you."

I thought about the last trainer who called me with news. "Am I going to like this news?"

"You should, you're heading up to Double-A. Congratulations! You earned it. Your flight leaves tomorrow, so you need to come in and get your bags and your medical folder."

"Wait. What?"

"Yeah, I know it's sudden, but you know how it is. The team's in Corpus Christi right now, part of an eight-day road trip. I'll give you the rest of the details when you pick up your stuff. I'll meet you at the field."

"Holy shit. What time?" I sprung out of bed.

"In an hour. Can you make it?"

"I'll be there."

"Cool, see you then, and congratulations."

And as I closed the cell phone, I also closed my time in A-ball. In a matter of eight hours, I would be gone. I would disappear from Lake Elsinore, leaving all my friends behind without so much as a good-bye. I thanked my host family, packed my bags, and caught a plane early in the morning to a new team in a new town with a whole new set of circumstances.

Chapter Twenty-six

In the cab, riding from the airport to the field in Corpus Christi I
decided to call my parents and tell them the good news—the first
call home I made since my assignment to Lake Elsinore. Like any
job, getting promoted is a good excuse to call family and boast. I
was excited.

I rang the newly replaced house phone. My dad, much to my
surprise, picked up with a tired "Ya?"

"Hey, Dad."

"Hey."

"How's it goin'?"

"It's goin'."

"Is Mom around?"

"Who knows."

"Well, I got some good news. I got called back up to Double-A."

"Uh-huh."

"Yeah, I'm on my way there now. Good news, huh?"

"I thought you were gonna quit," he said, in a queer, almost
disappointed way.

"Yeah, me too, but I'm back on track now."

"Uh-huh," he said hollowly.

One little note of excitement was all I wanted, but my words seemed to tumble into him like a deep, empty well.

This was one of the reasons I didn't call home. My dad was like any other father who pushed his son to be successful. He kicked me in the ass when I needed it, sometimes even when I didn't. He was my first pitching coach and first life coach. Consequently, he was the person I went to for help handling bumps in both roads. It felt like I lost a piece of myself when I started pitching without him in the stands. Then, when he began to vacate other portions of my life, he felt less like a father and more like an unstable person living in my house.

Back in 2005, when things were going bad and my demons had manifested into cloaked figures and regular ass-kickings, I called my dad to tell him I hated baseball. I told him I was sick of it and I wanted out. Essentially, I called him to be told I should keep pushing from the man who had pushed me to chase this down in the first place.

He didn't, though. He was bankrupt, no words to push himself along with and certainly none for me. He started screaming, his voice straining the speakers of my cell phone as the high pitches blared through. He told me to quit, "Just fucking quit! I'm sick of hearing you whine about it! Ain't got no chance anyway. Doesn't matter how hard you fucking try . . ."

It was so absolutely depressing to hear him say it. His passionate hatred for life could convince anyone it wasn't worth trying anymore. I kept playing as a way of refusing to accept his words as gospel.

That was then, and this was now. I didn't need motivation, I only wanted to share a victory. I was realizing, however, not only couldn't my father give, but he couldn't receive anymore either. He couldn't share this feeling or take hold of the success with me. The pain of not receiving joy from loved ones was something I had become accustomed to. The powerless feeling of being unable to give joy back, however, was not. I felt my promotion turn to ash.

"Are you proud of me, Dad?" I asked.

"What do you mean?"

"I mean, I'm playing professional baseball. I've been playing for a long time now. I know I may never make it to the big leagues, but I'd like to think you're proud of me regardless. I haven't given up."

"You don't need me to tell you I'm proud of you."

"I need to know. I need to know that what I'm doing makes you happy. I want you to tell me I make you happy."

"What does makin' me happy have to do with what you're doing?"

"I want to know you're happy, Dad. Please, just tell me you're happy."

The receiver hung silent, then, "Nothing makes me happy anymore, Dirk."

I held the phone like it was a brick as the cabby drove me down the cemetery roads of some forgettable, minor league tomb. The cab might as well have been a hearse.

"Can I talk to Mom?" I asked in a whisper.

Dad yelled for my mother. There was the sound of the phone changing hands, and my mom got on the line. "Hello?"

"Hey, Mom."

"Well, hello," she said, in a more typically cheery parental way. "How are you?"

"I'm okay," I mustered.

"How are things going?"

"Good, I'm on my way to Texas. Got called up to Double-A."

"You did! That's great!"

"Yeah. . . . It's where I want to be, right?" The words bled out as if I were deflating.

"You don't sound happy about it."

"Oh, I am."

"How funny. I know you don't like it when I talk about this, but I was reading in the *Mad Friars* the other day, and they said you weren't—"

"Please don't go there mom," I interrupted. "You know I hate that crap."

The Padres have their own team-specific media venue, which pumps out speculation and prophecy about kids coming up through the system. Like most minor league news venues, its reports are written to sell and hype as much as they are to inform. It's a fine example of how people in my line of work are sifted into the prospects and nobodies. My mom treats it like the Bible, while I detest it.

"If you called more often, I wouldn't have to read what they print."

"The people who write that stuff don't play the game, Mom. I do. If you are so concerned, then call me."

"You'd just yell at me for getting into your business."

"You are getting into it anyway, might as well get it from the source."

"You know I don't believe that stuff," she casually lied.

"Yes, you do, and so do other people. Do you know what it's like to be summed up by numbers and reports in the media? To be labeled? I can deal with the fact other people believe that I'm some kind of waste of space, but I'd appreciate it if you didn't. You're my mom."

"I don't understand why you get so upset about this. It's just words."

"You started the conversation off with, 'I know you don't like it but . . .'"

"Fine, let's change the subject, then. Talk to me about something else."

I sighed and shifted the phone from one ear to the other.

"What's the matter?"

"Dad."

"What about him?"

"Do you think Dad's proud of me?"

"What?"

"Seriously, do you think he's proud of me?"

"Sure he is. Why would you ask that?"

"Why can't he say it then?"

"Dirk, your father can't . . . He can't say a lot of things anymore." Her voice trailed away. I guess I didn't stop to think about how many things he no longer said to her.

"I don't understand that. Why can't he just get past himself once in a while," I pressed.

"You don't need to hear him tell you things to know he cares." She said it like a promise she hopelessly repeated to herself daily.

"He said that too, but what if I want to hear him say it. What about that? Maybe I just want to know I'm doing right by him, and I want to hear it from his mouth?"

She didn't respond.

"Now you're quiet too. Everyone's quiet. I'm doing something so many folks would die to do, and it's like he doesn't even care!"

Still only silence on the other end of the line.

"Why can't he tell me he's proud of his son for grinding it out? Why can't he just fake it once—"

"Are you done?" she interrupted. "I deal with this enough from him, I don't need it from you. I'm sorry you don't feel like he's being the perfect father. I'm sorry things aren't they way you think that they should be, but this is the way they are. So you are just going to have to get over it!"

Silence again, this time it was my turn. I spend more time in silence than I do in conversation with my parents.

I fought the urge to hang up. The cabbie looked back at me in his rearview mirror. I looked away from his eyes. Moments later, a calm, collected voice returned, "Honey, it doesn't matter what you do, you can't fix your father. He's not right, and nothing we can do is going to change that."

"I can't accept that."

"You don't have a choice," she said bluntly.

"Why?"

"Because some things aren't simple to fix. Not even when you get promoted."

I transferred the phone back to my other ear. I couldn't think of anything else to say.

"So, have you met any girls this season?" More banal small talk.

"No."

"Any good friends on the team?"

". . ."

"If you aren't going to talk then why'd you call?"

". . ."

My brother's rough voice rumbled in the background of the dormant line. Scratches echoed through the receiver as she moved her mouth from the phone to answer him. "I don't know, where did you put them last? . . . Well look there. . . . No, I didn't move them. . . . Why does your problem always become my problem?" She came back to our conversation with an exasperated tone, "I have to go, your brother can't find his pants, and he's got a meeting in a few minutes, and he's panicking."

"Fine."

"Everything's gonna be okay, Dirk, we are all proud of—I'm coming for Christ's sake, put some underwear on, then we'll worry about the pants! Gotta go, bye-bye."

She hung up.

Chapter Twenty-seven

The first thing any player should do after arriving with a new team is meet the manager. Even if you've been called up and sent back down to a club where the coaching staff is familiar with you, go pay your respects. The skipper might say nothing more than welcome, or he might lay out his master plan and your part in it in four acts. He's the manager; he can do what he wants. Some managers are moodier than others, and some have certain pet peeves, but almost all of them dislike being the last man on your list of priorities when you show up on their team. My advice: always appease those who have direct power to punish.

When I strolled into the office of the Missions manager, my hair had grown back down to my shoulders, popping out under my hat like the straw from a scarecrow's hat. I had a strong five o'clock shadow going and didn't even bother with a collared shirt. My eyes were bloodshot and my glasses were dirty. The manager, Randy Ready, stared at me as if I just walked in from the street to beg for change.

"Hey, how's it going?" I offered.

Randy eyed me. "Jesus, Hayhurst, you're takin' the law into your own hands looking like that."

"I was going to get my hair cut today, but I got called up and it ruined my plan. Honest." I've said truer things.

"Oh yeah, sure you were, right? How convenient is that, huh? Couldn't get your hair cut because a promotion got in the way." He laughed, openly skeptical.

I wasn't going to slip anything past Randy, least of all some limp excuse for weeks of haircut neglect. Randy understood baseball life too well. He knew all the trick plays and heard every excuse. The stuff he's seen during his time in the game makes my tales seem like nursery rhymes.

I've played under him before, and I know from experience he operates under the principle that with success comes leniency. It's a long season, and a good manager knows when to pick his battles. If a player does his job and keeps his nose clean, he'll make sure the police look the other way. On the other hand, if he sniffs out that guys are going through the motions, spending too much time thinking about things like hair, and not taking extra reps to ensure victories, he'll make sure the law is followed to the letter. He has his priorities, chief of which is developing winners. Somewhere down at the bottom is looking trendy.

I respected Randy for his desire to win, his views on professionalism, and, of course, his power to punish. I also respected him for other reasons. Some managers pushed the panic button when teams started to drop games. Randy always kept his cool. He never screamed at players, and he didn't have to. The ease with which he could tell a player how it was, what failure meant, and what he'd be forced to do if it continued were more sobering than high-volume verbal ballistics could ever be. True, he did get loud now and again, though he usually aimed it at an on-field official, getting him tossed like some form of baseball exorcism.

Abby, the Missions' pitching coach, sat on the far side of Randy's office. He stared at me in pretend shock, then took his turn welcoming me to the club with, "My God Hay, you look like Harry

Potter. Tell me he don't look like Harry Potter?" he said, gesturing to Randy while shaking his head. Randy smirked and offered a laugh that was more of a decorative exhale than anything. "You ain't gonna cast a spell on me are ya?"

"Okay, okay, I'll get it cut."

"Oh yeah, you will," Randy said. I had done nothing to help his team this year, therefore I had earned no leniency.

"Shit, you're looking like one of them fairy book people," Abby continued, again with the face of shock.

Things were not always what they seemed with Abby. Though his country drawl and old-fashioned disposition evoked a dim-witted Southern stereotype, he was anything but. He made a habit of rednecking up his speech, fumbling words and phrases, just to see if we'd catch it. He'd act surprised when the team called him out for it, like a teacher would feign shock when kindergartners corrected her for something she purposefully botched. He used it as a defense when he got in trouble, like when he'd cut in on boarding lines during team flights and aviation officials would reprimand him. He'd act as if he didn't know any better, airplanes were magical creations, and he was just a country boy after all. He'd never apologize, however, when he got that exit row seat.

Acting wasn't the only thing Abby knew. He was well acquainted with pitching and the numbers behind it. He kept track of everything a pitcher did on the mound, meticulously breaking down counts, averages, and ratios—analyzing, comparing, dissecting. All the backwoods Arkansas BS was a front. He was like the Columbo of pitching coaches, rambling his way into genius by pretending to be confused.

Thanks to his rich character, Abby had so many nicknames from his loving core of pitchers, it was hard to keep track of them all. Some called him Big Chicken because he looked like Foghorn Leghorn and spoke with the same inflection. Some called him Top Heavy because he had a boiler and a big head teetering on spindly legs. Some called him choice curse words. Well, Ox called him choice curse words, but he called everyone choice curse words. Most of us just called him Abby.

Rounding out the trio was Rick Poppollina, or Pops, as we called him. He was the Missions' hitting coach. A fiery Italian from Chicago, Pops had a firecracker personality that could go from zero to *go fuck yourself!* in four seconds flat. Pops was a player favorite. He spoke with a rough Chicago accent, and while Abby's methods were more subtle, Pops fixed people with a few good whacks of the bat. The more fired up he got about guys not hitting, the more he would replace the adjectives in his hitting critiques with cuss words. The players loved it. His intensity was great, infectious even, not to mention there was just something so amusing about swearwords said in a tough *Chitalian*.

"Hay, you need to get that mess cleaned up, fuh-uck." Though his tone was unmistakably condemning, he was smiling when he said it. He always let it be known when he was kidding. But if you didn't know it, you could tell he was angry by how long he held his *F* sounds at the beginning of his *F* bombs. Ff-uck is happy. Ffffuck—not happy.

"Good to see you too, Pops." He leaned forward in his chair and shook my hand.

Everyone had been met, which prompted Randy to move things along. "Alright, Hay, get yourself some threads. Get cleaned up. The boys will be here anytime now. Probably won't throw you in there tonight," he said, in reference to the game, "but, you never know." With that, he turned away from me and back to business. That was my cue to exit the office.

The next stop on my trip was Eddie's office. Eddie Tomagatchi was the team's trainer. His "office" wasn't really an office, though it did have a desk in it. It also had two training tables, a refrigerator, various boxes of cereal, one box of oatmeal cream pies, a giant drum of puffed cheese balls, trainer's tape, a jar of butt paste, hot tubs, a hot dog rotisserie, and a greasy George Foreman grill. His office tripled as the visitors' training room, cafeteria, and lounge. It was common for Eddie to work on a player's tender elbow while hot dogs tumbled end over end on the rotisserie behind him.

Minor league trainers don't simply tend to players physical needs, they handle all manner of things from broken bones to babysitting, like a cross between combat medics and third-grade teachers. They handle paperwork, travel arrangements, language barriers, and meal money, and they do it all in conditions similar to a Cambodian war zone. If there is one member of a minor league team who earns his paycheck, it's the team's trainer.

Eddie was one of the best. Coolheaded, quick-witted, and good with an ultrasound wand, he could get you loose, patch you up, and trade insults with you in his sleep. Not every trainer fits in well with the team, but the best ones were those who the players could trust for help on both sides of the lines. Eddie cared about his boys and wasn't above acting like one every now and then. Players knew who good trainers were, and it was generally circulated that Eddie, if players' opinion had anything to do with it, should be in the big leagues.

I walked into Eddie's office and coughed to make myself known.

"Hey, Hay, how are you?" he asked, looking up from a stack of papers. If Pops spoke in rough tones, Eddie spoke in short, chopped ones denoting his Japanese Hawaiian heritage.

"I'm good, buddy. Good to see you."

"Yeah, you too. Everything feeling okay? Your arm good? No issues?"

"No, everything is fine, pal. I feel good. Happy to be back up here."

"Do you have your folder?"

I fished out my team medical history folder and handed it over to Eddie. He flipped through it casually. I'm not sure what trainers look for. I can't read those things anyway.

"I have travel money for you. I'm sure you'll want that," he said, looking up at me again.

"Oh heck, yes! That's why you're my favorite person here, Eddie. We've only just said hello, and you're giving me money."

Eddie produced a sign-in sheet containing printed names and their correlating signatures for each player currently on the team. My name was not on the sheet, so Eddie wrote it in for me and I signed. He handed me a bank envelope with a few twenties inside. It's the minor league equivalent of passing Go.

Chapter Twenty-eight

My new, yet old, teammates started filtering into the park around 2:30 in the afternoon. I had good reunions with the guys I knew. The guys I didn't know walked up and shook my hand and said their names with a cordial smile. I said mine in the same fashion. It was all standard operating procedure.

Real introductions don't happen here. I may be on the team on paper, but I'm not part of the team until everyone feels comfortable with me. That takes time. It's kind of like being one of those people who document the behaviors of gorillas in the wild. You have to give the gorillas time to get acclimated to you, or they may tear your legs off and beat you with them.

It's tough to be the new gorilla even if you've played with a lot of the guys before. It was easy coming together with the Lake Elsinore team because we all started together. This squad had already gone through its formative period, and I'd have to ease in. The Lake Elsinore team was also younger than this squad, more immature and inexperienced, which gave me an instant leadership position. Here I was just another reliever. With a guy like Randy at the helm, it could be assumed this Double-A squad was also more rigorous and professional. Only time would tell, but I thought it best to act a tad more professional until I had a better read on things, which didn't take long to get.

While I finished trying on my new Missions jersey, I watched the team interact. The Latin players huddled together, speaking in hurried Spanish tones. A few position players sparked a card game and sat at the clubhouse's lone table arguing over the amount of plucks to go for. Others sat at their lockers punching keys on their cell phones while the rest stared up at a lone television screen watching ESPN commentators argue over the relevance of today's sports headlines. I pulled my pants up.

When I hitched up the waistline of my new pants, the cuffs of the legs came up as well, way up. The scrunched elastic foot holes sat inches above my ankles, around my shins, Greg Maddux style. I thought I picked out a longer pair. I took the pair off, checked the label—36 inches—and scratched my head, Then as if something could have magically changed by my reading of the dimensions, I put the pants back on again—still too short.

"They're all that way," Drew Macias said. Our first reunion in Double-A happened almost exactly like it did in spring training—me putting pants on. He had made this team out of camp and was happy to see me back on it. He walked over to my locker, watching me fumble around in my new uniform.

"What do you mean? These should be a good four inches longer."

"First, good to see you again. Second, the pants should be, but they're not. Grady made the Missions alter all our pants." He rolled his eyes when he said it and made a cuckoo gesture.

"Good to see you too, buddy, but wait," I said, eyebrows furrowed in disgust, "all our pants will look like this on me?" I pulled down one of the pant legs, which sprang back up when I let go. I jerked it down again, then tried to go through my delivery. When I kicked, my pants crawled back up my shin, again. Finally, I resorted to taking the pants off, standing on the legs, and wrenching the waist up in an effort to lengthen them.

"It sucks, dude. You know how Grady is about pants. When he came to town, he got pissed at everyone for not showing sock." There was an organizational rule forbidding pant legs the right to extend to the shoe or cover it, anyway—a rule that has irritated the hell out players since its creation. "So," Drew continued, "he had the Missions' tailor alter all the pants down to thirty-two inches to prove his authority."

"Isn't this taking it a little too far? I mean, I wasn't even here. Why do I have to wear Little League pants?" I felt like Huckleberry Finn in a pair of high-water overalls.

"It's stupid. I feel ridiculous in mine too! Guess we all get to rock the dirty mid look."

"I feel like a clown in these." All the stretching had gained me maybe an inch when I put the pants back on.

"We got guys with big-league time on this team, and they have to wear the same pants. One of the guys has a World Series ring!"

"One of our guys has a World Series ring?" I said in a whisper, forgetting about the pants. I looked around the room trying to spot him. I eyed the ring hand of all the big, burly players. Surely, the man possessing a World Series ring looked herculean, like a dude from a romance novel cover.

"Yeah, Wooten does. You didn't know that?" Drew looked at me quizzically. Most of the guys retained this detail from spring training. I did not, considering I was most likely preoccupied with fielding breasts or getting a ball up my ass.

"You know I don't know baseball heritage. I don't even know everyone on our big-league club right now." Fact.

Drew shrugged his shoulders. "Woot," he called, "show Dirk your ring."

One of the guys playing cards looked over at Drew, then nonchalantly extended his ring hand like the Godfather, revealing a ring the size of a grapefruit. I almost felt unworthy gazing upon it. Then I saw the owner. My notions that a World Series champ would look like a longhaired Adonis were slightly off because Woot looked more like one of the fat kids on the chess team. Short dark hair and a few extra tires, he sported a golfing visor, no shirt, and a pair of mandatory too-short pants. All things considered, he looked better in his pants than me.

Woot spoke in a high-pitched, nasally voice sarcastically declaring, "If you pay me, I'll let you touch it." He paused and thought to himself for a second. "Actually, I'm not doing too well this hand, so I could extend that offer to other things if the price is right." He looked down at himself and then back at me. "I won't charge much."

"World Series Champion, ladies and gentlemen," Drew said, laughing himself. He slapped me on the shoulder. "Welcome back. Enjoy the pants."

"Thanks."

A cry came from the other side of the locker room, "Goddamn it, you stinky little bastard! I'm going to sew your fucking ass shut!" Ox roared. He shot out of his seat and threw his glove at Manrique Ramirez or "Reek" as he was christened for just such behavior. Manrique laughed like a Mexican Tickle Me Elmo, delighted by his own stink and Ox's disgusted reaction.

"You won't be laughin' when I—" The stink settled in on Ox and derailed his monologue, his face shot several different directions, trying to find uncontaminated air. "Christ! Did something crawl up your ass and die?" Manrique waved his hand in a scooping motion to propel more of his stink at Ox. Players within the blast zone began to wilt as the stench crept through the locker room.

"It smells like a sick baby's diaper," one cried, falling.

"It smells like bad Indian food covered in burned hair," another said, exiting the area. Manrique laughed harder, delighted with his brew. More gloves were hurled at him.

"Wash your ass once in a while you dirty Mexican," Ox said. As soon as Manrique's mustard gas had cleared, Ox was back in the area to serve up some punishment

"Eh, eh, eh! Get off me, you fucking Yeti!" Manrique squealed.

Manrique was not a big guy. Actually, he was small and wiry and carried a look on his face that made it seem that he was perpetually caught off guard. Manrique was Mexican, as Ox so delicately noted. In locker rooms, race is not treated as politically sensitively as lobbying parities would like it to be. We are all one race, the baseball-playing race, and only recognize the colors cut into our uniform's fabric. We are the ultimate melting pot. We hand out slurs, low blows, and putdowns like candy in a multicultural parade.

"What did you call me?" Ox was doing his best to fight through Manrique's slapping hands to deliver some good kidney shots. Ox was not angry about the name-calling. He loved it actually. It was Ox's love language to be called names by his little Mexican brother. But Ox was still Ox, and when Manrique farted, farts that are mercilessly putrid, Ox would be the first to beat on him for it. Who would have thought a guy like Ox would be so passionate about air pollution?

Punishing Manrique for clearing the room with his emissions was not a very well thought-out idea. As Ox planted punch after punch on Manrique who was now scrunched up in the fetal position, the tension caused him to fart again, point blank on Ox. It sounded like a log going through a wood chipper.

"Goddamn!" Ox cried. He covered his face with the collar of his shirt. "You are one stinky motherfucker!" he said, releasing Manrique to block his nasal passages better.

Manrique laughed to himself, very pleased to escape his predators like a skunk.

"Nice going, Ox," came criticisms from scattering players.

"I'm going to fix this right now." Ox grabbed a shoe from his locker, then grabbed Manrique. "I warned you, didn't I?" Manrique squirmed while Ox tried to wedge a shoe into his ass.

"Good to see Ox hasn't changed," I remarked to Drew.

"Ox change? Impossible."

"Hey dude, how are you?" This was Jon Dalton. He'd come over to welcome me back to the league. He was wearing a pair of spandex sliding shorts and nothing else. He extended one hand to shake while the other was unmistakably stuffed in his shorts, fondling himself—perfectly normal behavior for Jon.

"I'm good, bro. How are you?"

"Great, I'm great," he said, tickling his Elmo. "Don't fucking live in the apartments up here, by the way."

"Okay. Why not?"

"Why not! Why fucking not?" Dalton was the coolest-headed crazy person I'd ever met. He was fearlessly rebellious, a tad hyperactive, but by no means stupid. He went to Citadel Military Academy, a full-on military school full of drill sergeants and hardasses. When he got out of line, he paid a healthy price for it. Consequently, he learned two things: first, if you are going to cut loose, get your money's worth in case you get caught, and second, don't get caught. He and the army did not mix well, though he deviously kept up appearances, toeing the line of trouble without paying the full price for it. Sure, he made a few mistakes here and there, but he learned from them, and the stories gained made it more than worth it. He was smart enough to know how to cheat the system, cautious enough to make sure he didn't get caught, and hyper enough to guarantee cheers and laughter from his teammates.

"Dude," he continued, "during our first road trip of the year, a storm caved the roof of our apartment in."

"What?"

"Yeah, my roommate and I came back, and the fucking living room was a pond. There were leaves and branches and bird shit all over the place. Everything was ruined."

"Holy crap! What did you guys do?"

"The apartment people moved us into another place, but a lot of our stuff was wrecked, which they wouldn't pay for."

"Wow, that sucks."

"You're telling me!" He stopped the conversation abruptly, then, "Hey, you got a dip on you?"

"No, I don't—"

"You don't dip, that's right. What are you, Mormon?"

"Why does everyone keep saying that?"

"I need a dip. Nice pants. Excuse me." He walked off, hand still on his piece. "Thompson! Give me a fucking dip. You owe me like forty!"

"I'm going to get dressed," Drew said, and he walked off.

"I'm going to look stupid," I said to myself, and stared down at my pants.

After batting practice, while the rest of the guys ran from the steamy gulf humidity for the comfort of the locker room's air-conditioning, I went to the pen to toss a light side session. I needed a tune-up after the trek I had to get here. Fifteen fastballs and ten breaking balls later, I felt like a pitcher again.

Soaking wet from the sauna-like conditions, I stumbled into the clubhouse to a party that had started without me. When I opened the door, I could hear the bass blaring. Five steps into the clubhouse and I could feel the steady pulse of a cranked sub-woofer. Grandmaster Flash singing "White Lines" permeated the sanctum, almost completely drowning out the laughter of the team. When I turned the corner into the main locker room, there was Dalton riding around on an electric scooter. Where this scooter came from or how it got into the building was beyond me.

The rest of the team had spaced chairs like cones on some kind of racetrack for the driver to weave in and out of while he sped around the locker room.

Ox was nearly falling over laughing so hard. Drew pushed chairs out into the middle of the track. The rest of the team stood off to the sides trying not to get run over. I remained in the doorway, unsure of my own safety.

Dalton rounded a corner, and ran over someone's shoes, getting them lodged in the front wheel. The scooter screeched to a halt, but "White Lines" continued. Dalton picked the shoes out from under the tire, then threw them into a nearby chair, shouting like an angry mother, "Whose shoes are on the floor?" Dalton was obviously upset that the rest of the team did not take track safety as seriously as he did.

He punched the throttle again and the scooter whirred into motion, sending him on a collision course with another chair. He narrowly dodged, jerking the scooter around and inches away from running over someone's Xbox, also lying on the floor. Like the scooter, I could not tell where the Xbox materialized from, as they are not commonly found in away-team locker rooms, but then again, neither are scooters.

"Oh, that was a hard one, watch out for the Xbox!" Each time he made a lap, or made up a lap, the team rearranged the chairs to make it harder. He snaked his way through as best he could, as fast as he could, sometimes kicking out to steady himself as he kept the speed up. Considering the track was only thirty feet by twenty feet with twenty-five chairs, a couch, a table, and an Xbox, he was pretty good.

Guys started throwing gloves and hats at him. The ones that missed were purposefully run over.

"Excuse me!" Dalton screamed as he barreled toward me. I sidestepped, and he flew into the hallway. Three seconds later, there was a crash in the training room, followed by laughter, followed by Eddie screaming. I turned to go investigate, but noticed no one else had moved to look, standing there as if it were all a normal occurrence. Woot walked in from the bathroom, looked around the clubhouse, then said, "Where's my scooter?"

I stood with my glove on my hip. If you haven't noticed by now, things are *way* more mature up here in Double-A . . .

Chapter Twenty-nine

The game started at 7:05 in the evening, and the Missions' relief core rambled out to the pen seconds before the anthem was sung. The visiting bullpen was indeed a pen; two mounds caged by chain-link fencing. Fans could poke us through its links or stare down at us from the seats above, pointing as if we were zoo animals on display. Composed partially of the right field fence, if the right fielder went back on a ball, he would only be inches from running into the relievers languishing just beyond the links.

Next to the pen was a swimming pool. So close was the pool, spray from cannonballs could splash warming pitchers. Cutting across the skyline was a towering bridge, under which freighters the size of the stadium passed carrying cargo. The stadium was a gem displayed majestically on the shore of the gulf. Playing on it reminded me how cool my job could be.

The relief core dragged the pen's chairs across the grass and up the fencing. We sat, kicking our feet up and catching our cleats in the fence's links. We watched the first couple of innings roll by, fans splashing next to us, ships passing by in the distance. The sun set and bright lights beaming out of a deep, Texas-sized sky illuminated the field.

Aside from a few new faces, the bullpen had mugs I'd come to know as friends through previous seasons. We'd been through a lot of battles together. Surviving the minors is a war of attrition, and we'd braved the odds at each other's side, something that, in a game of production or extinction, is worth honoring. There was a feeling of belonging by suiting up with these guys again.

Beyond our individual histories, the Missions' bullpen was a simple matter of ones and threes. One finger for the hard-sinking fastballs and three for nasty sliders. Everyone in the pen threw them, almost as if it were a fraternity requirement. If you had asked any of the boys about the suspicious absence of a changeup, they would have replied that changeups are for pussies.

I threw a changeup, incidentally.

We didn't talk much that night. I was new and so I kept quiet, which was fine because I had a lot to think about. I tried to remind myself I was on the track to being a prospect again, even though I didn't feel like one since talking to my folks. I told myself that their reaction was okay and that they didn't have to be stunned by a promotion to Double-A right now. If I put up good numbers, they will be impressed. Besides, I could still walk up to anyone in this stadium with my uniform on and make his day. Baseball had power, and I was its wielder.

When the last out of the game was made, I picked up the stray catch balls littering the pen. It was my job, as the latest addition to the Missions' bullpen staff, to wrangle up leftover equipment and cart it back to the locker room come game's end. While I herded balls back into their bag, fans predictably called down to me in hopes of receiving leftovers.

I put each ball back into the catch bag except one, a chewed-up fifty-five footer, the victim of a slider that ate dirt before it found a mitt. I placed that ball in my back pocket, earmarking it to give away. I finished equipment duties, grabbed the pen bag and zipped it shut, picked up my glove, and started walking the stretch of warning track toward the lockers.

The entire trip back to the pen, fans begged—leaning over the rails, calling to me for the ball, any ball, including the one in my back pocket. I walked by them, disciplined eyes straight ahead, ignoring. Their anticipation turned to letdown and then their letdown to anger. They told me I sucked for ignoring them, which incidentally I also ignored. I've spent enough time in this game to develop insult immunity when I don't meet fan expectations.

I was going to give the ball in my pocket out to someone; that's the whole reason I kept it separate. I didn't know who yet; I was waiting for someone to catch my eye. Passing out a free ball is tricky business. It can make one person happy and a whole bunch of others angry, like these fickle folks chewing me out. Everyone will say he or she deserves it, everyone has a kid at his first game, it's everyone's birthday, and everyone is a lifelong fan.

When I went into the underbelly of the stadium, onto the concourse running beneath the seats, I walked past a fenced section that exposed some of the stadium's innards to the fans. The fencing came together to form a gate where carts and supplies could enter. A security guard manned the gate from my side, keeping fans who lined the links of the section in check on the other. They, too, called to me as I went past.

On the far side of the gate, I noticed a boy in a wheelchair. When I saw him, I stopped. I can't read minds and I can't search souls, but I wanted to give this kid the ball in my pocket. It just felt like the right thing to do. Moreover it felt like something I needed to do. I pulled the ball free and walked to the gate.

I asked the security guard to let me through. He obliged, opening it for me. I stepped tentatively across the threshold. Immediately, programs and ticket stubs were pressed in front of my face. Parents called for their children, and whispers of urgency for something autographable and an implement with which to sign spread through the mass. They didn't want my autograph. They wanted the autograph of a baseball player, any player. I, however, wanted something more personal. I ignored them, walking through the spear tips of their pens to the boy in the wheelchair.

Standing there, looking down at him, I realized he was strapped into his chair. The expression on his face was not one of joy or expectation, but unintelligible emotion, continuously shifting while his head lulled side to side, sometimes gently, sometimes in thrashing spasms. His eyes focused on me as much as they did anything else, as if I were not there at all. He spoke no words, merely sounds and labored breaths.

I knelt and did the only thing I knew how to do in my uniform. They only thing I've ever been expected to do in it. I smiled and acted cheerful, like some fifties comic book hero talking to a Boy Scout. I produced the ball and held it out to him, as if it were words enough.

I expected him to take it from me, to snatch it up like every other child, yet his bent hands and crooked fingers continued to trace spastic patterns in the air. To him, I was not there and there was no ball—no souvenir, no magical bauble of white leather, no chance for a lasting memory. Spittle dribbled down the boy's chin and collected on a napkin tucked in the collar of his shirt.

His sister stepped in. She smiled graciously and requested the ball. I handed it to her. "Look!" she said to her brother in a sing-song voice. "It's a real baseball player and he's brought you a ball! Way cool, huh?" She rubbed his arm and placed the ball at his fingertips, but they did not grab hold. The ball fell to the ground.

The boy's face did not react to her excitement, nor did it cringe at the dropping of the ball. Rather, it contorted in a series of expressions, the ambiguous shifting of a face that could not cooperate with its owner. His sister picked up the ball, and in her hands it remained.

I looked at the both of them, then to the fans, and then to them again. Suddenly I was not there but standing in front of my father in his kitchen chair—his head in his hands while I stood awk-

wardly in front of him in uniform. I held out to him my accomplishment; I pressed it into his hands. Out it slipped, tumbling to
the floor, where it shattered. Unconcerned, my father looked on,
ever inward into a world none of us could understand, none of us
could penetrate.

Fans, parents, and kids alike, stared at me. All of them were
more than capable of receiving that ball, all willing to react with
the excitement I'd come to expect. I felt their gazes crush me, as if
I should be doing something I couldn't do.

I was imploding now, falling to pieces from the inside, until
the uniform I wore was a hollow shell moving on its own. I didn't
want to give the ball anymore. I wanted to give a part of me. I
wanted to tear my uniform off and wring out every last ounce of
magic it had within it. I wanted everyone to know how powerless
I felt in a costume that people believed could fix everything, yet
fixed nothing.

If I could have broken my dreams into pieces and sold them for
deliverance, I swear I would have. All I had was a baseball. And
while so many people would have fallen over themselves to get it,
and would have pushed, argued, and cussed me for not choosing
them to bestow it upon, I chose that boy, the one person in the stadium who couldn't take it. The one person I could offer nothing
to no matter how hard I squeezed the fabric of my outfit. It wasn't
fair, it wasn't right, and it wasn't going to change. His sister smiled
on, her patient face still watching me, ball in hand. I looked at her
but couldn't find any words. Then she spoke, saying, "I'm sorry."

She must have known her brother couldn't take the ball. She
must have grown immune to the broken joys. She knew the game,
and its most revered artifact were rendered meaningless by his
disability. She knew it because circumstances didn't change his
personality. She knew the hardship of trying to share something
close to her heart with a brother who could never relate. She knew
in some small way what it must be like to stand by and watch

events you could never change as they play out completely beyond your control no matter how many times you shook your fists at the sky above. Why on earth was she apologizing to me?

She was like my mother—apologizing to me for my own delusion. She was making the best of something she did nothing to deserve but couldn't fix. And no one, no matter what they wore or what they did, was going to step in and solve it.

I did not sign any autographs after I left that boy. Why should I? My name was as useless as my jersey, a scribble, a stretch of ink, and nothing more.

Chapter Thirty

I was operating under the assumption that after the game we'd head back to the hotel and go to sleep. You know what happens when you assume. It turned out, instead of catching some much-needed Zs on a nearby hotel pillow, I was riding another five hours on a bus as we made our way to the next town: Midland, Texas.

I had been awake for twenty-four hours by this point. All I wanted to do was sleep. My mind was so heavy with thoughts and my body with fatigue that even the notoriously uncomfortable seats of a minor league bus would be like clouds beneath my ass. However, this was no Lake Elsinore where I had bus-seating dominion. All the seats had been decided on, and I would be the guy standing in the aisle while everyone pretended to be sleeping, deaf, or dead.

I had to beg players to let me sit with them. Unlike the tour bus in Lake Elsinore, the bus here was older and smaller. Most of the guys I could pull the time card on were already doubled up. I sat with Cesar Ramos, another of the team's starters, and though he did not outright tell me he hated me for ruining his seating arrangements, it was clear he did not enjoy the company.

A side effect of spending way too much time in A-ball was that getting choice bus seats had spoiled me. I could no longer sleep with a man pressed up next to me, bumping my thigh with his, jutting his elbow into mine when he adjusted his iPod. I wasn't the trooper I was when I first signed, the player who could sleep folded in a suitcase, if necessary. Now I could not fall asleep without the luxurious space provided me by two open seats. I felt like a sardine wedged into a can. I sat there thinking about sleep, thinking about what it would feel like to get some of it, and wondering what it would feel like if I could never do it again. I began to envision hell as a place where people desperate for sleep were constantly jerked awake by a bumpy tour bus and seatmates who couldn't pick the right song on their iPod.

Eddie gave me eighty dollars in meal money, and I ended up spending it on a seat. I bought a pair of twin open seats from the team's strength coach, a man we called Juice. He had been in the back playing cards with Woot and Ward and had lost his meal money. He happily exchanged his seat for a chance to buy back in.

I took Juice's seat, but despite how hard I tried, I still could not fall asleep. I tried every awkward angle, leaning my head on the glass, trying to curl up over both seats, letting my legs dangle across the aisle. Nothing. Finally, when I got remotely close to slumber, I felt the urge to pee.

Exceedingly frustrated with my life at this point, I made my way back to the bus's bathroom. I had to climb back to it, picking my way over seat backs, trying not to step on other players' heads as I went. The aisles were populated with obstructions such as card games using coolers for tables. It was as if the bus were a casino on wheels, and as dingy and cramped as it was, it was still better than the Lake Elsinore Hotel.

The high rollers sat in the bus's rear, next to the bathroom door. To get in, I had to interrupt their game. They made me wait until the hand was over. Woot won on a bluff, to which he said, "I've been tricking people into thinking I've got something I don't for years now—just ask my wife." Woot got up and allowed me entrance into the bathroom. Before I entered, I noticed his scooter was parked in the rear of the bus as well. I had to pay eighty bucks for a seat and his scooter got one for free?

In the bathroom, I steadied myself with one hand, and relieved myself with the other. Trying to take a whizz on a tour bus is a lot like surfing. It's a delicate blend of balance and stream control. Not that it really matters if I miss, since by trip's end, the bathroom would be covered in pee from those less concerned than myself, but I was always taught to have pride in everything you do.

As I piddled, I heard scuffling outside the door. A thump hit the door, laughter, and then things calmed down. I tapped the last drop out, zipped up, and grabbed the door handle—it wouldn't open. It was being held in place. "Very funny guys. Oh no, I'm locked in the bathroom and I can't get out! Come on, this was a tired act in college."

"Hold on buddy, we gotta finish this hand; then we'll let you out."

I was pissed when I heard that, no pun intended. I shouldn't have to explain the short temper a person has when he's not slept for days. "Seriously you guys? What the fuck," I barked. I punched the door.

"Don't be a dick, dude, just wait."

I heard more commotion outside and some laughing. That didn't sound like a card game to me.

"Okay—just watch your feet when you come out." The bus casino allowed me to exit.

I pushed the door open cussing under my breath. I looked down at the floor as instructed. Bottles with dip spit had collected there, as well as some wadded up junk food wrappers and a scooter wheel. There was nothing to look out for, nothing that wasn't usually there. I took a step forward, eyes scanning the dimly lit floor of the bus. Still nothing.

"What the fuck am I supposed to be watching out—" The collective gasp of the team pulled my eyes up. There, about a foot from my face, dangling from the ceiling was the spread ass cheeks and ball sack of Jon Dalton. He was hanging from the bus's luggage racks completely naked, and I was on a collision course with his coin purse. One more step and he could have knighted me.

"Jesuscriss!" I blurted, and fell backward, tripping on the scooter wheel and falling into Woot. Everyone on the bus had scuffled back into viewing position and was now bursting with laughter. Dalton dismounted, landing in the aisle. It turned out he wasn't naked—he had on socks.

"Spider-Man!" a patch of players shouted. Dalton was laughing as he pointed at me, "You just got Spider-Manned, bud." He had one hand twirling his junk while he said it, as if he were thanking his sidekick for another job well done.

"I have no idea what to say to that," I said.

Woot pushed me back to my feet. Guys were still laughing, and I started to chuckle despite myself. I made my way back to my seat, completely unconcerned with anything on the floor. As I went some of the team smacked me in the ass for being a good sport. Ox smacked me so hard my ass almost fell off. Needless to say, I didn't get any sleep for the rest of the trip.

Chapter Thirty-one

Room service woke me in the Midland Hotel. In my delirium I did not think to put the Do Not Disturb sign on the door before crashing into bed. The maid knocked once, then opened the door, and popped in.

"No service," my roommate groaned.

"No serveeze?" the maid echoed.

"No service"

"No serveeze?"

"Si, no fucking serivico or whatever . . ."

"No serveeze?"

"NO FUCKING SERVICE, GO AWAY!"

She stood there for a second longer, casing our room or something; then she said, in a calm yet garbled voice, "Oh, okay, I come back later." She shut the door.

When I woke again, rain was coming down. It was pouring outside and in. The roof leaked. Buckets, dozens of them, strategically positioned under dripping hallway sections tried futilely to stem the flow. Some of the buckets were full to the brim, overflowing onto the floor, soaking the carpet, and forming large puddles that I foggily stepped into in my socks. The water was starting to leak into my room under the door, though, thankfully, nothing was dripping from our ceiling. Where the hell was I?

Time travel—that's a good way to describe it. After a thirty-six-hour travel binge, I was on a new team in a new town a couple thousand miles away from where I started the season. A matter of hours was all it took to remove me from the presence of my old teammates and crudely graft me to these new ones. That is how travel in the minors is though—harsh, immediate, and tiring, with a few hours on a plane, a few hours on a bus, and a few hours on a boat maybe if the roof keeps leaking. The most surprising part, however, is how fast a person adjusts and how quickly he forgets those individuals he played next to only days ago. I was no longer a Storm but a Mission now for however long it lasted.

I took the second shuttle bus to the field. I slept right up until I had only minutes to catch the shuttle. Dalton (now fully clothed) rode with me, as well as two other members of the pen: Boris the Blade, one of the team's closers, and Handsome Rob, the well-groomed, well-educated dean of the bullpen. Blade was the darker humored of the new pair, who enjoyed lighting the fuses of his fellow teammates and joyously watching them explode. He had a knack for sniffing out weak points. Handsome Rob, on the other hand, enjoyed judging the stupidity of fellow teammates and then pronouncing some insulting verdict. Rob was older, always well dressed, and spoke with an air of refinement. It was like being made fun of by Mr. Belvedere. Blade and Rob worked off each other well: one would instigate, while the other, too noble to instigate, would judge. I would have to be mindful of my behavior when around them.

After arriving, we strolled from the bus, across the walkway to the entrance of the hallway leading to the Midland visitor's team locker room. On opening the doors of the hallway, two crazed, angry dogs assailed us.

"Jesus Christ! What the fuck!" Dalton screamed.

The dogs, about the size of poodles, were locked in small kennels. They belonged to the visiting clubbie. Apparently, he let them run free when the teams were not present. When teams showed up, he locked the little ankle biters in tiny cages and, for some strange reason, placed said cages by the dimly lit clubhouse doorway. When the doors opened, the dogs ambushed anyone walking in with such ferocity that one would think they'd kill us all if they could get free.

Dalton did not like being startled. So he bent down to the cages and started barking at the dogs that barked back, biting at the gaps in the cage. The three of them barked at each other for a minute or so; then Dalton started kicking the cages screaming, "Shut the fuck up you stupid little rats! Grrrrrr, grrr rarf! Rarf! Rarf! Yeah, keep growling. I'll flush you down the fucking toilet!" He kicked the cages again.

"That's really working. Real mature," Rob said to Dalton, as the dogs continued barking with renewed fury.

"Rarf! rarf! Fuck you, dog. You want a piece of me? Grrrrr!"

"Are you really trash talking the dogs right now?" I asked.

"Wow Dalton, don't be such a pussy—they're just little dogs," Blade said. The dogs really were no bigger than cats.

"I don't care what size they are. What are they doing here?" Dalton asked.

"Scaring the shit out of you," Blade said.

"Yeah, you looked like Hayhurst did the other night when he almost walked into your dong."

Dalton relented on the dogs for a second and looked up at me. "Yeah, you should have seen your face when you got Spider Manned, Hayhurst. You looked like—"

"I just had a dong shoved in it," I interrupted, not amused.

"Oh, don't act like it's your first time," Blade chimed.

"True, but I usually get paid for the other times it happens." You have to roll with punches, or you'll just get more of them.

"How much do you charge?" Rob asked.

"If you have to ask, you can't afford me."

"Touché."

Dalton put his hand on the top of one of the kennels in order to stand up. The dogs nipped where he placed his fingers and scared him again, pissing him off even worse. "Goddamn fucking rats!" He started kicking the cages again. "SHUT UP!"

Dalton stood up and looked to the rest of us. "Where's the clubbie at? Who the fuck puts caged dogs in a dark doorway? I'm going to lock him in one of these cages." He marched down the remainder of the hallway and kicked the doors open. We followed.

Entering the clubhouse proper, Dalton could be heard yelling at the clubbie from around the corner, and every so often the words "dog" and "rat" could be heard. Blade and Rob went to their lockers and I to mine. On the far side of the lockers, more activity was brewing.

Woot was bent down behind yet another reliever's bare ass with a permanent marker. This reliever went by the name Ward and worked as the team's lefty specialist. Ward, like Wooten, was also a former big leaguer with years of experience. If his thickly accented voice didn't make it clear he was from the Bronx, then the sharp, quick-witted New York banter surely would. Ward had a mouth that (1) never stopped running and (2) was missing teeth. His ADD explained the first part, why he never slowed down and possibly his current, yet-to-be-discovered, exploit involving an artist and his ass. The missing teeth were due to bad dental care, despite the popular theory that someone knocked them out. He wore a mouthpiece to fill in the blanks.

Taking the job more seriously than a man inscribing another man's ass should, Woot made Ward move into better lighting so he could get a proper angle. The portrait was just as interesting as the canvas: Eddie, the team trainer. Woot drew a plump, round face with slanted eyes and short, buzzed hair. A mouth stretched from one cheek to the other, divided down the middle, of course. Though Eddie did not have acne, Ward's canvas did.

When the portrait was finished, Ward strutted into the training room, bare ass hanging out.

"Hey Eddie, check out this new tattoo I got." Ward bent over and showed Eddie Woot's masterpiece. To make sure there was no doubt who was represented, Woot wrote EDDIE over the work. "This way I can always remember you," Ward said.

Eddie was using the ultrasound wand on someone's arm at the time, but that did not stop him from attempting to kick Ward in the canvas.

"Hey, take it easy, you're gonna smear your face!" Ward protested.

Eddie launched rolls of athletic tape at Ward until he ran from the office.

"How'd he like it?" Wooten asked, as Ward scampered out.

"Oh, he loved it," Ward said, smiling broadly.

"Don't come crying to me the next time your arm hurts," Eddie said while standing in the doorway of the training room.

"I wouldn't do this to you if you'd just make me another PSP. You're freaking Japanese bro, you can turn this dip can into a Nintendo." Ward tossed the dip can at Eddie who batted it aside.

"Yeah, I could," Eddie said, "but I'm not going to make one for *you*."

"Awww, come on, bro, don't be that way," Ward said, smiling again.

"You draw a picture of me on your ass, and you want me to do you favors? I'm glad your PSP got stolen." Eddie turned back into the training room.

I was suiting up at my locker while the Ward Show was in progress. I looked over at Manrique, who was also watching.

"What's the deal with Ward's PSP?" I asked.

"He say someone broke into his room and take it. He's such a dipshit." Manrique let out a chuckle, which Ward caught wind of.

"What you are laughing at?" Ward said, staring down Manrique. "It's your cousins that took it. You tell them I want it back!"

"They not give it back, but they sell it back to you for a good price, since you're my friend."

Ward did not have a reply to that. Manrique, surprisingly coolheaded, trumped Ward's rampage of ADD. So, as Ward often did when he did not have a reply for a target outsmarting him, he switched targets. "Eddie, EDDIE!" he shouted at the training room door. "Reek admitted his family stole my PSP. I need the number for MLB security!"

"Good for Reek's family, I hope they enjoy it," came the shout from the training room.

Ward was on his feet and marching into the training room now. "Why are you so mean, Eddie? I've been the victim of a serious crime against my person."

"You drew my face on your ass!"

"Because I love you."

"Get out of my training room, you fucking jack-o'-lantern!"

"Oh that's low, bro, that's low. Why do you have to bring my teeth into this?" Ward feigned injury, though he was anything but. "Just when I was ready to forgive your people for what they did to us in Pearl Harbor, you go and say something like that."

Rolls of tape could be heard colliding against the wall of the training room. Ward came running out like a solider escaping gunfire. Aware of the events, Blade spotted an advertisement for a PSP in a Best Buy circular. He cut it out and took it into the locker-room pantry. Using tape from one of the rolls launched at Ward, he taped the ad to a milk jug in the refrigerator. Over the ad he wrote: Have you seen me?

I had relocated to the microwave in the pantry watching a bowl of Easy Mac spin in circles when Blade came in.

"Don't you think he'll be pissed when he sees that?" I asked.

"He won't see it."

"How do you know?"

"Have you seen his teeth? It's obvious he doesn't drink milk."

Chapter Thirty-two

Midland's park was brand new. Some of the luxury boxes weren't even finished yet. Yet, from what was complete, the place was shaping up to be a fine park. Everything from the dugouts to the scoreboard was miniature big league. The field was sunken, meaning it was carved out of the ground, placing the playing surface below the surrounding area's ground level. Grassy berms surrounded the park where fans sat out on blankets and towels. The bullpen was, like in Corpus Christi, a real pen situated beyond the left field fence. Instead of fencing on all sides, concrete walls twelve feet in height made up three of the four walls.

At the start of the game, Ox, Rob, Dalton, Blade, Ward, and I sat in the pen. However, since the weather was still poor, raining off and on with a constant drizzle since the start of the game, my fellow relievers decided to head into the comfort of the clubhouse. The game was viewable via live video feed in the clubhouse, and I would have gone with them, but someone needed to stay behind to play catch with our left fielder when the Missions came out to play defense. I, being the new guy, drew the short straw by default and was left in the pen to hold down the fort in the wet.

The game started to drag along, as it always does when you want it to go faster. Pitchers took their sweet time pacing around the mound, there were an excessive number of time-outs and foul balls. Officials came to talk weather. All I could do was sit in the pen while my parka turned into a wet blanket. Days like that sucked. It's not raining enough to get the game called and grant us an off day, but it's still soupy enough to ensure that we'll play in slop for nine full innings.

I kept my glove dry by wrapping it in a towel and placing it under the bullpen's bench. The rain wasn't coming down in buckets, or even big drops, but its persistent misting was enough to wet down everything, including the seats formerly occupied by my teammates.

With no one to talk to, I amused myself by flicking sunflower seeds through links in the fence, folding airplanes out of gum wrappers, and spinning paper cups into the ground to see if I could get them to stand upright on impact. I could just imagine my teammates right then, happily playing cards and drinking coffee from the comfy couches of the warm, dry clubhouse. They could probably see me, the camera zooming in on me while the announcers commentated on how stupid I was for remaining—those bastards.

I was right when I said something was watching me, though it wasn't the players in the clubhouse. It was something with eight eyes. A tarantula the size of a baseball cap had come out of its hiding place to escape the flooding. It had covered most of the distance between the wall and the bench when I turned to see it. I did a double take, and when I looked back the second time, I sprang out of my plastic chair, flipping it over into the muck in the process while yelling, "Holy fuck!"

The tarantula was huge. Eight beady eyes with thick brown legs. It's true: everything is bigger in Texas. It kept coming at me as if it were hungry for me. I grabbed my chair and held it out in front of me like a lion tamer. "Rarrrr! Yawh, Raarrrrrrrr! Get out of here!" I made pushing motions with my chair. The beast stopped, its long front legs hanging in the air motionless, as if it were deciding.

I hate spiders. Hate 'em. I don't think a lot of people can fault me for that as they aren't the cuddliest creatures in the animal kingdom. I realize this one, as big as it was, was only a fraction of my size, but fear makes you think crazy things. I thought that if it got too close, it could leap on me and bite into my neck or some other exposed fleshy part of my body. Then it would drag me off to its hole and finish me off. When the relief crew came back, they'd wonder where I went.

The tarantula stopped thinking and continued toward me. I shook the chair at it and called it names, but apparently tarantulas don't speak English and I didn't know Spanish. I tried kicking dirt at it, but the ground was too soggy. And if I threw the chair and missed, I would be defenseless. I was still in reach of the bullpen's complimentary seed bucket—another Double-A perk—which contained both packets of seeds and Double Bubble chewing gum. I grabbed the bucket and starting throwing gum at the monster. I only threw the regular flavor at it because the blue raspberry flavor is my favorite.

The beast spread its feet out and stopped as gum landed around it like artillery fire. I stopped. Maybe it was ready for a truce. It was hard to tell what it was thinking or what it was looking at because it could have been looking in any or all directions. It started to retreat! Victory. *"That's right spider! This is my house!"* My triumph was short-lived as the spider redirected toward my glove tucked under the bench. "No, get away from that! Bad tarantula!" I resumed firing gum at the beast but only served to speed him on his way.

Desperate times call for desperate measures. I dumped the rest of the contents of my ammo bucket onto the murky ground and went after the tarantula. Creeping behind it with my upside-down bucket, I skillfully slipped the plastic container over it for the capture. My glove was safe, but what was I going to do with the tarantula now that I had it contained? Payback.

Dalton was the first of my fellow relievers to return to the pen around the fourth inning. I sat casually with my legs crossed next to an overturned David Sunflower Seeds bucket, which suspiciously made tapping noises from within.

"Hey Dalton, would you be a pal and hand me some gum from the seeds bucket there?"

Dalton stood eyeing the bucket, which moved slightly.

"What the fuck is in there?"

"Why, seeds and gum, of course."

"No, there's something in there."

"Maybe there is, and maybe there isn't. Why don't you take a look."

Dalton tentatively stepped to the bucket, put one hand on the lid, and tipped the edge up to look inside. The arachnid shot out at Dalton, who dropped the bucket and ran to the other side of the pen. I got up and picked up the bucket, and with a scooping motion, I plucked up the tarantula and caged him once more, this time in the pail, not under it. I was mobile, in pursuit of Dalton with a bucket full of tarantula.

Dalton took a begging tone with me. "Come on man! I heard stories about those things jumping on people and biting them."

"You know I heard those same stories, actually." I started to close the distance between him and me with the bucket stretched out in front of me like garlic aimed at a vampire.

"Seriously, I'm not a fan of spiders, bud."

"What's not to like? You could always bark at it until I left you alone." I kept coming, Dalton moving toward the pen gate. The game was going on now, and if he left the bullpen, he would be in play. You could hear the spider clacking against the sides of the bucket with its hairy legs.

"Alright, that's enough . . ." Dalton whimpered.

"He just wants to be friends. Here, why don't you hold him for a while." I reared back with the bucket and made as if I were going to shovel pass the beast onto Dalton. I was faking it, but that's all I needed to do to run Dalton out of the pen with his hands up screaming like a schoolgirl.

"Now who got Spidermanned?" I called after him. "Make sure you check your bed tonight!"

The rest of the relievers passed Dalton on their return approach to the pen. They came in with quizzical looks on their faces.

"What's wrong with Dalton?"

"Look in the bucket."

Each one of them looked into the bucket and jerked back in surprise, all except Ox who peeked in and said, "Aww, look at that little fucker."

"What do you think we should do with it?"

"We have to stick that thing in someone's locker!"

"Hell no, I'm keeping it and training it to defend my hotel room," Ward said, probably thinking of his missing PSP.

Before we could decide how best to use our new pet, we were interrupted. There was no phone in the Rock Hounds' visiting bullpen, and Abby didn't use hand signals either. Instead, he equipped the pen bag with yellow walkie-talkies. One in the bag, the other with him in the dugout. The static-garbled sound of Abby's voice beeped in over the handset.

Ox picked up. "Go ahead, Abby."

Beeping, static, "Get Hayhurst up. Deago's only got about ten pitches left."

"Roger that." Ox pulled the talkie away from his ear and looked over to me, "Get 'er going, big dog."

"Ten pitches? Did he not know this move was coming, like, fifteen pitches ago?" I asked, moaning my complaint.

I popped up, slipped out of my wet parka, and took to the mound. Woot was in the pen now, standing behind the bullpen's dish, ready to receive. I tossed, trying to put a little more on each one, three pitches for every one pitch our starter threw.

After I reached max effort fastballs, I flipped my glove hand at Woot to indicate curve. A few hooks later, I pulled the glove back for changeup. Next, a flick left for slider. Who knew how many of these I'd use once I was out there? Maybe none, maybe all. I knew one thing though: it's always nice to have options, and I readied as many as I could before Deago burned up his few remaining pitches.

Two singles put runners on first and second. "This is his last hitter," came the call over the walkie-talkie. I started rushing, trying to get the most of what time I had left. I threw a slider in the dirt; Woot blocked it, but the ball was scratched and muddied. "Shit, can one of you grab me a new one?" I called to the boys still standing over the bucket. I was wasting valuable time. Just as a new ball was flipped to me, it landed in my glove to the sound of a crack on the field—grounder to third. Headley scooped it, threw it to Kazmar at second, who then threw to MJ at first—double play, inning over.

I took a deep breath and disengaged the rubber. I must have made forty tosses as fast as I could just to sit back down again.

"Hey! Your first dry hump in Double-A!" Ox called. He gave me a high five. The rest of the crew did the same.

"It was good for me, Woot. Was it good for you?"

"I've had better."

"Hayhurst's got the next inning. Hayhurst's got the next," Abby called in.

"Roger that, Top Heavy," Ox replied. He pointed to me, then pointed to the field. "Looks like you'll get some after all."

As I jogged from the pen to take the game mound in the fifth inning, I called back to the boys, "Hey, you guys be good to Spot while I'm gone!" They stood over the bucket drawing lots for whose locker they should hide it in.

"You just worry about pitching!" they called back.

Worry? I had wanted to get back up here so badly I was ready to quit when I didn't make the team out of camp. But I was back now, and I wasn't going to make the same mistakes I did before—all or nothing, with no half measures and no worries.

Two innings later, I had put two zeros on the scoreboard. I listened to the rest of the game from the warm, comfy confines of the locker room with my arm in a bag of ice and a tarantula in my locker.

Chapter Thirty-three

Before the bus took us to the field, it shuttled us to the local mall. The hotel was so far away from food sources that if we wanted to eat breakfast, we had to get up and take the bus to the mall food court. I had Chinese for breakfast and Cinnabon for dessert.

At the park, Pops came out to rag on the pitchers while we stretched. Most hitting coaches pick on pitchers and vice versa. It's part of an age-old rivalry that one job is harder than the other. Hitters will say swinging the bat is harder than throwing a ball, whereas pitchers contest the superior challenge is locating a ball while someone tries to strike it. Both sides are biased, of course, which means the fire will burn as long as the game is played.

Pops stood by us swinging his slender fungo bat like a golf club, trading insults with Handsome Rob about how pitchers got it easy.

"Yeah, you face the Yankees lineup and tell me it's easy," Handsome Rob countered.

"You ain't never faced the Yankees lineup. For all you know, you may go right through 'em."

"Right, I'm sure I'd still be here in the Texas League if I could go right through the Yankees. Great point, Pops."

"I'm just saying you could get lucky and get them out. There's so much room for error with pitching. You can make bad pitches and get guys out."

"And hitters can't take bad cuts and bloop balls in?"

"Sure, but that don't happen as much as bad pitches gettin' guys out."

"But if it happens three out of ten times and the bases are loaded those three out of ten, it hurts just as bad," Rob countered, in his high-society voice.

"You can argue all you want, but handling the stick is way harder."

Rob paused the tit-for-tat volley. He was pulling his arm across his chest, stretching it for warm-up catch, when an idea hit him. He stopped his stretch and walked over to Pops, a smile painted across his face.

"I suppose you would know Pops. Speaking of handling the stick, I heard you got a visit by the cops back in San Antonio?"

Guys slowed their stretching and began to watch Pops.

"You don't need to worry about that," Pops said, shifting from the confident arguer to an anxious worrier on the spot. We traded curious glances among each other. Pops' body language showed something was up.

"Oh, I heard the story," Rob pressed, "and I think you should tell it before you force me to."

Stretching came to a stop. Everyone eyed Pops with anticipation. A coach having a run-in with the cops was just too juicy not to hear. Pops looked around at all of us staring back at him. "Ff-fuck, alright," he consented. We crowded in. "First, it's not that big of a deal. It's gonna sound bad, but it ain't."

"What happened?" Blade asked, practically drooling.

"I'm sitting in my living room back in San Antonio, in those shithole apartments they put us in, talking on the phone. There comes a knock on my door. It's the fucking cops, right? I hang up, go to the door, and answer. I'm like, 'Hello officers, how can I help you?'"

"So they say,"—he shakes his head at the thought of it, while we're hanging on his words—"'We had a report that you were masturbating with your windows open.' I'm like, what the fffffff-fuck" His face looked genuinely shocked. The team started roaring, all of us, falling on each other.

"Yeah, you go right ahead and laugh. It was probably one of you that called 'em, you sons of bitches," Pops said, leaning on his fungo.

"Well, were you?" Rob pressed.

"Fffffuck no! Are you kidding me? I'm a grown man!"

"Grown men get urges," Blade countered.

"I don't give a shit what grown men get. I wasn't. I was totally shocked by it all. Oh, oh, get this, then the cop says, 'Sir, it's okay if you were, but next time, please be more discreet about it.' What's that supposed to mean? It's okay if you were, just be more discreet? They didn't fucking believe me, which pissed me off even worse. They didn't believe me, I'm some kinda perv."

"Did you tell them you weren't jerking it?" This was Rob again.

"Yeah, like a dozen times I says." Pops was arguing as if we were the cops in question. "But the more I talk, the more they don't believe me. So they says, 'How many times have you been arrested, sir?'" The team's laughter began again. We could feel Pops' frustration both now and then.

"I almost lost it right there. I ain't never been arrested. First you come accusing me of being some pervert; then you tell me to be a more discreet pervert; then you ask me what kind of criminal I am . . ." He was so worked up, he looked as if he might come to a boil.

"It's the mustache Pops. You can't trust a guy with a mustache."

"Those fucking cops had mustaches!"

"What did you tell them then?" Rob continued.

"I told them to get the hell out of my house. And as they was leaving, they told me they was sorry they upset me, but I should be more discreet! I could have—" He took his fungo and swung it through the air as if he were beating someone with it.

"But seriously, if it was one a you, I wanna know. I ain't mad." No one believed him. "I just wanna know so I don't have to worry about shifty characters peeking in my window."

"What if I peek in your window?" Blade asked.

"I don't doubt you would do something like that. People need to be calling the cops on guys like you."

"I peeked in your window, but I didn't call the cops," Dalton said, kidding him.

"That's fine. You keep on peeking. You ain't gonna see nothing, but if I catch your ass—" Pops took another cut with his fungo.

"If I'm not going to see anything, I don't think I'll bother to peek anymore."

Pops waved a hand at the smartass comments. "Seriously, if one of you did it, speak up. There's some weird-ass people livin' in that place." Nobody raised his hand. Pops scowled. "I don't believe it. One of you motherfuckers did it." He waggled his finger at the group while we laughed.

"Couldn't have happened to a better guy, Pops," Blade said, needling him some more.

"Ff-uck you."

Chapter Thirty-four

The relief crew spent a spider-free night in the pen. Having pitched an inning for the team, I officially felt as if I was one of the boys, As part of the family, I was privy to all manner of new information. Handsome Rob, for example, was dating a stripper he met at a place called The Palace.

"We aren't dating, okay."

"You're dating; you totally love her." Blade was at work again.

"You know, that's so immature, I'm not even going to respond."

"That's how I can tell you love her, because you get so bent out of shape."

"I am not bent out of shape. It's just an immature argument. I prefer to call it a working relationship."

"*Working relationship?* She dances and you insert dollar bills? What? Does she give you a discount for being with her? Define working relationship?"

"It's like Ox and the Puffy Taco."

"Whoa now, we don't need to bring me into this," coughed up Ox.

"Wait! What's the Puffy Taco?" I asked.

"It's one of our mascots back in San Antonio."

"Our mascot is called the Puffy Taco?"

"Our real mascot is Ballopeño, the Puffy Taco is like a side-kick."

"What the hell is a Ballopeño?"

"It's like a half baseball, half jalapeño."

"What the fuck?" I mumbled.

"Exactly."

"How does that have anything to do with the Missions?"

"No idea."

"So what's your connection to the Puffy Taco?"

Ox grumbled, but Rob happily filled me in. "The Puffy Taco is in love with Ox. It's a working relationship."

"What the hell does that mean?" Dalton demanded.

"It means, it's a summer fling and both parties know."

"Is that your *discreet* way of saying you're boning her?"

"Bingo."

"So you're boning a stripper." I nodded to Rob. "And you're, uh, boning a taco mascot?" I asked Ox.

"The chick that works the taco suit is a total cleat chaser. I'm not the first player; I won't be the last."

"So she's just your working relationship."

"Sounds like you're her working relationship," Rob said.

"She's not holding me down, that's for sure," Ox said.

"Yeah, Ox's not holding her down either. She and a few other guys went at it in the mascot dressing room," Dalton said.

"Could you imagine doing that," I asked, "with all those weird mascot heads watching you?"

Everyone looked at me funny.

"What?"

Ward opened the gate of the bullpen and walked in with a cup of coffee, as if he needed it. "What's so funny? What I miss?"

"Ox has a working relationship with the Puffy Taco."

"Sweet life, Ox."

"Save it, smiley."

"Hey! Heeeey!" interrupted a fan yelling down at us. We looked up to face a man holding a plastic beer cup. "Y'all suck!" He was standing on the brim above the fencing, surrounded by his buddies, all of them giggling like chimps.

"Beat it," Ox said, who turned back to the game.

"What's the score out there? Oh! Look, y'all are losin'. Y'all are a bunch a losers."

"Game's not over yet, pal."

"Y'all must be the bad players. That's why they stick you out here, huh? They keep the bad eggs away from the good ones."

The guy doing the talking looked as if he lived in his parents' garage. A thirty-something guy who probably raced demolition derby cars for a living and divorced his wife when he found her listening to Justin Timberlake music. He had a grease-stained hat; a pointy, ratlike face; and a hunting-themed T-shirt that said Shooting Deers and Drinking Beers, That's How I Roll. The guy had to have been several beers deep at this point, and making the most of it.

"Hey look," Ward started, "it's the Blue Collar Comedy tour. Tell me a redneck joke!"

"Hey, y'all do anything except sit the bench?" came the retort.

"Haven't I seen your face on television? Weren't you on *Cops*? Taking a break from beatin' your wife so you can come catch a game?"

"I ain't married," the man said proudly.

"No kiddin'?" Ward pretended to be shocked. "A classy fella like you?"

"Yeah, well, y'all are losin'."

"Yeah, I heard that one already. Get some new material. Hey, which one of you guys is the girl in this relationship. I hear most convicts take turns being the girl, so who's it gonna be tonight?"

"Fuck you, pal. I ain't queer."

"Fuck me? Oh, so you must be the guy tonight?"

The speaker was getting rattled, so one of the other chimps stepped in. His face was pocked up, and he had a Dale Earnheart hat on.

"You must be pretty bad to be down here in the minors," he started. "How far are you away from making it to the big leagues?"

"About as far away as you are from graduating high school."

"Shit, I'm smarter than you are."

"Yeah, you look it. What, you try to shave with a broken bottle? That's not a smart thing to do, bro."

"I'm better looking than you, and I got a better job too," the Dale Earnheart fan protested.

"Seriously bro, you look like your face caught fire and someone put it out with an ice pick, and being the greeter at Walmart is hardly a better job than this."

"Fuck you, pal,"

The third one stepped in. He was the largest of the three, a beer belly stretching the fabric of his collared shirt. At least it was collared, a feature that gave him an air of sophistication considering his company. "Talk it up buddy. It won't be funny when you get sent down."

"What, is it diabetes day at the ballpark?" Ward replied, pretending he had a big gut.

"Ha-ha. Maybe if you spent more time working on your game instead of your insults, you wouldn't be here."

"Oh thanks, coach. Hey, I don't go to McDonald's and tell you how to flip burgers, so you don't need to come here and tell me how to do my job. But since we're giving out advice, maybe you should spend less time eating the product and that shirt wouldn't be strainin' to hold your gut back."

"I might be fat, but at least I ain't stuck in the minors, losing."

"Yeah, we might lose tonight. We might win tomorrow. But at least we wake up with a chance to be something, which is more than I can say for you, pal."

"Shit, I can be anything I want to."

"Oh, so you *want* to be like that? Sorry, I didn't know you were living your dream."

The trio was not as well prepared as Ward was. They probably thought we would sit there and take it as most players do. Surprise! They took a moment to conference on how to reply. Putting them on the run, Ward wasted no time.

"Hey tubby, did your wife make it home alright last night? We didn't talk much when we were together, but tell her I had a good time. I never drank champagne from some of those spots before." Ward could have gone on all day, but before the trio had a chance to come up with something, a stadium usher came by and asked them to back off the railing and take their seats. Defeated, they took this as a sign to call it a day.

"Y'all still suck, stupid Yankees," they said, a final parting shot as they disbanded.

Ward looked at us and started laughing. "Did he just call us Yankees? Hey! Heeeeey," he called back, "don't drink too much, since I wouldn't want you to be too drunk for your Klan meeting." The group continued walking.

"Yankees? Really?" Blade shook his head. "This is the only state I know where people will make fun of you because you aren't from it. Like people here think they are hands down better than you because they are from Texas."

"Those were some fine examples, let me tell you."

"Consider where we are. It's Midland, Texas, where the hottest thing to do is take your sister on a date to the mall food court," Rob said.

"Well I hate this place," Ward said with a smile. "Manrique's family steals my PSP, Eddie makes fun of my teeth, and the guys from *Deliverance* tell me I'm a loser. I just don't know how much more I can take, bro."

Chapter Thirty-five

We didn't find any spiders that night, but we did rack up another loss. Including the game I pitched in, that made three in a row since my arrival. Sometimes players correlate new faces with losses, but the team didn't connect my arrival to its bad luck. In fact, it didn't seem as if the boys cared too much about the results, content to enjoy each other's company and have a good time at the park. After the third loss, Randy pulled the team together for a meeting before the next game's stretch, to make a preemptive strike.

He walked out of his office and stood in the middle of the locker room, his uniform pants on, tailored to stop at his shins, and an old T-shirt that looked like it dated from his playing days. He pulled a piece of paper from his back pocket and cleared his throat.

"At this level, I'm a teacher, but I'm also an evaluator," he said, prefacing his remarks while unfolding the paper to reveal some notes written in shorthand. "So, I'm going to take my experience in the game and address some things I'm seeing.

"I'm not saying we are a bad club, fellas, but right now I think we are a little snakebit. I don't like the smell of things, or where they're going. We had a good April, with fifteen wins and nine losses, and here we are in May at 3–6." He glanced over the notes, letting the room fill with silence again, then looked back up at us.

"Look, I think we need to have a certain amount of discipline in order to play consistent baseball. We're gonna lose some games, but how we go about it is what I'm smelling. I'm sniffin' around here and I'm starting to see, come game time, we aren't ready to play. Guys aren't taking preparation seriously, and that's a reflection on me. I pride myself on getting you guys as much information for the game as I can, so I expect you to put in your work and be prepared. Take your ground balls, get your cuts in, get your mind right, and be ready to go all nine, from the first pitch to the last. I don't think we are getting our priorities in order, so . . ."

Randy laid down a few new rules curtailing time allowed for shenanigans like Xboxes and scooter racing. Then he placed a limit on card playing and television watching before game time.

"Look, the partying, the nightlife, I don't care if you're doing that stuff as long as you are doing your job. I know it's gonna happen, some guys can operate while doing it. However, I will say this: no matter how good you are, you will not be as consistent a professional baseball player if you are a consistent partier, especially not if you are in here loud talking about it while I'm sniffin' around." He let the last part hang for a while, looking around the room. Some guys shifted uneasily. I hadn't been around long enough to know the scoop, but Midland didn't exactly seem like an after-hours hot spot.

"Our body language really sucks right now," Randy continued, again with the piercing stare. "We've only played thirty-seven games. It's May tenth, yet I see bodies telegraphing that the season's over.

"Here's how it works. A couple of guys start showcasing negative body language when things are down, soon other guys start gravitating to them when they take their lumps. It spreads. Guys start feeling sorry for themselves, and there's no room for that. This is Double-A baseball, men—it's a separator. You got scouts coming in and out of here all the time, looking for guys who can rise to the occasion. Every day's a clean slate with me, and it's gotta be that way with you . . ."

Another glance to the notes. "I've already heard guys whining about this today, so I'm going to address it. The *I'm tired, the travel's hard in this league* stuff . . . fucking get over it. Grind it out for the five months. You know the forecast, you have to have the mind-set for it. Didn't get enough sleep? Didn't get a chance to get up and eat? Bad accommodations? Sorry. That's the way this game goes sometimes. Still gotta compete. Still gotta play the game hard. I'll tell you this, men: if you're a pussy, this game will call you out on it real fast. It will cut you down."

He folded up the paper and put it back into his pocket. "My suggestion: back to the basics. Be ready to pitch, be ready to hit, be ready to make the play. Be ready to compete. If you got things getting in the way of your commitment to the game, get 'em out of the way. Baseball has got to be the priority right now. We have got to play with a purpose to have success, individually and collectively. All the little things we were doing early on to be successful, I don't see us doing them right now. To me, that's lack of focus. We have got to get our focus back.

"It's a grind, it's a motherfucker, but come six thirty, you gotta be locked in, men. We won't always bring our best to the park every day, but we gotta compete with one hundred percent of what we got."

He looked around the room, serious faces staring back at him. "Hey, prepare, compete first pitch to last pitch, lay it all out there, and at the end you can say you did the best you could—

that's the only way to go about it. Play to win, that's the only way I know."

"Questions or concerns anybody?" Randy asked.

No hands went up. Message received.

"Alright. Stretch in fifteen." He walked back into his office. The room sat silent for a second and then Tourney stepped in.

"Hitters, I'll have the film of your at bats ready to watch by tonight. If you wanna see it, stop by my hotel room and we'll review it."

"Hey Tourney, make sure you put the Do Not Disturb sign on your door if you're gonna be doing something you don't want us to walk in on."

"Yeah, and shut the blinds for God's sake!"

"Very funny, very fucking funny." Pops tromped back into the coach's office.

Everyone would take Randy's words differently. I'm sure I was no exception. While the other guys suited up to hit the field and made resolutions to cut back on their nightlife, I remained at my locker, thinking about his message and the experiences that got me to his team.

He was right. This level is a separator, not only of physical talent, but of priorities too. People play the game for different reasons. Looking back, I knew I played for a chance at something better, for the glory, for a fix, for an ego stroke, and for validation. But the first and main reason, the one that hooks us all: I wanted to make it to the big leagues.

The nice thing about pitching, I decided, was while I was doing it, I always knew what the goal was. Get an out; get a couple of outs. Life, on the other hand, wasn't so clear. The trouble was baseball was my life. The two were connected somehow, that much I knew. Yet I didn't know the proper formula and was tired of the explosive result they yielded when mixed. I wanted to separate them, keep them safe from each other. I decided to take the lessons I had learned—forget the loose ends—and disappear under the waves of baseball.

When I started this game, I had a dream of playing in the big leagues. Everyone who signed a contract did. It's the basic player motivator, and like Randy said, maybe it was time I got back to the basics.

Chapter Thirty-six

When we made it back to San Antonio, I took the advice of Dalton and Pops and passed on living in the team apartments. Having my roof cave in or someone lurking in my window didn't sound appealing. Instead, I decided to get another host family. It worked so well in Lake Elsinore, why not in San Antonio too?

I got hooked up with an older guy who was out of the house a lot. He let me rent a room dirt cheap and insisted I finish the groceries he couldn't eat when he left town. Never married, he had all the cool guy toys that single men of means can afford, like big screens and cool trucks. It cost me about $200 a month, everything included, and I got to watch *SpongeBob* on the fifty-two incher in my underwear during home stands.

The baseball chaplain who found my host dad also found me a car. All I had to do was make a few appearances at his Little League practices in return. That and promise I wouldn't do anything naughty with a girl in it, and I was fine. He made it sound like I could actually get a girl in it with me, which was very flattering.

Randy's speech about getting our focus back worked for a little while. We came home and swept Corpus Christi, but the mojo didn't last. Soon we were dropping the majority of our games in each series we played—Frisco, Springfield, Arkansas, and Midland again. All of them took more from us than we from them, and before we hit the second half, we had fallen from first in our division to last.

If I had to place my finger on a starting point for our downward spiral, I'd have to say the bullpen. The most frustrating thing in baseball is to watch a hard-earned lead slip away, but it seemed to be our specialty. We blew saves with the greatest of ease, making Blade, typically unflinchingly sarcastic and fearless, worry about his future. Then Dalton caught the "blew flu." His symptoms were walks and wild pitches. He couldn't keep the ball in the strike zone, and when he did, it got lit. I contracted a mild case of homeritus and nearly gave up back-to-back-to-back home runs if it wasn't for Drew, who climbed over the centerfield wall to save me. Rob and Ox began bleeding runs, not massive leaks, but enough to cost us W's.

Then the virus mutated and spread to the hitters. Soon we didn't have any leads to blow. We didn't have any runs, hits, or balls in play. I thought the hitters' limbs would begin to fall off or their bats spontaneously combust. Pops dropped F-bombs like the *Enola Gay*, though the only real casualty was the equipment in the dugout hallway, as frustrated hitters took cuts on it after striking out. On more than one occasion, hitters tossed our lumber onto the dugout floor, kicking it around and screaming at it to try to wake it up. If you were a fat chick looking to score, this was a very good time of the season for you.

The virus resulted in several amputations. A few guys were released, most notably, Woot. Skip, the legendary designer of our bus boob billboard, was also released, losing his job as the utility man, a moment that left more than just Skip in tears. White Chocolate was lost in the shuffle of utility outfielder. Our shortstop was sent back to High-A, followed shortly by our second baseman. A stud left-handed starter was taken off the forty-man roster, claimed off waivers, and disappeared into another dimension. And Chase Headley, or should I say, Chase the magnificent, went up to play third base in the big leagues.

After a few pieces were removed, some patchwork inside the wound was made. Guys changed roles. Blade lost his job as the closer, and Dalton lost his role as setup man. Some position players auditioned for other spots, and new batting orders were devised. Guys who didn't see a lot of playing time started seeing more.

We kicked around the Texas League trying to find our new identity. Sometimes it feels like a team expects to lose, and I guess that was a fair assessment of us at the time. We felt like losers and played like it too. At one point, after eking out a win, Handsome Rob made the comment, "Did we win last night or just run out of time before we could lose?" Diego, the pitcher I relieved in my first Mission appearance, actually threw his glove in the air after a series of consecutive fielding errors were committed in front of him. He swore to the heavens in Spanish as a pile of unearned runs buried him under a losing streak.

We started to give up on each other. Then the season seemed to slow down to a painful crawl. I would sneak into the clubhouse, eat chips and salsa, and play web boggle with the clubbie to pass the time between outings. The travel seemed to take longer, and we got grumpier. Yet, just before the feeling got so bleak that we wrote the season off, some new faces came up.

With so many players going here, there, and home, we had spots open. Fellas from the cast of characters in Lake Elsinore came up. Frenchy and Tiny were both promoted and filled in holes in the starting rotation. Anto, the stud first-round-hitting standout, came up to play second and raked at the plate. Chase, who was never meant to be a permanent solution in the bigs, came back to the oohs and ahhs of his Double-A mortals. Edwin Moreno, aka "El Gato," a soft-spoken Latin teddy bear with a bazooka for an arm, was acquired and fell into the role of closer.

Inspired by the fresh infusion of talent, some guys started to recover. Blade's fever broke and so did Dalton's. Soon the turbo sinker/slider pen was back in fighting shape, contrasted with the addition of the poo-throwing smoke and trickery of Stubbs, the balding lefty. Ox was cured after picking out a new Godsmack song to exit the pen to.

New fielders, new pitching, new rules, and new results all worked to stop the bleeding and even producer a win or two. Then a few wins became multiple. Then we began to catch fire. We hadn't gelled yet, but it was easy to see we had all the makings of a tremendous team.

Just as things seem to go bad in a viral way, teams can get infected by a positive bug. We started coming back to win games. We held leads. We trusted each other to be successful. We expected victory. It probably sounded arrogant, and maybe it was, but when all our cylinders were firing, we were the best team on the field. I guess being a good team was just a matter of belief and consistency. If we kept the flame fanned, we would have a chance to get back into the race for the playoffs—maybe.

Chapter Thirty-seven

Despite our team troubles and a few lumps of my own, I pitched strongly. I don't know whether it was my sweet new ride or my bachelor pad, but I was the poster child for consistency. I gave up a few runs here and there, but I was nothing like the old Dirk who lingered in the pen for weeks at a time before the coaches found enough courage to throw him out there. I noticed I was having success in every role I was put in. I didn't ask any questions about why things were going so well, but I didn't have to. Sooner or later, people start asking them for you.

A week or two into the second half, Abby began pulling pitchers into his office to have little discussions with them about their seasons thus far. He closed the door behind some of them, and left it open for others. When it was my turn, he called me in saying, "Hey, Hay, why don't ya come on in here for a second?" I obeyed, entering the room. He did not shut the door, but gestured for me to take a seat. I plopped on a chair he had next to his desk while he began pulling cards that looked like miniature spread sheets out of a stack. He produced one with my name written across the top.

He looked over it as if he was reviewing my resume, his glasses sitting low on his nose, staring at the numbers while taking big breaths. He folded his legs, leaned back into his seat, and then shifted his gaze from the card to me.

"What's on the sheet?"

"Yer numbers for the year. I like to keep my own records on how guys is pitching. Things like first pitch strikes and how often each pitch is thrown, how often you're in a certain count." He looked back down to the cards and ran his finger down a column.

"I'll tell you what Dirk, you're having a real good year. One of the biggest things for me is the first pitch strike, and you're throwing it. You throw a first pitch strike more than seventy percent of the time—that's real good."

I knew things were going well for me since my promotion. I knew that my ERA was the lowest it'd been in years and that I wasn't getting pulled out of games as often. I also knew I was walking fewer guys. Those were about the only stats I kept track of, the only stats I felt really mattered to me, personally. I couldn't control wins or losses, and strikeouts are great when you can get them, but outs—no matter how they come—are the goal. I was throwing harder too, which I'm sure Abby didn't care about, but it made me feel slightly more macho. Over all, I felt better.

"I know the organization is big on getting hitters out on three pitches or less and yer doing well with that. . . ." His finger continued tracing the numbers. The television was still on in his office and a muted *SportsCenter* played highlights in the background. I peeked at the screen as he searched his numbers.

"Your slider's come a long way," he said, looking up at me. "I can tell you was working on it in the off-season. I said that to the Brass, I says, 'Hayhurst's been a working on that slider.' You know something, I think it's made yer curve better, too. It's tightened it up."

"It feels better this year."

"It *is* better." He looked back at the notes as he spoke. "You've been throwing all your pitches for strikes. Avoiding hitters counts, staying ahead of guys." Now he looked up at me. "You are definitely my most improved pitcher from last year—and people are noticing."

I smiled and put my head down. I didn't know what to say.

"What do you think is the biggest difference from this last year to this?" he asked, pointing at me with one hand while placing the cards back on his desk with the other.

I took a moment to reflect. I thought about how my mental approach changed and how I might explain it in a way that didn't seem as if I had developed a marijuana problem or had wanted Abby to join a cult or, at the very least, convince him I needed a therapist.

"Well," I began, "I won't say I just don't care about what happens out there, because I do. I want to win when I take the mound. However, I don't care about what I can't control once I'm out there. I mean, the way I figure it is, I'm going to go out there and give everything I've got. I'm going to go right after guys. It's all or nothing. I guess this year I'm fine with the nothing part. I'm not afraid of failing.

"Does that make sense?" I replayed the words back in my mind. It made sense to me.

"It's all or nothing, huh?" he repeated back.

"Yeah. Like I was afraid to ante up before, but now I'm not."

"Hmmm . . ." Abby murmured, his face scrunched up in a confused manner.

I wondered if I'd said something wrong. Part of Abby's job as pitching coach was to turn evaluations of me into the Brass. I hoped I didn't volunteer any incriminating information by saying I didn't care about my results.

"Let me ask you something," Abby said. "Why would you

ever go out there with any other mind-set?" In his matter-of-fact country accent, he made it sound as if the things I just spoke were blatantly obvious facts everyone in the game already knew.

"Well, I . . . uh . . ."

"I mean shit, what were you thinking all those other years?"

". . ."

"You have to go out there and go right after guys; you can't be scared to—"

"Look," I said, "it's different for everyone I suppose, but I put so much stock in what it meant to be a baseball player, I became afraid to fail at it. I'd be out of a job, and out of an identity. I thought I'd lose everything without it."

"Well hell, Dirk, we're all gonna be done at some time or another."

"I know. I guess I thought I'd be done sooner rather than later."

"Maybe, but don't you think you'd be done sooner by not doing your best?" Again he used the commonsense country tone.

"I know what you're saying, but I want you to understand, I wasn't able to get to this point until I was okay with the idea of baseball coming to an end. I could miss every bastard spot, walk the bases loaded, challenge hitters, and lose. I could take risks and fail, and then I'd be out of my job."

"Or you could succeed."

"But I was only thinking about the failure part, what I had to lose. Now that I'm not concerned with it, I don't think about it."

Abby mulled over my words for a moment, then sat up from his chair. "You know baseball isn't a hiding place, don't ya?"

"What do you mean?"

"I mean, this is a profession, not an existence. You can't hide in it, no matter how well yer doing. I've coached a lot of guys, and some of them have all the success in the world but no means to enjoy it. When they're done, they ain't got nothing even when they have everything."

I stared at him, waiting for more information, but it did not come. He shuffled his notes, then smiled at me quite pleasantly and said, "Well, whatever yer thinking about now, keep thinking it. Keep doing what you are a doing. Yer havin' a great season so far, and there ain't no reason you can't keep having it."

"Thanks, Abby."

"Alright then. Send Frenchy in wouldya please?"

Chapter Thirty-eight

We had been to Frisco, Texas, before, when the team was laboring to get through games without completely breaking down. Now, after our rebirth, we were back for another round. Frisco was one of the best teams in the league, and if we were to have a shot at playoff baseball, we'd have to beat up on the Rough Riders.

Easily one of the nicest ballparks in minor league baseball, Frisco's park is the gem of the Texas League. The outfield fences are giant LCD display boards that show hundred-foot advertisements, stats, and graphics. Big-league parks don't even have such things. In fact, the entire park benefits because it is a minor league stadium. It does things its own unique way. The architecture of the facility reminds me of a high-class horse track, with custom loges featuring balconies, outdoor ceiling fans, and exposed walkways. It's like proper ladies with large hats and fancy, one-time-use dresses should be alongside gents with tall leather boots and coats with tails, not dudes in frayed ball caps sucking down Budweisers.

All the stadium seats are angled toward the center of the field, meaning there is no bad seat in the house. A waterfall and swimming pool occupies the space behind the right field fence, and the bullpen has spent more than one night ogling the ladies occupying it with a set of binoculars. A display board the size of a small house towers above left field. However, as distinct as the field is, the one trait I found most unique was its bullpen.

The bullpen in Frisco is located in the stands—literally in the seats. A set of stairs actually climbs up into the stadium's bleachers down the right and left field line allowing access to the pen. Surrounding the pen are seats on all sides. I have never experienced anything like it. Being thrust into the stands and surrounded by fans sets the table for unique fan-player interaction. Our last trip to the park, a group of high-school-aged kids came down to heckle us. They wrote signs that said You fucking suck, You're going nowhere, and You aren't never going to make it! The grammar gaffe on their part opened up the door for us to hammer them. The end result was security confiscating their signs and tossing the kids from the stadium. We asked if we could keep the signs, security obliged, and the relief corps hung them in the locker room as motivation.

Indeed, the park was a fantastic place to come of age in. If the team could rally against the Rough Riders, then we could feel good about our chances for the rest of the season. It would be a good test for us. This was a big series, big for a lot of reasons, though just how big would not be as simple a story to summarize as a line score . . .

Another notable feature I discovered during my last visit was that the grounds crew's clubhouse was close to our own visiting clubhouse. The grounds crew had an Xbox in their clubhouse, something I told myself I would go and play during the nights I knew I wasn't going to pitch. Our first night in town, I was on the shelf and unusable for relief, so I made the most of it. I felt like such a rebel, playing video games when I should have been out watching the real one, but honestly, sometimes sitting through game after game can be boring as hell.

During the first couple of innings of the game, I paid a visit to my favorite field workers. Outside their clubhouse was a dry erase board with tombstones drawn on it, each stone inscribed with a name. The last time I was in Frisco, I asked what it meant. The stones represented the names of individuals who were either fired or quit. There were more stones this visit than the last. It's hard to comprehend why or how people got fired from grounds crew— it wasn't exactly rocket science—but most of the crew members were high school age and preferred wearing giant-sized foam hats, aviator sunglasses, and playing Halo in between prank calls to Mexican porn numbers. In fact, that's what they were doing when I stopped by.

"Hey, guys," I said, peeking my head around the corner. I had my spikes on, and I'm sure they could hear me coming as I click clacked my way down the poured concrete hallway.

"Hey, bro, what's up!" The ones I knew from my last visit got up and shook hands.

"Nothing man. I came to get a round of Deathmatch in with you guys while I wait for this game to end."

"Absolutely! Let's light it up!" said my pal in sunglasses, holding a bag of corn chips. There were empty boxes of Mountain Dew cans and beef jerky wrappers. I felt like I was inside a sixteen-year-old's car. They were watching some reality television show at the time when I sat down. Folks on the screen had videotaped their amateur wrestling moves, involving idiots jumping off trailer home rooftops onto the bodies of their opponents, but missing and cracking their skulls open. It was damn good television. The crew flicked the channel and soon the screen went Microsoft green.

"Let's rock and roll!" I said.

"You want to put some money on this one?"

"Let me get warmed up first, and I'll think about it." They were always trying to get me to bet.

Around this time, the team mascot, a giant, fuzzy prairie dog walked by the door, stopped, looked at us, shook his head and walked away. The Rough Riders mascot was not rough or a rider, he was a giant orange with a tired act.

"You guys like your mascot guy?" I asked.

"He's a total assbag," the dude with the corn chips said.

"Why's that?"

"He acts like he's a Hollywood star, Mr. Big Shot. Like his act is the most important thing on the field."

"Yeah, get this, man"—sunglasses dude smacked me in the arm—"he had a meltdown because I drove him around the field too fast, and he didn't get to maximize his exposure time. What the hell? He's a fucking orange prairie dog!"

"Do any of the players mess with him?" Players have a long history of screwing with mascots. Mostly, this involved buckets of water and the drenching of fuzzy suits. Some mascots thrive on it and use it as a chance to entertain the crowd. Others hate it and want to be left in peace while grinding out another day of acting like a Lumber King, or a Prairie Dog, or Beaver.

"No, some team tried it once, and he had a conniption. He had our front office write a formal reprimand to the team that did it."

"Wow, what a puss. You know, I've had some pretty good run-ins with mascots. There was this one dude, he was a Hawk or an Eagle or something, and he drove around the field on some kind of mini motorcycle." I talked while the game started, and soon we were all firing rockets at each other, explosions echoing down the hall.

"The first night of the series, when this dude came rolling by, everyone in the pen smoked him with cups of water. He got real pissed about it, and later on in the game, he came over to the pen during one of his acts and yelled at us in his mascot hand-move-ment, mime language. We were like, 'Dude, we know you're a man in there. You can talk to us. It's okay.' So he started screaming at us about getting him wet and how we better stop or else, which, of course, made us do it again the next night."

"Of course," the crew said. I blew one of them up and watched his body fly into a wall like a Jack Russell terrier.

"So we did it again the next night, worse, aiming for the face mesh part of his costume. We almost knocked him off his bike. He decided he would get even by making water balloons and soaking us during the game, when we were getting warmed up to go in."

"No shit? Did he?"

"Yeah, he soaked one of our guys—the wrong guy. The dude he hit with the balloons was a maniac with a full back tattoo and a thing for German death metal, and he almost went over the rails to kill the mascot." The crew laughed as I went over the rails and fell into a deep chasm to my doom while trying to avoid a grenade. "The next night, when the mascot rolls by, our dude gets up and charges at the mascot. He didn't tackle him, but he caused him to wreck. The mascot gets up and mimes that he wants a piece of our boy. Nothing happens there, but that night, more water balloons come raining down on our pen."

"Damn it!" a crew member cried. I had stuck a plasma grenade to his character's back and he blew up, giving me the lead.

"What did you guys do to get even?"

I finished the game before finishing the story. I lost, but it was close.

"Oh, yeah. Well, the next day, we got there earlier and got into the mascot's dressing room, like the one your mascot has down the hall here. Our dude who wanted to kill him took a dump, scooped a turd into a bag, went into his dressing room, and ground it into the mascot's helmet."

"That's awesome!"

"Yeah, it was hilarious. The mascot didn't even come out that night. Ruined his whole show, but you know, he had to have put it on before he figured it out." The grounds crew looked around at each other and smiled deviously. "You didn't hear that from me," I said.

"Hear what?"

"We playing again? No rockets this time?"

"Yeah, what level—"

Suddenly, Dalton's head popped into the room. "Jesus dude, been looking all over for you, Abby wants you in the next inning. You gotta get loose, like now."

"What!" I said, springing to my feet. "Holy shit! I thought I was down tonight!" I dropped the controller and ran out the door, rounding the corner so hard my cleats slipped on the smooth concrete causing me to wipe out and eat floor.

When I hit, Dalton stood there laughing at me. "I'm just kidding dude, you're fine. Abby didn't call. Gotcha."

"You son of a bitch!" I said, rolling over.

"Oh my God, that was one of the best things I've ever seen!"

Chapter Thirty-nine

On day two of the series, during pitchers' stretch, we dodged batting practice balls struck by the Rough Riders as we loosened in right field. Back and forth we went, jogging with high knees, shuffling, and doing tall leg kicks while calls of "heads up!" echoed across the field, informing us that another ball was coming in hot.

Juice, the team's strength coach, seemed preoccupied with something other than our stretch. He stared longingly across the outfield grass at a hot young blond girl who was shagging balls with the Frisco team.

Strength coach is a peculiar job. Though it has the word coach in its title, it's not truly a coaching job in the minors as much as it's a babysitting job. The strength coach makes sure players stay in good shape, but in the minors, where the food is fatty, the travel hard, and the desire to spend extra time in a gym weak, it's all about compromises.

Since a strength coach doesn't do much coaching, he isn't respected by the team as a hitting coach or a pitching coach would be and isn't paid like one either. The strength coach finds himself more player than coach. Most strength coaches are young, younger than some of the players they're asked to oversee. They want to have a good time, get rowdy with the young bucks in uniform, and at the same time be respected as the coach title suggests. It's a fine line, and if you act like a player most of the time, don't expect to be treated like a coach when your ego gets hurt.

Juice was named so because he was a big ball of muscles. Since bulging biceps and monster quads were associated with illegal substances, we nicknamed him as such, even though he was as clean as the virgin snow. Minor league coaches and staff are subjected to drug tests just like the players, FYI. Juice spent most of his college years pumping iron and learning about the body. It would only make sense that he was built as his title suggested. However, for such a tough dude, he was a little sensitive, a trait we exploited whenever possible.

Juice obviously liked the girl he was watching. She worked for the Rough Riders, and that's how he met her. He took her out just a little while ago, and they got their groove on, something Juice didn't keep to himself. Now seeing her on the field surrounded by minor leaguers made him uncomfortable. He suddenly wished he'd been more discreet.

"Is that your girl over there, Juice?" Blade asked.

"She's looks like she's having a lot of fun next to number 24."

"Yeah, I hear he swings a real big bat."

"Chicks dig the long ball, Juice. You know that."

"Shut the fuck up," Juice growled.

"Oh man, sensitive! Sorry Juice, if you would have told us you were in love, I wouldn't have brought it up."

"I'm not in love with her."

"Then you'd be okay if I asked her out?"

"She'd never go out with you," Juice said. I forgot to mention, he was a little vain. It's hard not to be that big and not dig your looks just a tad.

"Wow, dude. I may not look like you, but it looks like she digs guys in jerseys."

"How many guys on the team do you think she's been with?"

"That's enough. Keep running your mouth, and I'll rip your fucking arms off and beat you with them."

The guys stopped stretching and stared at Juice. Blade smiled. "Did you just say you'd rip my arms off and beat me with them?"

"Shut up!" an angry Juice warned.

"You did! You did just say that. You seriously said you would rip my arms off and beat me with them. I've had a lot of threats in my day, but wow."

"Juice, she's got you whipped, bro," Rob said.

"No, she doesn't."

"If you are willing to dismember another dude for her, I'd say you're whipped."

"Fuck you, guys. You're all a bunch of savages anyway."

"Us? All of a sudden you're better than us?"

"Heads up!" Another ball came screaming in, and Juice picked it up and fired it back into the fence.

"Jesus bro, fucking relax. We don't need you going all *Hulk smash* on anyone."

"I can't believe you think you are better than us, Juice. Us— your family," Blade continued.

"I just don't need your comments about my girl."

"We don't need you getting all pissed at us. You should be tearing off the arms of number 24 over there."

Juice turned around and stared down the guy lingering in the area of his lady. He wasn't even talking to her.

"Wow, you are rattled, bro."

"No, I'm not."

"I think she's bad for your career."

"Just shut up and get on the line. You got half poles today."

"I don't think I can do the running today, not in this unsafe work environment." Rob again.

"Shut up and get on the line."

"Why? Because if I don't, you'll rip my arms off and beat me with them?"

Juice dropped his head and smiled a bit but tried to fight it back in favor of his inner alpha male.

"There he is! There's happy Juice. Come on out happy Juice; come on back to us!"

Juice smiled and suddenly all was well again. He took a deep breath, and the crowd of pitchers started laughing with him. "Repeat after me, Juice: bros before hos. Say it." Juice shook his head. "Say it, Juice!"

"Bros before hos," Juice mouthed.

"That's more like it. Now that we got that squared away, seriously, can I ask her out?"

Chapter Forty

"Alright, Kangaroo Court is now in session, any fucking swear words from this point on and it's a buck." The crowd sat silently, with the oldest guys in the middle acting as judges. Ox, Rob, and a position player, Brett Bonvechio, to made up the, panel representing each of the two major player groups. "What do we got first, Drew?"

Drew dug into the box and pulled out a folded-up paper. "This is to Manrique from team. Max fine for having the worst smelling . . . uh, can I say ass?"

"Yeah, if you're reading, it's legal."

"Worst smelling ass on the team."

"How do you plead Manrique?"

"No guilty. Is not my fault I'ave bad gas."

"Yes, it is. You eat all the stuff you know you shouldn't eat, and then you don't even try to be considerate about it once you start ripping," the prosecution responded.

"What you mean? I eat what you eat—same spreads."

"No, you don't. You come in here with your carne asada with extra beans every other day. If there is a Mexican place in the area, you'll sniff it out."

"What you want me to do? I'm Mexican. I eat Mexican food."

"Well, take some Beano for Christ sake! Make an adjustment."

"Valid point," Handsome Rob said.

"It's not like I'm trying to fart on you." Manrique threw his hands up, as if innocent.

"Actually," I said, raising my hand. "That's not entirely true." Earlier in the season, I was passed out on the bus during a long trip home from Arkansas. I had finally fallen asleep after fighting to get comfortable with the bus seats for what seemed like hours. I went under with my head careened back, sucking air like some old man who passes out in church services. Manrique thought it would be funny if he climbed onto the seat backs, dropped his pants, and laid a bare-ass Mexican food fart right into my open mouth. I woke up dry heaving. It was so ripe, I thought we'd crashed into a manure truck.

As soon as I contradicted Manrique, everyone in the room started to laugh. Kangaroo Court with this team was a treat. It was unfortunate we didn't do it earlier in the year as it always proved to be a good bonding moment. But with so much travel, movement, and adversity, it was difficult to fit it in. Now that the team was coming around, making a race for the playoffs, we felt comfortable enough to loosen up. Sure, we'd collect some fine money for a trip to the bar, but we were bonding.

"Dirk offers another valid point."

"Yeah, every time I tell you I'm going to kick your face in about your stinky butt leakage, you giggle about it. You know what you're up to. Max fine. Hell, I'd double max fine, if I could."

"I agree," Rob said. "Max fine."

"Yeah, I'm tired of smelling you, too," Brett said. "Max fine."

Manrique threw his hands up again. "Fine, but I am going to fart twice as much now on purpose."

"I'm going to beat you twice as hard!" Ox retorted.

"Okay, next offense," Rob said, moving things along.

Drew fished another fine out of the fine box. "This is to Chase Headley for referring to himself in the third person. Witness: team. Suggested fine: double max."

"Whoa now, that's ridiculous. I've never referred to myself in the third person."

"Yes, you did, Chase. I heard you," a witness shouted. "I heard you say it after you got back from the big leagues that 'Chase Headley is only one man'."

"I've never said anything like that."

Another position player spoke up. "I heard you say that if you were in the big leagues, you would have hit that ball into the upper, upper deck. *'But here,'*—the witness made quotations with his hands—'Chase Headley has to understand the balls aren't as good, and Chase Headley will have to settle for standard home runs.'"

"Whatever. You guys are just making stuff up." And they were, but the crowd was laughing and Chase was the only person on the team to make it to the big leagues from inside the organization. He was a shoo-in for Texas League Player of the Year and was having a phenomenal season—no way we could let that go his head. He also got a big-league paycheck, whereas the rest of us had to be content with our minor league pittance. We couldn't let him hog it all to himself.

"I heard him do it too," I said. "I heard him say that 'Chase Headley knows what the fans want and Chase Headley will deliver.'"

"Wow, Chase, you can take the player out of the big leagues, but you can't take the big leagues out of the player, huh?"

"Erroneous! Erroneous on all counts!" Chase declared, smiling.

"Yeah, this is only the minors, Chase. I know it's not San Diego, but you don't have to keep reminding us how easy it is for you. The least you can do is stop the third-person routine."

"Go ahead, fine Chase Headley. See if he cares," Chase said. More laughter.

"Alright, Chase pleads guilty to not being here all year. Ten bucks for going to the 'show' and not taking us with him."

The next fine was for someone wearing the wrong hat out to batting practice—simple two-dollar matter. Then there was a fine for a guy getting drunk and ruining his wingman's night out by throwing up on the potential beef. The crowd roared with laughter as the story was told. The party being prosecuted argued he did the offended a favor by shielding him from the grenade he was about to take home. However, said the court, since the offended was in a slump, the accused was indeed guilty for standing in the way of his wingman's career development and, thus, the success of the team. It was a very wise ruling.

Manrique was fined a second time for his gas, but the fine was thrown out under the statute of double jeopardy. I was fined for playing video games with the grounds crew during a game, which I fought as best I could, losing the case only when I admitted that I lost the Deathmatch to the grounds crew—a poor representation of our team's video game prowess.

"This next fine is for Juice for threatening to rip off someone's arms and beat him with them. Witness: bullpen." Blade retold the story that got Juice heated up again and, consequently, jeered by the entire team. He was fined two dollars, one for each arm he threatened to rip off.

"This fine is for Lunchbox, from Hayhurst, for asking what is on the other side of the sun. Suggested fine, one dollar," Drew read.

The crowd of peers looked to me; then Rob spoke. "We are going to need to hear the story on this one." Lunchbox shook his head in disgust.

I told the tale about how I was sitting on the bench in the dugout in San Antonio. Lunchbox comes in in a huff. He sits down next to me and asks me if I know a lot about science. I say yes. He asks if I know a lot about the sun. I say I know a little. Then, in a moment of genuine seriousness, Lunchbox looks me in the eye and says, "So, do scientists know, like, have they figured out what's on the other side of the sun?"

"You mean, what's on the inside of the sun? Like the center?" I replied, thinking of gas and pressure and whatnot.

"No, like what's around back of it, like behind it, the other side."

"You're asking me what's behind the back of the sun?"

"Yeah, do scientists know that?"

"Yes, Lunchbox, we are, planet Earth, like half of the year. We orbit it."

Lunchbox stared at me in wonder. "What do you mean, orbit?"

"Are you serious? We circle it, all the planets do. It's how we get our calendar."

"That doesn't make any sense," Lunchbox said. "If we orbit it, then how come in all the science books the planets are all lined up in a row on one side?"

"That's because it's a diagram. It's not to scale."

"What does scale mean?"

I stopped there to let the crowd take it all in.

"Lunchbox, what do you have to say for yourself?" the judges asked, not shocked at all after playing with him for a few months.

"Hey, it's not my fault. I'm not Mr. Science Nerd like Hayhurst is." Everyone in attendance laughed, which made Lunchbox laugh as well, thinking he had won the room over. I wanted to point out to him that everyone was laughing at him. But I think Rob said it best when he said, "I'm going to take that as a guilty plea, but

I'm going to waive the fine, since I don't think it's fair to fine him when life has already done it."

Soon after, the court session broke down into a storytelling free-for-all with random fines sprinkled in for spice. It was one of the first times the team, as a whole, communicated, laughed, and socialized. Then the doors of the clubhouse opened and in walked the Brass. Grady and Kevin Towers, or "KT," the infamous general manager of the Padres, were in town to inspect the players and their progress. Having them here meant the eyes of the real Grim Reaper of baseball were on us.

If there was one person to impress in the organization, one person superior to all others, it was KT. He spent almost all his time with the big-league team and rarely appeared in our part of reality.

The room didn't quiet down, but the jovial, relaxed tone began to escape as KT walked about the place, shaking hands with a few individuals, like Chase, and greeting others. He walked right past me as if I didn't exist, and for all intents and purposes, I didn't. I looked at Ox, whom he also didn't bother to acknowledge, and said, "I have not spoken to that man one time in my entire career here."

"Don't sweat it. He doesn't talk to a lot of guys. I think I've met him once."

"I just don't understand why he wouldn't at least say hello or just point and say my name like Grady. I don't think he even knows my name."

"You have to *make* guys in his situation know your name. It's too easy for them to ignore you."

"What do you think I've been trying to do this year, Ox? I've tried to put up the best numbers I can."

"Numbers and reports are one thing, bub. There's no substitute for firsthand impressions." With that, Ox slapped me on the back and went off to punch Manrique. He was right though, there is no substitute for seeing someone get the job done first-hand. If I pitched well while KT was here, if I could make him remember my name, it could take my career from nonprospect to prospect.

Chapter Forty-one

From my perch in the pen, I searched the stands behind the back-stop trying to pick out exactly where the king of the Brass was sitting. He had to be dead center, picking apart the game and all its little details, writing them down in notes to be used in the real-life fantasy draft of the Padres of the future.

That night I got my turn to pitch, as I hoped I would. I clip-clopped down the steps of the bullpen and hit the right field grass on a jog heading in to finish the seventh. When I made it to the mound, I kicked some clay out from where my stride foot lands, licked my fingers, and smacked the rosin bag.

My audition started out well. I K'd the first guy swinging. I felt pretty badass about it because I did it when it mattered with the right people watching. You can always say a pitcher is lucky when he gets hitters to mis-hit a ball, but there is no arguing that K's are impressive. At least I felt impressive, which was a mistake because it went to my head.

I tried to look elite on the mound, as if I could manufacture some ace-style mound presence. I hear about how big leaguers have a swagger to them, and I tried my best to produce it, even though I wasn't sure what it was. I think I flexed my bicep while pretending to look at the ball.

Knowing this was a big opportunity, I felt like I was on some baseball pageant, and instead of asking me about my personal interests in baking and world peace, they asked me to get hitters out, not let anyone score, and look pretty doing it. I gave up a single to one of the league's hottest hitters, and I felt my tiara and scepter start to slip away, but recovered by popping the next hitter out. I escaped the inning, no runs scored.

Escape was not what I wanted, however; I wanted impressive, stellar, and, above all, memorable. The Brass could write this inning up anyway they wanted, that I got lucky or that I made my pitches. I needed something unquestionably good.

Randy sent me out for the next inning. I didn't expect to return because I wasn't the typical eighth-inning guy, but I was glad for another chance to prove myself. I trotted out to the mound like some purebred racehorse. When I finished my warm-up pitches, my catcher, a tall blond giant of a guy, walked out to me to discuss my sign preference for a runner on second. "Second sign, shake first?" he asked.

"Yeah, that's fine." In spring training we do some other outs-plus-one-oriented bullcrap because the coaches demand it of us, but when game time rolls around, we do what's easiest.

"Okay," he said, "this first guy has a real long swing. I think we can get in on him, so let's start off there and work away."

"You're the boss, Mort. Just tell me what you want and where," I said, a tad cockily.

"Okay, let's go with your two seamer, then."

"Oh, you want Mr. Nasty then, huh?" I said, now fully cocky.

"Mr. What?"

"Mr. Nasty, the old bat eater."

"Uh . . . whatever."

"You got it baby." I bobbed my head up and down.

He flipped his mask back down over his skullcap, packed his mitt, and retreated to the dish. I dug in on the mound.

Indeed, the first hitter was tall, long armed, and equipped with a formidable piece of lumber. He extended his hands out over the plate for a few mock swings—excellent plate coverage, as promised. Mort, squatting behind the dish with the umpire hovering over his back, flashed a single digit, then swirled it as if he was stirring coffee—a two seamer. I had no objections, nodded my head, and took my hand to the ball cradled in my glove.

I wasn't rushed to get ready to face this hitter; I wasn't tired from the previous inning; and I wasn't even working against arm fatigue. Everything was in my favor, as good as I could ask for. I had my best stuff in an optimal scenario, making for a perfect audition. This encore inning was my chance to impress. I wound, kicked, and snapped my best two seamer into flight, aiming to jam the hitter just as I did in the windswept plains in High Desert. The long-armed, jammable guy with the slow bat turned on my boring bat eater and crushed it well over the left field fence, over the railing that separated the parking lot from the field, and into the darkness of the world outside the game.

I stood on the mound kicking dirt as Long Arms jogged around me, excited, party-themed music blaring over the stadium's speakers. A volley of fireworks shot up and boomed above us, crackling back to earth in the night sky. Fans roared, some took the opportunity to scream out how much I suck. Mort stood behind the plate with his mask in one hand and a shrug on his shoulders. The umpire handed him a ball, which he tossed out to me about the time Long Arms crossed the plate and clapped hands with his compadres. As he walked into the dugout, I realized he was the guy standing next to Juice's girl in the outfield during the previous day. I suddenly wished Juice had ripped his long, home-run-hitting arms off.

One pitch, that's all it was, and I told myself not to worry about it. *Everyone gives up home runs, and a home run on the first pitch is a fluke, you know that.* Recover and then focus on the next pitch, that's the key, that's what shows a true competitor. I tried to man-ufacture a stable bridge of internal propaganda to take me from a negative to a positive. I could strike out the side and look great now, maybe even better than I would have otherwise looked with-out the run, the dark stroke of a solo shot serving to bring out the bold, bright, punch outs I'd soon record.

The next hitter singled to left; then I threw a wild pitch, grant-ing him second. Then I gave up a double and he scored. *Goddamn it!* I screamed internally. Suddenly, my inner arrogant voice was crucifying me. *What the fuck are you doing? You are blowing this big chance!* I scrambled around the mound, full of anxiety trying to pull out bad thoughts, but there were just too many of them. Just when I thought I'd could still salvage it, was too late.

Randy called time out and made his way from the dugout to the mound, one hand extended to the bullpen. My night was over. I cast my eyes to the stands, in an attempt to search out what those great decision makers thought, hoping to read a face or an expression. KT chatted idly on his cell phone; Grady dragged a pen across a notebook. I could feel the words he penned, words I had no idea about but safely assumed as bad, branding me again. A whole year of numerical success was now a paragraph of doubt based on eyewitness failure.

In a game of getting people to like you, I had missed a prime opportunity, and I cursed myself, and the game, and my luck, and whoever the hell else would listen as I made my way back into the dugout. I placed my glove down like a teacup, grabbed a drink, tried my best to breathe without letting the anger escape. I held myself together, though I could split the earth with my disgust.

When the inning changed, Drew came in, patted me on the shoulder, and said, "Short memory, dude." It's something the best relievers have, but unfortunately, the Brass, who only see you pitch once or twice a year, do not.

Chapter Forty-two

I spent a lot of the night angry, frustrated, and paranoid about my career and what was being written about it. I felt it clear as day because for so much of the year I had let it go. Feeling its return was like being wrapped up in the nostalgic confines of a straitjacket. I blew a great opportunity, and I knew it. It stewed inside me, sickening me. I needed to get it out of my system, but I had no one to unload on. I learned a long time ago teammates don't want to hear you whine. They have their own issues to deal with, and they know nothing, no words, no medicine will make the cold bite of failure heal faster. I think it's one reason why so many players tip brews, to help relax, to help forget, to celebrate a better time, or to talk of the of ones to come.

My mother was up. She worked nights and didn't get off till after midnight. I could call her and talk about the issue. Who knows what she'd tell me, but it was better than talking to myself. I certainly didn't have anything nice to say.

Standing outside the Frisco hotel in the cool night air, I scrolled to her name in my cell phone, then dialed. The phone rang a couple of times before she picked up.

"Hey, babe! Wow, what's the date? I thought you'd lost our

number," she answered. The sound of late-night cable television dribbled in the background.

"Hey, Mom."

"What's up? How are you?"

I sighed. "I pitched like shit tonight."

"Oh, well, that sucks."

"Yeah, I did it in front of the Brass, the decision makers."

"Well, how bad was it?"

"Home run, single, wild pitch, double, 'nother run. I didn't even get an out." I had already forgotten any positives.

"Ouch."

"Yeah . . . I'm terrible. It's nights like tonight when I feel like I'm only ever going to be mediocre."

"Well, I don't know what to tell you," she said. "I was reading online, and it said you were doing pretty well."

"Well I was, and I think I made the Brass take notice, but I had this opportunity to—"

"Hey, can you hold on?" she interrupted. "Your brother wants the phone."

"What?" I said, slightly irritated at the mention of my brother and his demands.

"Just hold on. . . ." She put the phone to her chest, but I could hear muffled conversation between my brother and mother.

"You know, just once I'd like to talk about something that's going on in my world without him getting in the way," I said, though I wasn't sure if anyone was listening or if anyone ever did for that matter. It wouldn't take much to promote me from irritated to pissed off.

"*Alright, hold on!*" I heard her strain. Then to me, "Your brother wants to talk to you."

"About what?"

"I don't know. Stuff."

"What stuff?"

"I can't tell you; he has to do it."

"What am I, the principal?"

"Just hear him, okay?"

"Fine." My mom transferred the phone to my brother.

"Hey," came his rough, tarry voice.

"What do you want?"

"Did Mom talk to you?"

"She told me you wanted to speak to me, that's all."

Some shifting of the phone, background noise fading away, a sound of a door opening and closing, and then the faint fuzzing of wind over the receiver. "Look, I uh . . ." He took a deep breath and started up again, "I've been going to some meetings, some AA meetings and . . . Well, I've been sober for a few months now and my sponsor told me I should call up the people I've hurt, you know, while I was drinking and apologize. He said it was part of the process."

"Apologize?"

"Well, ask for their forgiveness."

I'll admit, I'm afraid of my brother. I thought of him as a monster and talked to him only when I absolutely had to. I had my career goals, and he had whatever the hell he had, which I stopped caring about a long time ago when he decided the best way to resolve our differences was to get shit faced and beat the fuck out of me. I spent most of my formative years weathering the storms, picking up the pieces, watching him kill my father and frustrate my mother, and the last thing I thought about, right after dealing with my own failures, was forgiving him of his.

"Look, Brak, I pitched like shit today, I don't think I want to deal with this right now."

"Just hear me out, okay? I have to ask you because it's part of the steps, for my sponsor."

I got a better grip on the phone. Then something deeper and meaner than breaking down on a ball field took hold of me. "Is that it?" I accused. "Is that your way of asking me to forgive you for all the shit you've put us through? A fucking phone call and *somebody put me up to this BS?*"

"No, it's not like that."

"Then, what's it like?"

"I've already talked to Mom and Dad, and I realize now that I've got a disease, Dirk. I'm an alcoholic."

"No shit."

"But I'm working on it. I'm getting help. I have a counselor and a sponsor and—"

"And this sponsor is going to fix it? What about all the other law-mandated counseling you went to in between trips to the bar? What about the other help that was supposed to stop you from beating the hell out of us?"

"This is different."

"Doesn't feel different to me."

He sighed and labored to keep himself in check. I could tell I was frustrating him. I wanted to. I wanted him to explode. I wanted him to yell at me and turn into that monster I knew so well because I felt like one. I felt disgusting and broken, and I didn't want to hold it back. I didn't want to forgive, and I didn't want to hear about it. I took plenty of blows from him, and it was his turn to take some of mine.

"I expected you to be skeptical, I understand. I know I've hurt you and a lot of people."

"You know? You don't know anything, Brak, I wanted to kill you. Seriously, I thought about it. I thought it through. I could claim self-defense and no one would bat an eye after all the trips the cops have made to our house because of you. I've lain awake hoping for you to wreck your car and die. That night you broke my head open and I had to lie to the police about it. That night you chased me around with a knife. When you grabbed the wheel of the car when I was trying to get you home and almost wrecked us. Every time I talk to Dad, every time I hear Mom yell, every time I think about home. You break and you destroy, and all we can do is try and hold it together."

"I know."

"No, you don't!"

"YES I DO!" he roared. "There were nights I wanted to be dead too! There were nights I wanted to kill myself, Dirk. Do you know what the fuck it's like to feel like that? Of course you don't. You think your fucking baseball struggles are everything in life, running from one side of the country to the next while I fuck up back at home. You've never known the shit I have. What's the worst you've dealt with, huh? Make a bad pitch? Christ!"

"The worst I've had to deal with is you, Brak."

"Great, then think of me the next time you pitch like shit. It should make you feel much better."

The phone sat silent for a minute while he collected himself. I had beaten him, but it did not satisfy as I hoped. "I know this is my own fault," he said, somber, focused. "There are no excuses. That's one of the first things AA teaches you, and it's true. There are no excuses; you have to accept responsibility. I accept my actions, but you are part of this."

"How am I a part of this? I didn't make you start drinking."

"Yeah, but you have the power to forgive me for it."

"Why should I? Because your sponsor needs me to do it so you can get your AA merit badge?"

"Goddamn it Dirk. . . . No, not because of AA, but because I don't want to struggle with this anymore. Because I'm tired of fucking up. I want to have control of my life again. I'm not good with words like you, but I'm asking you the best way I know. I need you to give me another chance."

"I don't know if I feel convinced."

"It's not all about you, Dirk! It's not all about how you fucking feel! I may be a drunk, but at least I'm not an arrogant son of a bitch."

I had a strong notion to dismiss his words. Who was he to tell me anything, least of all what I was? Yet, as rough and tarry as his argument was, he was more right than I'd like to admit. The brotherly thing to do was forgive, even if it was messy, even if it didn't feel good. But the way he so easily called me out as arrogant while touting this redemption of his pissed me off. He suddenly had an undeniable sense of direction. He knew what he wanted, where he stood, who he was. He accepted the circumstances, and he seemed stronger for it. I'd never heard him talk that way, or level any argument against me that wasn't drunken gibberish. I felt jealous and spiteful. I wanted him to stay lost because I felt he deserved it. But here he was, found, and I could just hate him for it.

I was so angry that I would let him kill himself to satisfy my pain. The realization of my thirst for destruction hit me hard, so hard I almost threw up. I dropped to the pavement of the sidewalk and grabbed my head. Who was the monster now? I felt tears welling up in my eyes.

My brother spoke but much more controlled. "I've hit the bottom, Dirk. I mean, if I go any lower, I'll be dead. Just like you wanted."

"That's not what I want, Brak."

"What do you want then?"

"I want to know how you got to this point, how this transformation?"

"I had some help."

"I know that, but you've had help before."

"This may not make sense to a person like you, Dirk, but I guess I realized that the best of a person isn't discovered in great accomplishments. I haven't done anything like you have. I've always been the failure, and I hated that feeling. I hated the comparison. That was why I drank. I realize now though, the best part of a person is how he deals with the low points in his life, not the high ones. I don't expect you to understand that, I mean, you've always been the successful one. . . ."

"I do understand," I said.

"Well, . . . I think about that stuff and it makes me feel stronger, like I can still do something with my life."

I thought about his words. Neither of us talked, and the situation calmed.

"So, what do you think?" he continued. "Think you can forgive me?"

I labored for each syllable as if I had never spoken the language before, but I got it out. "I think so. It's not easy, but . . . you're right, it's not all about me."

"I understand it's hard, and I am sorry for all of it."

"I know you are. I know it's a disease, and I forgive you, but it's going to take awhile before I forget."

"Don't ever forget. I can't. The minute I think I've got it beat, that I'm beyond it, I'll fall into it again."

"Then I won't forget."

Chapter Forty-three

We won the game I pitched in, despite my best efforts to blow it. We also won the next game as well, but if you talked to the starter about it, you'd have thought we lost.

I opted to be Frenchy's road roomie when he got called up. I was paired with a position player before he arrived, and that's never as fun as having another pitcher to plot and scheme with. When I got back to the room that night, Frenchy was on his cell phone, not exactly yelling at the person on the other end of the line, but not in perfect agreement with that person either. His face was still wearing the scowl he left the game with when he got pulled, something I understood very well.

He looked at me standing in the doorway, waved at me, then got up and left the room for the sanctum of the hallway. Though I tried to stay out of his business, I caught most of his conversation through the cheap hotel door. Up and down he paced, sometimes barking at the phone, sometimes whimpering. The barks were for his parents, while the whimpering was reserved for his girlfriend. He started today's game, and it didn't go as well as he'd have liked it too. Three runs over five innings of work, could've been way worse, but he expected perfection. Can't say that I blame him;

he'd been cruising most of the year, pitching like baseball was a video game and he had the cheat code.

Perfectionism is a funny thing. It won't allow you to cut yourself even the tiniest bit of slack. It will insult you when you fail to achieve it and berate and belittle you until you're your own worst enemy, an enemy you can never defeat. It'll make you mad at those who try to tell you positive things. It'll push people away. In the end, what was once a strong drive to do your best is now a wicked master who's never satisfied.

I remember the times I did what he was doing now. Hell, I just did it—having a bad outing and then dialing friends and family for someone to dump on. This was the first time I'd been present for someone else doing it. I may not have been the pitching prospect Frenchy was, but I can sure whine like one when I fail.

When his cell phone died, Frenchy came back into the room. He flipped the dead phone onto the couch and collapsed on the cushion next to it. He stared at the floor for a second, then picked up where his battery left off, using me as a captive audience.

"I just don't understand what my problem is. It's like I can't pitch anymore," he said, staring at the wall as if it were a projector screen where his mind reviewed all the bad he'd done today. "Back in High-A, I was so much better than I am now. . . ." He detailed a list of reasons, assumptions, and best guesses for his failure. Then, he began beating himself, calling himself stupid, worthless, incapable. It was as if he were a lawyer arguing for the death sentence—his own death sentence.

He ended his venting by fishing for compliments. I didn't bite. He'd just tell me I was wrong for pooh-poohing him anyway. Intent on wallowing, he took my silence as affirmation he was indeed a lost cause, which started the process anew.

I had a lot on my mind today. I needed that outing in front of big decision makers to be good and I didn't get it. My brother, who

I felt would be better off dead, informed me how jaded my view on life was and asked for forgiveness. Now I was listening to a guy who got a win tell me he sucked. I didn't feel like rehashing it, not from a kid with more talent than myself. "Frenchy," I interrupted, "listen to me. You're twenty-one and in Double A. It was a solid start. You pitched fine. We all saw that. But the worst part about your outing was that crap you pulled in the dugout and the stuff happening right here."

He looked at me quizzically, "What do you mean by that?"

"I mean it's over, and you are an emotional wreck about it. You are dumping this problem on everyone around you. This is what brings a team down, especially after a win. Your self-pity and negativity will make the boys avoid you, ostracize you. Throwing your glove, throwing a fit in the dugout after giving up runs, marching around mad hours after the game is over—it's immature, bro. What, you honestly believe you're above having struggles?"

"No, but—"

"This is a man's game. You need to act like one."

Frenchy's shoulders fell; his head followed. The words struck a chord, and it made me feel guilty for speaking them. Frenchy was my friend, but sometimes friends need to talk to each other that way. Still, having been in his shoes, I knew it's never fun to hear a friend say you're whining.

"I don't think I'm telling you anything you don't know, but hey, we all fall short of our mark from time to time. It's how we handle that fall that makes us the players we are. It's not all about accomplishments, but how we soldier through disappointments." And those were some of the best words I'd ever said to another person in baseball, and they were not mine. They were my brother's, a person who never played a day of baseball in his life.

Frenchy stared at the floor for a second or two. Then his head started to bob, and he said, "You're right man. You're right."

"I have pitched *way* worse than you did today. How about my second inning yesterday? I know that terrible, sick, bad-outing feeling you get when things don't go right. I know what it's like when failure burns you up inside. I still deal with it. But I also know now all that negative self-talk is you punishing yourself."

"Punishing myself?"

"Yeah, sometimes when we fail, we punish ourselves with negative self-talk so we can feel like we paid the price to feel good about ourselves again. But winning and losing doesn't make us heroes or failures. You can be upset about your imperfections today if you want, but, imperfections are part of this game. Beating yourself up doesn't make you any better at this sport. It just drains you, and sooner or later you start to believe the voice telling you how bad you are. Sooner or later, you don't care about anyone else but yourself, and you won't listen to anyone else no matter how relevant that person's words are. You become your own enemy, and your words turn into something more than words.

"Take what you can from this and move on. It's really all you can do. Besides, you're a lot better than you think you are right now."

Frenchy leaned back on the couch to let the words settle in. I did the same from my chair.

I spoke to him as much as I did to myself. They weren't my words, but they were my experiences, boiled down and pieced together like some bullpen gospel. I had taken more than my share of lumps in this game, and while I thought I had nothing to show for it except a string of yawn-inducing numbers, it turns out I did. I had wisdom, something far more valuable.

"That's some great advice," Frenchy said, leaning forward again. "Seriously dude, that may be some of the best advice I've had in a long time."

"It may be some of the best advice *I've* had in a long time too."

Chapter Forty-four

The next night in the bullpen, in between chats about how Martha Stewart would be the perfect clubbie, a lady about Martha's age came and petitioned us for a baseball. "There is this cute little girl down behind the dugout who really should get a baseball," she said. She had enough gold jewelry around her neck to make Mr. T jealous and spoke with an air of refinement.

If Martha Stewart were a clubbie, she would fold our uniforms up like swans, serve us Independence Day–themed cupcakes with sprinkles on top, and make us wear galoshes over our spikes so we didn't get the clubhouse floor dirty. She wouldn't beg us for baseballs for cute little mystery kids.

"I'm sorry, we can't give these balls out," I replied.

"Oh my, I'm sure you're not supposed to, but she's so darling. You really should see her. All the other kids have gotten one, and her precious little shoulders slump in disappointment each time she sees them with one. It's torture, I must say."

"I know, I know," I said, unmoved. "Unfortunately, that's how it works sometimes. Honestly, though, we really aren't supposed to give these out." Nor did I want to give her one, I must say. I've heard the darling little kid excuse so many times now I'm convinced the world is completely populated with pageant winners and child actors. If she would have asked me to give her a ball because there's an ugly, bulldog-looking kid with a tail by the dugout, I might've had second thoughts based on originality.

"I understand, *of course*, but she's not even my child. I just can't bear to witness her suffering."

"She's not your kid?"

"No, but her parents won't ask, so I thought I'd take it upon myself."

"That's just weird, lady. I mean, she just didn't get a ball; what's so bad about that? If her parents aren't concerned, why are you?"

"I will buy a baseball from you if you insist on being so difficult about it," she said, irritated with us. I guess mostly me—well, all me.

"If you're going to buy her one, just go to the gift shop."

"I don't *want* to buy it. I want you to take this opportunity to make a little child's dream come true," she said, nobly, like some knight of baseball injustice.

"But I'm not even going to give it to her. It's going to go through you. What if it doesn't get there?"

"Do I look like the kind of person that lies?"

I took my time thinking about it, which made her extremely offended. "Lady, life's not fair, and sometimes we don't get what we want. I used to get good grades on my science papers, and when I brought them home to my parents, they'd beat me with a belt. I asked them why, and they'd tell me that 'because life's not fair, this is the only way we can teach you, son.' The way I see it, this little girl has it easy." That never happened actually—I never got A's on my science tests.

"Your parents should be ashamed," she declared.

"I got a whole bag of baseballs now, so they must have done something right." The lady stared at me in confusion, then threw her hands up and walked away declaring I had a terrible attitude.

An inning later, a mother and her son approached the pen.

I pretended to look out at the game, a boring one in which our starter dominated, effortlessly mowing through the Rough Riders. I faked interest in the on-field events, but in my mind I thought about going in to play Halo.

"Hello," said the mother—another mother and her precious child who deserved a baseball, no doubt. I heard them speaking, but I didn't immediately react. None of us did. Following the noble lady, a group of obnoxious teens came knocking at the pen and then some frat kids who tried their hand at heckling. Someone threw peanuts at us and called us monkeys in our cage. Then came more good ol' drunk Texas boys. If we'd have said yes to everyone, we'd be out of balls. As it was, we were already out of patience. I thought the mascot was supposed to handle crowd-control issues, but it occurred to me he didn't come out for the game today. Then I remembered that the grounds crew looked more cheery than usual . . .

"Hello," said the mother again. "I have a little boy here who would really like to meet you."

The boy jutted out from behind his mother's leg. Shy blue eyes pressed down, timidly stealing glimpses of me from under the brim of his oversized ball cap. He had thin wisps of blond hair on a pale face and a smile waiting to blossom, if he could only find the courage to let it. If only someone would help him. His mother nudged him forward, but he resisted, comfortable in Mommy's shadow.

"Hi there," I said to the boy. I didn't have to hand out souvenirs, but I could still talk with the boy. My words, however, made him cling to Mommy's leg like a shy koala.

"Tell him your name," his mother said, and he did, in a squeak of voice.

I repeated it back to him, adding, "Nice to meet you."

The strong, silent type, he opted out of the conversation. I left my comfy Rough Riders bullpen chair and went to the railing in pursuit of the boy who had contentedly buried his face in his mother's leg. "Hey there, buddy. Why so shy?"

He let one eye free. "It's okay. You can talk to him," his mother said, trying to encourage him not to suffocate on her kneecap. I steadied myself on the railing, squatting like a catcher, awaiting his attempt. "Tell him how old you are," his mom coaxed. He didn't speak, but offered me three tiny digits, instead.

"You're a slider? That's what it means when you wiggle your fingers like that. Are you a slider?"

"I'm three," he said, letting the other eye free.

"Oh" I replied, "you're *three*. Okay," I said, holding up my fingers back to him. He giggled and flashed a smile he'd been waiting to offer. He let go of Mommy's leg and faced me now. I smiled back at him.

We were about to have a good chat about the life and times of three-year-olds when his mother's hand came down on my own, grabbing my wrist, and pinning it to the railing. My personal space was violated. I looked at the mother to scold her. *Your kid's cute, but there are dozens of cute kids here every night whose mothers want me to play Santa, and they don't grab me when I'm in arm's reach.*

"Thank you for doing this for my son," she blurted. "Thank you for taking the time to speak with him. . . ." Her eyes began to crack, and drops formed at their edges. Her next words did not come out in the cheery tone she used to coax her son to speak, but fractured, in heartbroken gasps. "He has liver cancer, and it's terminal. . . ." she mustered. She tried to keep control, but her words came rushing out like water shattering a dam. "He doesn't even understand what it is, and I don't know how to . . ." her head dropped. She passed her hand across her face as she heaved. When she brought it back up, her makeup was smeared. "I'm sorry. It's just . . . he's always wanted to meet baseball players."

I looked back at the boy smiling at me. He didn't seem concerned with his mother's tears. Maybe he was used to them by now, even though he didn't understand what brought them on. His hat sat loosely over his head. A pale face framing eyes of bright blue hid underneath the bill. His skin, from the little legs that extended from his shorts to the free hand not covered with a tiny baseball glove, was ghostly white in the middle of summer. He was three years old, and he was dying.

I looked at the bag of baseballs. I looked at the boys in their chairs just feet from me. I looked at my jersey, to the field, to anything that could make this situation better. When I glanced back to the mother, she had not looked anywhere else but to me.

"What can I do?" I would gladly give him a ball or anything else I could give away.

"Just be a real person to him," she said. "That's all I ask."

I looked down on the boy. "Wait here."

I requested the attention of the bullpen, recounted the tale, and pointed to the child. Without a second thought, we scooped the boy up and placed him in the pen with us, in the middle of our pack, surrounded by players. We turned our chairs to face him, begged him to tell us about adventures of his young life, and offered him the gum bucket like a bowl of Halloween candy.

He loved baseball. He also loved cartoons, playing at the playground, and eating candy, which he shoved into his mouth until it was so full he could hardly answer. He liked school and he didn't like girls. And he was going to start T-ball soon, but he proudly declared that he didn't need the tee.

"That's one step ahead of me," I said. The pen chuckled, the boy smiled.

"Are you going to be a big leaguer when you grow up?"

He nodded his head up and down, unwaveringly certain. We nodded in approval.

He ate almost all our bullpen gum. He tried seeds, but they were too much work to eat, so we taught him how to flick them at fans instead—he liked that. We let him try on our gloves, which swallowed up his hands like beach towels. For an inning or two, he was one of the guys, complete with a pair of pants that went up to his shins and a newfound appreciation for nice legs.

When it was time for us to give the boy back to his mother, before lifting him back over the fence, we produced a baseball and a pen to sign with. Each of us stretched our names across the leather in lovingly crafted scribbles, punctuated at the ends with our numbers. We handed the ball to the boy, pressing it into his tiny hands. His face alight, mouth gaping in awe, he looked up at us in wonder, as if we had handed him a treasure from the heavens.

He spun and stretched his arm with the ball for his mother to see. "Alright!" she said, clapping her hands together. She reached for it to take a closer look, but the boy pulled it back to his chest. It was his baseball. His mother laughed.

"Okay, bud, let's get you back to Mom." We hoisted the boy, still tightly gripping his ball, and deposited him on the other side of the fence.

"Did you say thank you?" she asked.

"Thank you!" the boy said, with a big smile.

"You're welcome, buddy," said Ox.

"Thank you all so much," the mother said, her face wet from tears.

"It was our pleasure," said Rob.

We won that night, but the game did not matter. Wins, losses, and numbers behind them were rendered meaningless by two perfect innings spent in the bullpen. Something else, something bigger than baseball that can't be recorded took place. Something no one will read about in the box scores. Something only uniforms with real people inside could make happen.

Baseball and life—such funny things that don't always make sense. Yet, in those moments spent with that child, watching him live in the game in a way none of us who played it could, every-thing made perfect sense. I'd wondered all year how the power of baseball should be wielded. And now I knew. Baseball doesn't have any intrinsic power. It only has what people give to it. For some, the man who plays is a superhero, and he can do great things. For some, the man who plays is an obstacle who must get out of the way. Is baseball as important as food, knowledge, care, or a dry pair of boots? Is it as important as some of the things that pass us by in everyday life? I don't think so. Can it inspire, motivate, and call us to do something greater than ourselves? Absolutely. The burden of the player isn't to achieve greatness, but to give the feeling of it to everyone he encounters. It was wrong of me even to try to separate life and the game. They were intertwined, meant to be, one affecting the other, one teaching the other, even when the mixture occasionally blows up. It takes a real person, one who un-derstands himself, to use the tool of baseball for something good. For that person, as long as he has a jersey on his back, he has a chance.

Chapter Forty-five

The Missions took three out of four from the Rough Riders. We had proven to ourselves we could handle one of the best teams in the league, mix fun with talent, and still brew up victory. By the last month of the season, we had a clear-cut sense of ourselves, an undeniable purpose, and a taste for winning. We went after the league with a vengeance.

If ever there was a time for montage music to be played, it was during this time of my baseball career—something sweet, rocking, and all together satisfying. The boys from San Antonio found ways to win, manufacturing them out of raw will and determination. We took early leads, made astronomical comebacks, and occasionally just did some good, old-fashioned ass-kicking. Come the last week of the season, we mathematically clinched a spot in the playoffs, an accomplishment you'd swear impossible had you seen us play only a month or so earlier.

When we locked our spot in for postseason ball, we were rewarded with Tott's champagne and watery domestic beers, not for drinking, but for soaking. The bottles and cans sat packed in ice-filled coolers like clubhouse centerpieces. As we filtered in from the victory, we all grabbed hold of bottles and popped the corks of our Tott's champagne rifles, but did not dare spill a drop of the liquid in celebration until Randy had a chance to address us, pronouncing us victors.

He came in, pleased, but under control and focused, with a bottle of champagne in his own hands. We stood, elated and giddy, some with jerseys untucked, others with hats spun backward, others in just socks. "Hey, couple things, guys," Randy said, gesturing with one free hand, armed with a thumb-capped bottle in the other. "We are, as of today, the second-half winners. On behalf of the staff and myself, I'd like to say congratulations. You earned it. You kept fucking grinding it out, and you earned it." Then, he smiled at everyone, spread his feet and started shaking his bottle. "But"—we armed ourselves as he spoke—"you still got work to do!" He let it rip, hosing us down. We followed suit, turning the center of the room into a fountain of cheap champagne. Our clubbie watched the floor accumulate hours of future cleaning as we danced around like natives, wrecking the place.

The work Randy referenced was a little thing called winning the Texas League—no easy feat. We did, however, do our best to make it look that way as we swept Frisco in three games to clinch our berth in the championship series. Before ten days had passed from our last champagne spraying, we were in the locker room again, standing in front of Randy with another round of bottles, awaiting his words.

Randy came in for the second time, a thumb pressed over the top of his bottle. "Alright, we got everybody?" He looked around at us, all of us ready to imitate firefighters. "Look at you guys— you're already on this shit, aren't you?" What could we say. We had a taste for winning, and much to the chagrin of our clubhouse manager, we got to trash the place like idiots every time we won three games. "You guys keep pushing, just keep pushing. We got one more series. Someone's gotta win this shit, might as well be us!" That was his cue, and we wasted no time dumping booze like abolitionists. When we were finished, our clubbie stood in the middle of the mess and shouted, "I hope you beat these fuckers so I can watch you wreck someone else's clubhouse for a change!"

After we finished dumping everything we could on everything we could, we mingled about, talking about the coming championship series. Those of us who were still around to recall the colossal defeat of the Cal League spoke about how the coming game would be a second chance. Other players, first timers to veterans, spoke excitedly about the chance to play for some jewelry. The only person who seemed slightly bummed was Chase because he knew a September call-up was a very real possibility, and even though winning the Texas League would be grand, collecting big-league paychecks was a lot more exciting. We double max fined him.

Being in the playoffs is an experience all to itself. During the regular season, if a team doesn't win a game, it can be written off as another day in the grind where developing prospects is the focus, and wins and losses a side effect. In the end, the only level that really matters is the big leagues, and no one will remember how terrible the minor league teams were that gave birth to a big-league star. Teammates on those squads get along as best they can because they have to tolerate each other while they reach for individual goals.

The playoffs, however, are when a minor league team is really, truly a team. There are no prospects. There's no time for worries about being outshined for a promotion or lack of playing time. All that matters is winning, in any way possible. Players root for each other because all interests are suddenly entwined. There's a ring to be won, and no one can strip you of the title of champion once you receive it. It's an experience that bonds players together in a way that a regular season can't. And like so many other experiences that reach our hearts and our desires, it has the ability to crush you, unlike any regular season defeat can.

We were on a one-way course with destiny, a chance to define ourselves as capable players even if the media in its infinite wisdom only thought a handful of us were worth a damn. We could win something for ourselves and no one else. We could be champs. To do that, we would first have to beat the Springfield Cardinals, the best team in the league. The Missions, the former worst team in the league, would take on the best team in a battle for the Texas League crown.

The Cardinals came to our house for the first two games of our possible five-game set. Chase the Magnificent smacked a home run in his urgency to end the series, get a ring, and go to the big leagues. We rolled over the Red Birds, 6–2. The next night, the Birds answered back in similar fashion, beating us with the same score, 6–2. I pitched two innings of relief in a losing effort, allowing one of the runs that cemented our defeat. When we left San Antonio for Springfield, the series was tied.

In game 3, Frenchy beat the Birds like a drum. He punched out six, allowing one run, and managed to collect two hits for himself at the plate. We won 3–2, thanks to his masterful performance, and I could have almost punched him in the head for ever doubting his ability.

Come September 15, we were leading the series 2–1 and had a chance to win the whole thing.

Chapter Forty-six

Next to Hammond Field the Cardinals' home in Springfield is a park. It's small, and clean, and green. There is a walking track that winds around tufts of soft grass, artistic mobiles, and blooming flower beds. Stay on the path long enough, and you will come to a fountain.

In search of a calm before the night's coming storm, I stopped at the park before entering the stadium. I walked the trails, admired the art, and watched bees float from flower to flower. Then, like I did two years ago, I plopped on the grass and lay out like I was making a snow angel.

There were no screaming fans, no hot dog smells, and no Baseball Reaper. A cool breeze pushing clumps of clouds through the blue sky stretched above me. I was floating with them, tumbling off to some place, blown by the breeze. Tonight could be the last game of the season. Another season finished—a season that I almost never started.

The sounds of laughing children broke the silence. I sat up and searched for the source. Ahead of me, the park's fountain, apparently time activated, had begun shooting spouts of water from dozens of water jets. Up the squirting water went, like water fireworks, before coming down and splattering on the smooth stone surface beneath. The fountain was built flush with the ground level. If you walked the path and stepped on the fountain at the wrong time, it might squirt you, a scenario the kids thrived on.

Like tribal warriors chasing after elusive prey, they ran the width of the fountain, shirts off, screaming as they went. Some anticipated which holes the next burst would come out of, some ran recklessly, lunging at each spout as it came. Some stood still, soaked, knees knocking and arms tucked in, with chattering teeth forming a smile.

The jets seemed to play with the children, staying just out of reach or biting them from behind with playful nips. The children kicked and swatted them, sometimes standing on them, sometimes shouting at them for escaping. Around and around they danced, until the jets built to a crescendo and erupted in a steady fountain of water, drenching the children completely before coming to a stop.

Parents stood outside the splash zone, forming an audience to watch the children play. They happily lived through their children, ready with dry towels for exhausted, soaked heads. I sat in the grass, content to watch, though I did feel tempted to join. This was not my moment though—this was theirs—and all we spectators could do was enjoy watching those few living it.

When the fountains stopped, I ran my hands across the tops of the grass blades. *What would the children do if they caught the water?* I thought. Of course, they never would. They could never hold on to it. The water would never come home as a trophy or a pet. Catching the water was never the idea. Experiencing it was.

Chapter Forty-seven

The crowd was teeming, even before the Cardinals took the field. Springfield, Missouri, fans knew baseball. They knew what was going to happen tonight, and extra motivation via some stadium staff cheer squad was unnecessary. En masse, they formed a sea of organized crimson—red hats, red shirts, red towels, face paint, signs, foam fingers, and plastic megaphones. The energy was almost tangible, waves of sound pressing our uniforms as we walked to the field. The Cardinals' faithful were a formidable tenth man, and we felt like true baseball players in their presence.

I was happy, I admit, to be shielded from them in the pen, which felt more like a bunker than a cage this day: three walls of concrete and one of chain-link fence protecting us from the madness about to go down.

Some players think a big game requires an extra shot of intensity. Truth be told, big games require players to slow down. Emotions are already running at intense paces. Anxiety is in high supply. Big games are won by those who can keep control of themselves. Intensity can be a liability. Some exhaust themselves worrying about the game before it starts.

Mike Ekstrom, or "Ek," our quiet, unassuming, right-handed fourth starter, who spent most of the season buried in a book or quietly taking in the day's events, went through his stretch motions while the crowd brought itself to a boil. Whether it was his enigmatic persona or a focused sense of duty, the crowd, the day, the magnitude of it all, seemed to bounce off him.

This was the first time Ek would pitch in the playoffs. Our sweep of Frisco did not require us to call upon his services. The break we had while Springfield won its series allowed time for our rotation to reset, bringing our 1, 2, and 3 back around. Now game four was here, and it was Ek's turn.

Autumn had begun its slow creep across the Missouri landscape. The air was cool, and the wind carried a chilled bite, reminding us we were in the playoffs. Bulbs flickered on the stadium's scoreboard. Its massive LCD board flashed bios and compared lineups. The PA announcer read off our batting order in a less-than-enthusiastic voice while the Imperial March from Star Wars played in the background. Then the order for the home Cardinals was read, each name evoking raucous enthusiasm from the crowd. A montage of highlights showcasing the St. Louis Cardinals lineage was played on the big screen. Legendary music, playing over clips of great Cardinals moments in the past showed in the hope of blessing the future. The lights were lit, the anthem was played, and the crowd roared like a lion. We were not impressed.

In the first inning, we scored three and Ek blanked the Cardinals. Come the second, we scored four more. We knocked the Birds' starter out of the game before he could record six outs. Ek snubbed the Cardinals again in the second inning, and by the time the third rolled around, we were comfortably in the driver's seat, seven to nothing.

In the pen, we scampered about the place like flighty schoolgirls. I think we would have held hands and bedazzled our jersey pants if we could have.

"Hayhurst, you gonna get shit-faced?" Dalton asked.

"No. I am not getting shit-faced." I rolled my eyes.

"But you're still drinking, right?"

I'd made a promise to the boys. If we won the whole thing, I'd have my first drink to commemorate it. I vowed I'd never drink while my brother was doing it, but now that he had had sobered up, I could finally raise my cup with my teammates, something I'd been waiting for a long time, at the very least, to experience. The boys loved this little extra incentive, and to be honest, I liked it too. For so long, drinking was something I looked down upon for the chaos it sparked in my family's life, but this was one chance for me to see it used to celebrate something great.

Even though I was okay with joining in with the boys in what would be the best moment of my baseball career, I was not cool with getting trashed. One would be enough, thank you very much. Besides, I heard it tastes like piss.

"If we hold on to this, I am," I confirmed.

"Oh, we will, baby!"

"So you aren't gonna get wrecked to commemorate it?" Dalton asked.

"No, dude."

"Well, I am!" Dalton cried. "I'm gonna get shit-faced and watch *Road House*!"

"*Road House*?"

"*ROAD HOUSE*, BABY! *ROAD HOUSE!*"

In the fifth inning, I went into the clubhouse to take a whizz. The clubhouse attendants were busy hanging up plastic over our lockers, thick, clear tarps to protect our personal belongings from the streams of poorly aimed champagne. I watched them work, taping it to the ceiling, covering every exposed section of the walls and lockers.

I know it's sacrilege to the baseball gods to believe a game is won before it actually is, but it was hard not to think it when the locker room was already prepped for the victory party. If there was any doubt, a banner reading 2007 Texas League Champs! was stretched across one of the walls. I permitted myself to believe it was really going to happen.

I returned to the pen in the top of the sixth, in time to watch our left fielder hit a home run, putting us up eight–zip. Ek pitched seven scoreless before being relieved by Rob, who put up a zero of his own. The offense never stopped, and by the time the ninth, the last inning of the year, rolled around, it was twelve nothing.

Blade would receive the honor of closing the game out. He would also be the person crushed at the bottom of the pile of ec-static Missions uniforms when we came roaring onto the field to celebrate. When he left the pen, we cheered him into his destiny. All we needed were three more outs.

With so much anticipation flowing through the pen, we were borderline ridiculous. We practiced approaching the bullpen's exit gate and opening it, like a fire-drill escape exercise. No one wanted to be the last person onto the field when we won it.

"I want to be last," Ox corrected.

"What? Why?"

"So I can jump on and crush you motherfuckers."

"You might kill someone."

Ox smiled at the thought of it.

"You can go first," I said.

When the inning started, we stopped worrying about exit strat-egies and stuck ourselves to the fence. A season of getting outs just to have a chance at getting these.

"Come on, Blade!" we cheered, but he couldn't hear us from the pen.

The Cardinals, who spent the entire game rolling over to our onslaught, suddenly decided to muster some resistance. They sin-gled, then hit a two-run blast to put them on the board.

I'm sure Blade wasn't happy, but I felt almost charitable about it. I was glad to see the Cardinals didn't get shut out in the last game of their season, on field, during the championship series.

However, my mercy transformed into concern when Blade walked the next two batters and allowed another single.

We were still up ten. In any other situation, there would be no cause for alarm. But this was not any other situation. This was *the* situation of the year. The emotional, ecstatic anticipation turned into neurotic what-ifs.

The pen phone rang. Abby wanted Moreno up. No sooner did he start throwing than he was in the game, and the score was 3–12 with no outs. A wild pitch brought it to 4–12 and a single, 5–12. Our first out was made after the fifth runner scored, but if the Birds kept this up . . .

Seven runs was still a huge deficit to overcome with three outs. The law of averages was still in our favor. That didn't stop the bull-pen from graduating to a full-on freak-out. Just a minute ago, we were cruising with a ten-run lead. Now we watched the Birds put up five without recording an out, and there was nothing we could do but watch from the confines of our square in the outfield.

When the score hit 7–12, I started to kick myself. All that talk about having a beer, all the talk about winning, all that talk of *Road House*! What was I thinking? I felt sick, like all the happy butterflies in my stomach had just died gruesome deaths. Panic hit.

"What the hell did we do?"

"THE BALL BAG!" Dalton screamed.

Some idiot, probably me, had packed the ball bag. A universally accepted no-no that always seemed to warrant punishment from the baseball gods, which I almost started to believe in. Thinking about winning and acting on those thoughts were different. Packing up your equipment in expectation of a predictable ending usually ensured the unpredictable. It was more than stupid—it was heresy!

Dalton grabbed the rosin from the ball bag and threw it back into the bullpen. When another hit was recorded, he took the ball bag and dumped everything out. I stood in front of the pen's chain-link fence, squeezing the links with my hands.

"This can't be happening . . . not again," I mumbled.

"Come on, Moe! Come on, baby!"

Cheers arose. Futile cheers that came from our bullpen but were trampled over by the Cardinals' war machine in the stands. They had come alive now, cheering their hearts out for their hometown boys. They were marvelous and horrifying in their intensity. There were no mathematical probabilities to them; no deficits too deep to overcome. I watched the scene on the field play out, completely helpless, feeling like I did those years ago when I watched the Cal League championship slip away.

Turning to the boys I said, "If we lose tonight, we'll lose tomorrow. There is no way we come back after a heartbreaker like this."

"They will have all the momentum," Ox said.

"If we are going to do it, we have to win it here."

El Gato wound and delivered. The ball was struck, a deep but tilting foul. Venable had a bead on it. We grabbed the links of the fence as we watched him track it, squeezing the fence like a throttle:

"Come on Will! Come on Will!"

The ball came down. Venable's body was out too far to stay balanced, and he went down with the ball, glove out across the grass, reaching to make the catch! Two outs.

"HELL YA!" we cried in unison. We shook the fence to vent our energy.

"Attaboy, Willy!"

"One more fellas, one more!"

"Come on, Moe! Come on, baby!"

One more. That's all we needed. The Birds were down to their last out, but baseball has a way of making one little out impossible to get. In an attempt to confuse it, our catcher called time and walked out to the mound. There was nothing he could say that wasn't obvious by the situation, but the conversation wasn't important. He could very well talk about candlesticks or fried chicken. He was stalling.

We were slowing down the Birds. They were riding a surge of adrenaline, a fire fueled and stoked by the crowd. Our battery was trying to put it out by starving their need for action. A long enough lull and the energy would dissipate, and the Cardinals would once again be aware of their dilemma.

The umpire, not immune to the energy, hurried our pitcher along, though he resisted as long as he could. The players reset. The crowd's engine turned over, firing up again. Moreno looked for the sign. Fastball, just what he wanted. Leg kick hand break, and then the ferocious uncoiling down the mound to where he let it loose.

The ball was struck by a hitter who had batted around. He topped it, sending it spinning across to third base like a bouncing boobie to Chase. Chase scooped, stepped, and threw it across the infield. The ball seemed to move in slow motion, spinning like any other and, at the same time, unlike any I'd ever seen. It seemed to stand still, as if the field, the stadium, and the whole earth itself moved around it. It carried the expectation of a 147 game season on it, the culmination of every drop of sweat, every sacrifice, and every hope. Thousands of eyes watched, dozens of hearts pushed, and one outstretched glove caught the ball that ended the 2007 Texas League season. We had won it all.

I made it to the gate first, but my emotions were driving me at a reckless pace, and I couldn't get the latch open. All the practice I put in, and I was rendered impotent like a freshman fumbling with bra hooks. I began punching and jerking on the fence, finally resorting to kicking it open.

The rest of the pen was on top on me. Suffering from the same adrenaline stupor, they would have pushed me through the fence or simply knocked it down had I not gotten the gate open. When it flung wide, we burst through like a raging river. Across the outfield we ran, screaming wildly.

I was in a full sprint, my arms raised in a V with both fists clenched as I crossed the infield dirt. Ox and Dalton tore off their jackets and threw their hats as they ran. We were set to collide with the mountain of teammates already forming on the pitcher's mound. Arriving last, we landed on top of that screaming pile of uniforms. Underneath, we could hear cries for mercy from the crushed. They begged us to relent, crying they couldn't breathe, that something was going to break if we didn't get off. Ox got off, jumped back on, and rolled around on the top like a pig in mud.

The voice of the announcer, the same one who called our names to the demonizing tones of Darth Vader, announced us as champions. The crowd mustered hollow congratulatory applause. Then the announcer took a cheer offering for the slain Cardinals, and the place erupted one final time for the fallen.

A stage was erected on the field, directly behind home plate. Our team was called together and presented a trophy, the prize of the Texas League. We clamored to touch it, to feel the tangible proof of a championship. League officials made speeches, coaches offered magnanimous words, and pictures were taken. Microphones and the people who wielded them chased around key players for marketable insight, but no one wanted to linger on the field. There was a celebration waiting for us in the locker room, and we wasted no time getting to it.

As we entered the locker room, champagne bottles were again handed to us like rifles. The stereo blared hip-hop, and guys squealed and screamed like children ready for birthday cake. We popped the corks of our bottles and held our fingers over the barrels, awaiting firing orders. Randy entered when we had all gathered and attempted to give us a victory speech, but he didn't get far before streams of champagne cut him off because every trigger finger was an itchy one.

We soaked one another, chasing each other around as if the bottles were squirt guns. We drenched teammates, walls, furniture, the ceiling, members of the press, mascots, and everything else we could blast. Drew took a champagne bottle and sprayed it as if he were riding a pony. Lunchbox acted as if he were jerking off with his bottle. Ox sprayed it up Manrique's ass, and I sprayed mine on the wall thinking it was my fellow players because I had my eyes closed. Dalton ran around naked, and Blade, knowing he wouldn't get his arms ripped off, sprayed Juice in the face, then dumped the rest down his shirt back. When the pressure in the bottles ran out, we tackled each other and dumped the remaining gulps on each other's heads.

Randy fought us off as long as he could before we cornered him with the watercooler. Ice cold, it took his breath away when we dumped it over him. Abby, less mobile than his managerial counterparts, stood his ground and was demolished—standing with his eyes closed, hands out like a blind man while a river of booze splashed down on his head. Pops happily called us all manner of swears and curses, which only served to cement the inevitable dumping of an ice chest on him by his hitters.

When we ran out of bubbly, we moved to beer cans. We sprayed it from the lid, slopped it like paint, spit it out of our mouths, and dumped it on heads and down pants and shirt backs. We even punctured the cans and let little annoying streams squirt out like baby sprinklers. Ox tried to catch as much of it in his mouth as he could.

When the waterworks stopped, we peeled off, picked each other up, and stumbled around, staggered by the surreal quality of our victory. Hugs, shouts, arms over shoulders, punches to shoulders, chest bumps, hugs again, until there was nothing left for us to do except take it all in. There we were, a pack of grown men, big kids, and wild warriors standing in the locker room so far from our homes. We had done the very thing we only whispered about in spring training, back before teams were made. We were a family now, baptized in the power of a championship. We posed for personal pictures with our arms around shoulders and our pointer fingers up, declaring we were number one. We stretched the Texas League Championship banner out in front of us and surrounded it, soaking wet, hair matted to our faces, reeking of cheap booze for the best family picture of the year.

After showering and changing into dry clothes, we made our way to the hotel for the after party. There was beer there as well, but the meant-to-be-drunk kind. There was also pizza, chips, our freshly acquired championship trophy. Fortunately, Dalton was clothed again.

The guys took turns having their pictures taken with the monstrous Texas League trophy, complete with a fresh engraving declaring the Missions as 2007 champions. I took my turn next to it, though the real prize was something far less tangible, something that felt like redemption.

A promise is a promise. Drew poured me a tall, plastic party cup, like the kind I refused at so many forgettable college parties, filled to the brim with New Castle. With my chalice in hand, I walked to the center of the converted conference room. I interrupted the party, asking for the attention of my teammates, raised my cup and declared, "Here's to you guys! A hell of a good reason for a first!" With that, I inhaled the entirety of my cup in one gulp, slammed the cup onto the table in front of me like a Viking, then gagged, cringed, and coughed. My teammates shared a laugh at my expense, then showed their approval by screaming, "Get him another one!" Twenty-three fresh beers were immediately pressed into my face.

"That's okay," I said, waving them off, "I think I'll take it easy from here on. It really does taste like piss."

Twenty-four hours later, I was on a plane back to Ohio. The season was over. No long good-byes, no sobs, and no last-minute declarations of love. It was done, the institution of minor league baseball shut its doors, packed up, and closed for the season. The next time we'd see each other would be in the spring, when we'd duke it out for a chance to do it all again.

Chapter Forty-eight

One Year Later

I could tell them anything. The people who didn't know me, which was most of the people in attendance, had probably heard the fantastic tales perpetuated by baseball books and movies and would take me as an authority on the subject, eagerly swallowing whatever concoction I fed them. My friends and family would believe me because of the inexhaustible supply of fantastic tales I'd already told. Stories about baseball just have that effect, I guess—it goes down smooth. But this wasn't the time to goof around, even though my uncle thought it would be cute to toast my last night as a virgin with, "Don't swing for the fences on your first at bat, buddy—just manufacture runs, steal a base or two, bunt." My family has a way of spicing up any occasion, including my wedding.

"First," I began, "I'd like to thank all of you for coming today. I'm so very pleased Bonnie and I could share this special day with you. I know you wouldn't have missed it for the world, but we appreciate it all the same." Especially since their showing meant a guaranteed gift.

"Second, I realize many of you here today don't know me,

which is a regrettable side effect of my career. In fact, I'd say most of you know more about my job than you do about me. I've been told by several of you that you've been following my stats on the Internet and rooting for me. Thanks.

"I'd like you to get to know me though, beyond my stats, and, with my wife's permission of course, I'd like to tell you a story about me and baseball, a real one that I think we can all relate to." Unlike my uncle's hitting advice.

Most of my wife's relatives—the bulk of the guests—flew in the day of the wedding and would be leaving the next. They didn't know me, though most thought I was a nice young boy because reports they received about me told them so. What they did know, for certain, however, was I was a big-league baseball player, something that always seemed to dominate my conversation regardless of the occasion. Though I did spend most of the nonceremony portion of the evening being cordially threatened by the males in my wife's extended family over what would happen if I didn't treat her right, I also spent an inordinate amount of time getting big league ticket requests and contract speculation fired at me by fingers folded into the shape of guns.

Making it to the big leagues was no small feat, especially considering how distant and impossible the goal once seemed. Me meeting a beautiful, caring, and capable woman was no small feat either. As it would turn out, both of these occurrences had their roots in the 2007 championship season.

At the time, meeting my wife wasn't quite as celebrated as winning a championship and discovering some of the mysteries of baseball. We were introduced through the wonders of technology, over the Internet. We spent the last two months of the season, even the night of the championship party, talking on the phone and exchanging e-mails. Our first live meeting came days after I returned home. When we finally met, the heavens opened up, doves flew in her wake, and I knew right then and there she would be the reason I moved out of my grandma's. It was love, and the following season, I proposed.

Speaking of the following season, I pitched my way back onto the Triple-A roster out of camp. I put up good numbers in the spring, even good enough radar reads to warrant Earp talking to me about something other than my nuts. Though I was sent off to Portland, Oregon, with a message from Grady that I might have to come back down to Double-A and pick up some spilt innings, it never happened. I pitched well enough to avoid that scenario, well enough in fact to earn an invite to the Triple-A All-Star team. (I turned it down to go home and help my wife plan our wedding, FYI.)

Abby and Randy moved up along with several players from the 2007 championship team. Reunited, we had another season of adventure, but then again, they are all seasons of adventure. Come the end of the year, the Portland Beavers selected me as the Community Player of the Year, an honor given to a real person who moonlights as a baseball player. And then one unassuming night in August, I was called into Randy's office, the door was shut, and I was told I would be exchanging my minor league uniform for a major league one.

My relatives, much fewer in number, sat together at their tables. They were already bored with me and preferred to lavish my wife with attention, resulting in the males of my own family threatening me over what would happen if I didn't treat her right.

My mother, brother, and father, along with my agent and some mutual friends, were grouped together. My closest, nonbaseball friends sat at the wedding party table. My grandma sat at home watching Judge Judy because she refused to come. She said that my wife had the voice of a whining dog and that she hoped she was dead before the day of the wedding. That's okay, she was just upset I was leaving her for another woman, and I'll take that as a compliment. She's still single now, and if you're interested, she loves bird watching, is handy with a gun, and is a fantastic cook. Bless her heart. Naturally, my wife and I sat together, happy as could be.

Officially sworn in as new family additions with everyone comfortably seated in front of food and beverage, I thought I'd introduce myself and my intentions with an experience that helped me put the game into perspective, even at the big, brightest level. This is what I told them:

I was sitting at my locker when a big hand fell on my shoulder. It was the hand of Trevor Hoffman. I turned around, nervously, and offered a pathetic squeak as baseball's save leader pawed me.

"What you doing kid? Writing a book?" he asked, staring down at me as I typed away at my laptop computer. I started keeping a diary at the start of the 2007 season.

"Uh, as a matter of fact, I am," I replied, shutting the lid to keep my thoughts private.

Hoffman sat down next to me, which was as flattering as it was terrifying. I hadn't been in the big leagues long, but it didn't take me long to realize that this level had more unspoken rules about time and behaviors than any other. Young guys were weighed and sifted by older guys, and depending on the disposition of the older guys, the scales weren't always balanced.

Young guys in the bigs aren't only auditioning for the front-office Brass, they are auditioning for their teammates at the only level that really matters. New guys know from climbing up the many rungs of A-ball, they are to be quiet, seen, and not heard, and when they are seen, be doing something productive or entertaining. In my short amount of time at the big-league level, I wasn't doing either. I had my butt handed to me on several occasions. In fact, my biggest highlight, the one my mom called to inform me I made *SportsCenter* for, was giving up a home run to Manny Ramirez.

"You like writing?" Hoffman asked.

"Yeah, it's a good release," I said, trying my hand at humor, "speaking of which, if I keep pitching the way I am, it may be my next career."

Hoffman smiled, but he was not looking at me when he did it. To me, this conversation was a once-in-a-lifetime event. To him, it was small talk, something to pass the time while he waited for whomever he had business with to finish taking a crap.

"Did you major in English in college?" he asked.

"No, no, I didn't."

"So you just kinda picked this up then?"

"Yeah. I started doing it because I thought the experiences we have in baseball are too valuable not to be recorded."

"What's the book about?"

"It's about one season in the minors. It's about baseball. Maybe it would be better to say it's about what baseball isn't."

"What it isn't?" Hoffman asked, now giving me his full attention.

"Yeah."

"What do you mean by that?"

"Well, baseball is a lot of things, but it's not everything. It can't make your brother sober. It can't make your family stop fighting. It can't make peace or win wars or cure cancer. It makes or breaks a lot of people, like many jobs where the folks who do it find their identity. I don't know if it should be as valuable as it is, or maybe baseball is valuable, and we players just don't use it the right way. I guess that's what I want to figure out in the book."

This was probably one of those moments I should have kept to the seen-and-not-heard rule. Hoffman was talking to me, on his own accord, and I went into deep water. I could have just said it was about baseball and smiled like a kid in a parade while he waited for the sound of a toilet flush, content with the scraps from his table. When people asked, Hoffman could say I was a nice,

harmless kid who majored in English. I would tell folks I talked
with baseball's all-time saves leader, who was a nice, personable
guy. We could both ride off into the sunset, another conversation
neatly wrapped up with a bow and forgotten. Instead, I just told
the person who was baseball's walking synonym for "save" that
our identity shouldn't rest in our job.

Hoffman looked at me, evaluating and judging me like those
big leaguers with time and power do. "I agree," he said, and the
words struck me as if someone had taken me out to be shot but
fired blanks instead. "Baseball's brought me everything I have,
but I agree, it's not as important as a lot of other things in life."

"Yeah. I, uh . . ." I swallowed hard. "I mean, I believe that if
you take baseball out of the world, it would keep spinning, but if
you took math or science, or love, or art, or teachers, or doctors,
or some of the other things we take for granted away, it would
stop. Baseball is such a small thing, comparatively speaking."

"I've never thought of it like that, but I'd agree with you," he
said. "Though, you can't deny it's still a great tool."

"That it is, if you know how to use it," I added. A bold comment for a rookie to make, but one that would spark more conversations than I ever thought I'd have with my childhood hero.

Every now and then, when the pen was quiet and I was feeling
courageous, I would pick Hoffman's brain on a subject about life
and baseball, and he would always give me, some rookie with less
big-league time than the watercooler, a real, thoughtful answer.
Come the end of the year, after the last game of the season, while
everyone packed up their bags and readied to escape the dismal
conclusion of the 2008 season (we lost 99 games), I felt compelled
to approach Hoffman one last time. With a half-a-dozen baseballs
I had snuck from various sources, I asked him whether he would
mind signing what would become my groomsmen presents. He
obliged, and while he stretched the ink of his name across the
balls for me, I asked, "Do you remember a few years back, dur-

ing spring training, coming out to speak with the minor league pitchers?"

"Yeah, I think so."

"Do you remember being asked a certain question about psychological routines and inculcating yourself?"

He looked at me funny, then smiled, "Yeah, I do remember that. You were the one who asked me that huge question. Now that I know you, it doesn't surprise me at all!"

I didn't know whether I should feel flattered or embarrassed that he remembered. "Yeah, about that, I just want you to know you turned me into a laughing stock."

"I'm sorry kid. I remember that question, and to be perfectly honest, I didn't know exactly what to say to you. I mean, you have to understand, when you reach this level, there is so much pressure surrounding you, it's easier to let people down than it is to meet their expectations. This game puts us on a pedestal, and showing our human side doesn't always go over well with those keeping track. I'm sorry I made you look bad."

"That's okay—it made for a good story," I said dismissively, as he scratched his name across the white leather. "Do you think it would be better if it wasn't like that, if we weren't placed on pedestals?"

"Sometimes."

"Do you think people like *you* could change that?"

Hoffman looked up at me, "I think all people could change that, not just me." He handed me the last ball.

"You know," I said, "there weren't many players I cared about while I was growing up, though I always kept track of you. You were one of the players that inspired me to chase my dreams. I was excited to get up here, if for no other reason than just to say I played on the same field as you.

"But when a person gets to the big leagues, he realizes that the people in the bigs are just people. Heck, some of the guys up here are dirtbag savages just like the knuckleheads in the minors. Not everyone lives up to the expectations, and not everyone is safe on his pedestal. I guess that's just life, but I want to tell you Hoffy, you met every one of my expectations, for whatever it's worth."

I took a moment to look out at all my guests, listening to me tell them a story about life in the big leagues, which was really just a story about life, and smiled.

"I'm sure a lot of guys had kissed Hoffman's butt in his career. Guys do that to big names in the industry, but that wasn't why I said it. I said it because I wanted to tell a person who was great in the game that I respected him more for who he was than what I thought he was. I knew him as a real, genuine person, and that's what I valued. Baseball wouldn't make my marriage work, just like it didn't make so many other things work, but a man of integrity can make any profession seem heroic by how he lives while doing it.

"Hoffman told me I paid him a very high compliment, and he was very flattered. Then he said words that I will never forget. He said that the conversations we'd had touched him. He said they made him think about baseball in ways he'd never thought about it before. He said, with absolute sincerity, that the best part of me wasn't in the locker room or on the baseball field, but beyond the lines. Just like the best parts of us aren't in our jobs or stations. He said there was more to a person than just what they do, and that only a real person, not an icon or an image or a jersey, can take a job that puts a man on a pedestal and use it for something selfless."

I stopped there and let the words settle on my listeners. Relaying the story was the easy part. The next part was a little more spontaneous.

"When I signed my contract to play professionally, I thought that was the best moment of my life. When we won the Texas

League, I thought that was the best. When I put on my big-league uniform, I thought the same. Then there was that moment, the one I just told you about with Hoffman—truly, an amazing experience I will never forget. Yet, as amazing as it was, it pales in comparison to this." I reached down and picked up the hand of my wife.

"I may be a big leaguer, and that is something I have always wanted to be, but I will always be a man first—a man in love with this woman right here. And it takes a man, not a uniform or a title, to do that. It takes a man to care about people. I am a man, a very lucky one, who's just married a woman way out of his league, even if it is the bigs!"

Silverware struck glasses, and my wife stood up and laid one on me that made everyone hoot and holler. Cups were raised in the honor of something much bigger than a minor league championship, even though there were far fewer fans present. Flowers were thrown, even though no one checked for velocities. A garter was caught, but no one was called out.

Just before my wife and I left for a very special All-Star break in which I planned to bust an extremely long slump, I felt another thick hand grab me from behind. I turned to face my father. He wore overalls to my wedding, and Mom combed his hair. His hand fell from my shoulder, slid down my arm, and grabbed my hand. His calloused, crippled digits labored to form a firm shake. He wrung my hand, and then for the first time in God only knows how long, he pulled me in for a hug.

We embraced for a few seconds, with me in my wedding uniform and him in his overalls. Then he said words I'll never forget. "I'm proud of you Dirk. I've always been proud of you."

Thank you, Dad.